PASSIONATE
AND PIOUS

MONIQUE MOULTRIE

PASSIONATE AND PIOUS

Religious Media and Black Women's Sexuality

Duke University Press   Durham and London   2017

Printed in the United States of America on acid-free paper ∞
Text designed by Courtney Leigh Baker
Typeset in Whitman by Westchester Publishing Services

Library of Congress Cataloging-in-Publication Data
Names: Moultrie, Monique Nicole, [date] author.
Title: Passionate and pious : religious media and black women's sexuality /
   Monique Moultrie.
Description: Durham : Duke University Press, 2017. | Includes bibliographical
   references and index.
Identifiers: LCCN 2017022557 (print)
LCCN 2017036780 (ebook)
ISBN 9780822372240 (ebook)
ISBN 9780822369998 (hardcover : alk. paper)
ISBN 9780822370048 (pbk. : alk. paper)
Subjects: LCSH: Sex—Religious aspects—Christianity. | African American
   women—Sexual behavior—Religious aspects. | African American women
   clergy—Sexual behavior—Religious aspects. | Mass media in religion. |
   Sexual ethics for women.
Classification: LCC BL65.S4 (ebook) | LCC BL65.S4 M685 2017 (print) | DDC
   261.8/357082—dc23
LC record available at https://lccn.loc.gov/2017022557

Cover art: Nicole Miles, *Sunday Kind of Love*. nicolemillo.com.

To my grandmother **MILDRED CREWS CARTER**,
whose spirit of perseverance and generosity is a guide.

To my life partner, **EUGENE JAMES SE'BREE**,
who shows me daily the Divine's tangible presence in my life.
I'm glad you chose to share your life with me.

And to the memory of my mother, **TOMMIE CREWS**,
a soul who lived and loved freely.
Thank you for always being proud of me.

CONTENTS

This project began as a conversation with my doctoral adviser Victor Anderson as I tried to explain the questions I had been pursuing since leaving my rural Virginia community for college. From that conversation came a dissertation on Juanita Bynum and her importance to discussions of black women's sexuality within religious spaces. I remain grateful to my extraordinary graduate mentors at Vanderbilt and Harvard (Victor Anderson, Linda Thomas, Lewis Baldwin, Bernadette Brooten, Marla Frederick, Sue Houchins, Sharon and Walter Fluker), who pushed the work at its earliest stages. In my quest to research Bynum, my doctoral cohort buoyed my efforts by sending me links, sharing their stories, and being a support network that held me accountable to finishing the pursuit, so I also must acknowledge the PhDivas (Natasha Coby-Earl, Nichole Phillips, Amy Steele, Kimberly Peeler-Ringer, Keri Day, Tamura Lomax, Kimberly Russaw, Tamara Lewis, Angela Cowser, Lisa Thompson, and Bridget Green) and my doctoral brothers (Charles Bowie, Christophe Ringer, Brandon McCormack, TL Gray, and Asante Todd). My graduate education also brought me friends from outside my immediate community, and I remain thankful for their presence in my life (Haywood Harvey, Jason Cogswell, Lynda Jordan, Albert Smith, and Ipsita Chatterjea).

While the human resources that sustained this project were crucial, it is equally important to acknowledge the numerous funders' financial support for this project over the years. The Forum for Theological Exploration believed in the merit of my project, as did the Southern Regional Education Board and the Roothbert Fund. As the project grew into a book, I was fortunate to receive generous support from the Ford Foundation, Harvard University, and Georgia State University that provided the needed time and resources to complete the work.

I would be remiss if I did not thank Jade Brooks and Miriam Angress and the team at Duke University Press for their deep faith in this work at every stage. I would also like to thank my colleagues at Georgia State (both the religious studies and African American studies faculty) for being sage counsel and sounding boards for my ideas. Barbara Revkin literally provided me with a room of my own, an invaluable space to write and live while in Boston. I am also grateful for the mentorship of pastors Dennis and Christine Wiley, whose work with black churches, black women, and sexuality is a model for all.

This manuscript started off as an ode to Bynum and slowly morphed into something more as I realized the successors to Bynum's movement were more salient in contemporary black women's sexual decision making. Along the way my research was greatly enriched by women who shared their stories with me. I am deeply indebted to the women who joined my focus groups in Nashville; Chatham, Virginia; and Boston. I spent years as a participant observer in the Pinky Promise Movement and Wives in Waiting groups, and I hope these women can see how seriously I took their stories. Whether or not your narrative made it into the final manuscript, know that your lives have inspired this project in tangible ways, and I hope the work reflects the deep questions of faith you shared with me.

Finally, I want to acknowledge my forever friends and family who have made my journey through the academy endurable. Ayana Burnett, my soror and friend, has always reminded me of my wise mind and my worth. Nichole Phillips has supported me through graduate school and the early years of our teaching careers, providing me with copious prayer and laughter. James Logan has encouraged me to see the greatest possibilities for myself and to actually do the work to achieve them. Almeda Wright's inspiration to keep on task brought order to my leave year, and her friendship has sustained me through my best and worst years.

I conclude with thanking my family for their years of sacrifice for me. As I started writing this manuscript, my biological mother was diagnosed with brain cancer. Her illness and subsequent death brought me back home every month for a year and a half. My time at home grounded me and pushed me to keep going. In my deep loss I grew in unexpected ways, and my family supported me in ways that are immeasurable. My grandparents Mildred and Thomas Carter raised me in a home of love with purpose and pride in my accomplishments, and my aunts and uncles have provided financial, emotional, and comical support over the years, reminding me not to take myself too seriously. To my Nashville family, the Eppersons, thank you for embracing me and for loving me unconditionally.

To my beloved partner, Rev. Eugene James Se'Bree, you were my strongest and most vocal support during this project. There is not a word present that I did not discuss with you first. You are the mirror that reflects God's love for me and shows me the best parts of myself. As my life partner and best friend, you provided steady encouragement even when completing this project took me a thousand miles away. I appreciate your generous spirit, your keen insight, and most of all your love. When your daughters moved in oh so many years ago I did not know the impact their presence would have on my research. It is for them that I now write, with the hope that Chandler and Jioni will have alternatives to struggles with their faith and sexuality. May they understand our sacrifices and know our love for them as they embark on their life paths.

FOR ALL THE SINGLE LADIES

Black Women's Stories of Faith and Sexuality

Only the Black Woman can say "when and where I enter, in the quiet, undisputed dignity of my womanhood, without violence and without suing or special patronage, then and there the whole Negro race enters with me." —ANNA JULIA COOPER, *A Voice from the South*

Sexual stories about black women are all around us, but they almost always rely on key myths, while few stories told by black women about their own sexual lives are available. —TRICIA ROSE, *Longing to Tell*

When I was seventeen, two of my teenage female friends were brought before the church to "repent" of their sin of getting pregnant. I remember watching their tears flowing as they stood before the entire congregation with their parents, two sets of highly regarded church members. As if it were yesterday, I watched as our male chairman of the deacon board made their sins known publicly (neither was visibly pregnant at the time of disclosure) to the audience, who then voted to strip these young women of their privileges as members, removing them from youth choir, for example. I watched in horror and confusion as no one dared speak on their behalf or at least bring the sexually responsible fathers-to-be up with them to share in this public shaming. Although we attended separate high schools, we all saw each other often at the numerous church events extending beyond our Sunday worship together. I could not fathom these young women's plight, nor could I stomach the audacity of a religious community asking them to apologize to God and to our church. On that Sunday my decision to be a questioning Christian was bolstered.

When I got home I asked my grandmother, the woman who raised me in that particular Baptist church and who was also an esteemed leader in the church, why these young women had been singled out when we both knew, deacons, ministers, and others in that same church had children outside of their marriages. I had never witnessed these men brought before the church, not even when the church gossip ran high. She stared at me with confusion and said, "Of course not, they are all men!" Her response, while still true today, was jolting to my sensibilities as she reminded me of the patriarchal double standard with which I would live if I chose to remain a black churchwoman. This book's major questions started on that day as I pondered how a church that gave me absolutely no direction on sexuality except to abstain from intercourse until marriage could then have any stake in any of my future sexual decisions. I learned that day that many black churches are willing to pay attention to sexuality as long as it is to impugn black women's sexuality as an evil that needs to be controlled. Before I learned what sexism, womanism, and patriarchy mean, I learned that day that the God of my tradition did not expect men to accept responsibility for their sexual conduct or even sexual sin. Yet I was not defeated by this new reality; I was encouraged to ask more questions, to challenge what did not seem godly, and to think critically about a God and a tradition that was worthy of my devotion.

In this work I continue to ask questions and rebel against the sexual messages given to black women by religious communities. Black women are given a variety of messages about their sexuality, and I explore their sexual beliefs and how they make sexual decisions. Whether black women are viewed as hypersexualized and in need of restraint or asexual and too holy for sex, there are plentiful conversations about sexuality, but few are informed by black women's actual lives. By highlighting how black and white feminists have responded to these pervasive stereotypes I propose that womanism, the discipline interrogating the multilayered oppression of women of color, is the best means for probing how single black churchwomen make meaning from their varied history, lived experiences, and faith perspectives.[1]

Investigating religious messages directed at black churchwomen is a topic of great import given their influence through the recent increase in faith-based sexuality ministries. These ministries include Christian televangelists, Christian women's and singles conferences, and Christian media (e.g., videos, audiotapes, and live streaming on the Internet). It is rare to see analysis of these media in any discipline, but such a discerning analysis is required particularly as these ministries have become a "multi-million dollar industry—with books, classes, internet and gospel radio dating services . . . and conferences," all ostensibly to help black churchwomen navigate their sexuality and spiritual walk with God.[2] Recent scholarship on televangelism focuses on prosperity gospel advocates and typically ignores the other messages, yet faith-based sexuality ministries are often as lucrative—and therefore as influential—as those that promote prosperity.

These messages and ministries also beg to be examined because of their collective effect on women's lives; as the anthropologist Marla Frederick astutely notes, black women are making decisions about their sexual practices based at least in part on their adherence to televised messages.[3] Often these messages correspond to those they receive in church (especially since many church leaders are seeking to emulate the formula of televangelism). What is different is that these alternative religious spaces offer an abundance of ways to market that same message. A pastor's sermon may be forgotten after Sunday service, but televangelists, e-vangelists, and faith-based sexuality leaders are in constant communication with a supporter via emails, text messages, journals, meditations, and even messages throughout the day via Instagram, Facebook, and other social media. This mass communication provides a vast market to interrogate.

Exploring the faith-based sexuality market reveals a new phenomenon in the modernization of sexuality. If Foucault is correct and sexuality is a constantly evolving modern invention, then new categories are created by contemporary discourses.[4] Notably, Foucault is discussing the invention of the homosexual, but his larger argument reflects the steady progression of discourse that is bolstered by power structures to create seemingly stable categories like homosexuality or in the case of this project black Christian sexuality. Philosopher Ludger Vieflhues-Bailey analyzes the predominantly white evangelical group Focus on the Family as evidence of the proliferation of

Christian sex products, and he argues that these products create a "Christian heterosexuality."[5] However, the Christian heterosexuality he speaks of is specific to the lived experiences of white married Christians. The faith-based sexuality ministries familiar to single black Christian women do not share this same history; thus Prophetess Juanita Bynum creates a genre that gives single black Christian women a space to talk about their sexuality and spirituality. This space allows them to ferret out which sexual messages to follow, modify, or ignore. Using womanist ethnography to explore the category of black Christian sexuality, I provide a womanist sexual ethics for contemporary times that is focused on agency, desire, and responsible sexual decision making.

Black Christian Sexuality

The category of black Christian sexuality is distinctive in many ways from the Christian sexuality that Vieflhues-Bailey presents. While there is an emphasis on sex the way God intended (typically construed in white evangelical literature as heterosexual, married, with the wife submissive to husband), black faith-based sexuality ministries construct black Christian sexuality as a sexual identity and category that place these standards in line with black female lived experience. Despite their conservative theological views, black evangelicals entering the faith-based sexuality ministry market adjust the white-dominant message to reflect a history wherein a woman's purity is not automatically considered the property of her father, a woman's purity can be denied because of stereotypes of her being sexually available, sexual pleasure can be discussed, and a woman's path to a God-given marriage is not guaranteed.

Perhaps this difference in starting points also reflects a distinction in the evangelicalism experienced by participants in faith-based sexuality ministries. The overall industry of evangelical sex products typically targets whites, evident in the cover art, illustrations, and, more important, life experiences discussed. Sadly even scholars of American evangelicalism tend to use *evangelical* as a universal category that excludes black and Hispanic Protestants. While there is much in common among evangelicals, such as belief in the inerrancy of scripture, spiritual rebirth as a criterion for entering heaven, and an expectation of certain types of behavior, there are different denominational histories, theological perspectives, and class and political differences.[6] Historian A. G. Miller notes that while it may be difficult to determine exactly how many blacks identify as evangelical, black evangelicals are certainly most visible in religious media, which is also true of faith-based sexuality ministries.[7] Black evangelical ministries also must deal with the reality that more of their membership is single, and thus their ministries cater to these audiences.

Among all U.S. women, black women make up the smallest population of married women. If the predominant religious message they are hearing and seeing is that sex is for marriage only, then there would seem to be some angst among black women. How do they make sense of the church's teachings in light of their ongoing singleness? In what ways do they account for the dissonance? I expected to discover many women, who after embracing their singleness, discovered that their sexual desires had not abated. Aware of heterosexual female ministers' and religious leaders' narratives of sexual temptation and frustration, I anticipated that their followers would be the masses of single black churchwomen who were happily married to the Holy Spirit while disappointingly sleeping alone.

This research focuses on heterosexual relationships as a means of weighing in on the secular "marriage debate" that seems entirely dedicated to heterosexual black women. One question in this debate is *Why aren't more black women married?* Heterosexual black women are also signaled because the majority of discussions around sexuality in black churches are focused on homosexuality. Heterosexuality goes unnamed, unchallenged, and often underdeveloped as a concept of both theological and practical concern. This focus on black female heterosexuality is an effort to shine scholarly attention on an area that has been understudied in religious studies. I concur with the religious historian Amy DeRogatis that evangelical attention to sexuality has overemphasized same-sex desire as a problem while carrying on simultaneous discussions about the "proper practice of heterosexuality."[8] Equally my decision to study black female televangelists and e-vangelists corrects the gap in scholarship on American religious broadcasting, which has tended to focus primarily on white men. In those rare instances when scholars do diversify the field, they typically expand it only enough to include the voices of black men.[9] Even the recent scholarly interest on singles ministries has focused on white male religious leadership. Thus, for the community of self-identified single black women on the margins of the margin, investigating the experiences of female leaders in their movement is a necessary balancing move.

FIGURE INTRO.1.
Hands of Praise, by
Frederick Moul-
trie Jr. Used by
permission.

The black feminist scientist Evelynn Hammonds postulates that black women create whole worlds of sexual signs that must be interpreted by their specific cultural contexts.[10] For black churchwomen this decoding means hearing through the silences and expectations of sexual virtue that certain readings of Christianity impose. By listening through the silence, it is possible to learn of an entirely parallel culture that suspends expectations for a new and more complicated reality. The black historian Darlene Clark Hine was one of the first theorists to discuss black female sexual silence in terms of culture. She refers to silent women's participation in a "culture of dissemblance," a culture created to protect black women by seeming to disclose only what they wanted to disclose of their sexual selves, thus allowing women space to utilize their own resources of resistance against tropes that castigated their sexuality.[11] This seemingly silent culture was not actually silent about sexuality. In fact there was a great deal of discussion of sexuality going on as women refigured their images and created empowered definitions of themselves.

Many critics of this culture of dissemblance suggest that it merely reaffirms the Victorian notions of morality present in the dominant culture that was Christian-centered and heteronormative, but perhaps there was more was going on than just colluding with a dominant historical pattern. The philosopher and gender theorist Judith Butler argues that agency is always located within structures of power, which means that actions and subversions often participate in the very same oppressive structures.[12] This challenges feminists from classifying as agency only what seems to be resisting domination. When applied to this study, a discussion of agency highlights how black churchwomen were and are refiguring heteronormativity to fit their unique circumstances. Thus while some view as hypocritical black churchwomen's open castigation of premarital sex yet jubilant celebration when a child is born from this contemptuous union, this can also be read as an understandable response to the complexity of relationships within black women's groups.

The structures of power that black women are navigating also include historical stereotypes that manifest in public policy and public opinion. The two main stereotypes of black women, as Jezebel and as Mammy, are represented in these women's everyday experiences of the Christian madonna-whore binary. Of these the image of black women as Jezebel, the evil seductress known for her excessive, unbridled sexuality,[13] has historically trapped some black women in sexual exploitation because they were not deemed "women" who required protection, as did white ladies. Yet slavocracy mandated that another myth of black female sexuality emerge because the slave system could not have functioned if all black women were sexually licentious. The Mammy stereotype was created to explain how black moral degeneracy did not influence white women and children in their care. According to this stereotype, "Mammy" was generally considered asexual; she had learned to quell her uncontrollable sexual desires so that she could attend to the needs of her surrogate white family. The Mammy image served as the cornerstone of the "cult of true womanhood," and black women who desired societal respectability often donned this persona. The black women's club movements and black churches in particular adopted and adapted this persona through a "politics of respectability" that downplayed black women's sexual expressions.[14] Black church members became experts at disciplining the body by teaching that respectable behavior was evident in following biblical restrictions on premarital and same-gender sexual relationships.

This discipline is perpetuated even now, through the policing of female bodies and the silencing of black female sexuality, as reflected in my content analysis of various faith-based sexuality ministries. Unlike televangelist culture, which seldom refers to sin or hell and instead gets consumers to focus on becoming their best self, faith-based sexuality ministries believe in speaking on these unspeakable topics. They approach black women's sexuality with a religious fervor and quite openly insist that God cares whether you are living a sexually pure life (e.g., avoiding biblically proscribed acts of sexual immorality). Typically a ministry's discussion equates personal sin with sexual sin. This fits well in the logic of televangelism and growing e-vangelistic enterprises that focus on individualistic faith and personal values.[15] Despite this emphasis on personal sin, a large number of my focus group participants did not seem to adopt the rigid conservative values and customs of previous generations. They tended to reject public shaming of persons in sexual sin and instead promoted an ethic of loving reproach in which they privately chastised persons to follow God's will. Yet a new culture of dissemblance occurs when women attend singles conferences and ministries and openly discuss their sexual desires and demands for pleasure. Within these spaces they are articulating their own conceptions of sexuality, even if they seem only to reiterate the dominant messages. Thus I examine three dominant messages about black Christian sexuality: that sexuality is sacred; that sex is reserved for marriage and is always between a man and a woman; and that there should be no sex among singles, forcing Christian single women to control their sexual desires while being depicted as asexual—all messages that are the foundation of faith-based sexuality ministry's rhetoric.

I discuss these dominant messages about sexuality using the frame of womanist sexual ethics. Arguably the leading womanist authority on sexuality is the theologian Kelly Brown Douglas.[16] In her groundbreaking *Sexuality and the Black Church*, published in 1999, she notes that although Christianity historically saw sexuality as negative due to the influence of Platonic thought, which sees flesh and spirit as distinct, one corruptible and the other pristine, the incarnation of Jesus Christ suggests a very different interpretation of the body and, ultimately, of human sexuality. Douglas states that the fact that Christ was embodied calls for an appreciation of the whole human body as a gift from God. She also highlights the African religious heritage that views human sexuality as divine and offers from the womanist tradition the notion of loving our bodies (completely) as a way of reflecting God's love. Rejecting the dualistic demonization of body/soul requires black churchwomen to acknowledge sexuality as a sacred act.

This dualism is clearly present in not just the sacrality of sexual relationships but in the assumption that proper sex occurs within a heterosexual marriage. While Protestants tend not to have a universal opinion about any particular church doctrine that rivals the canonical nature of Catholic Church teachings, an exemption to this lack of universal consensus is evident when considering the pronouncement that sex should occur within a marital bond. When pressed for a rationale for this particular hierarchy, many in religious leadership point to biblical instructions on marriage, yet upon examination of the messages it is rare to get clarity about why a particular brand of biblical marriage is being promoted over others. For example, the Bible clearly indicates the prevalence of polygamous marriages, marriages between family members, nonconsensual marriages, and marriages conducted as financial transactions, so an advocate of biblical marriage, which is contemporarily coded as a union of one man and one woman, requires being selective about biblical marriage.[17] Yet this stance is common to all the faith-based sexuality ministries. Each ministry promotes sex within marriage as the one and only way, but this message is as old as the Protestant Reformation. Subsumed within this "one" way is in fact the variety of ways the Bible discusses marriage, especially in the New Testament, where Paul is the orchestrator of a grand scheme to get persons married before they burn with sexual passions. If Paul highlights celibacy as the ultimate gift and suggests marriage be avoided so that one can focus on the work of God, why then do our contemporary religious messages reverse this notion and make marriage the example of spiritual maturity? More important, why do black religious spaces embrace this one biblical interpretation but challenge so many other scriptures?

Douglas's work is helpful to understanding the sway of marriage for post-emancipation black churches. She contends that churches prescribed their members' sexual behaviors, especially those of black women, whose pre-nuptial sexual freedom was replaced by marital fidelity.[18] Enslaved women were often denied the right to marry and to control their sexuality, so when they entered churches after slavery many were no longer sexually "pure." By emphasizing marital fidelity and strictly sanctioning all premarital and extramarital activities, religious leaders also reinforced a gendered bias that actively restrained black female sexuality while merely recommending restraint for black males. Church commandments that sanctioned sex only in marriage often excused the male offender because it was thought that his "sin is individual," whereas the woman's sins were deemed to be larger as she "sins against the family and race."[19]

This double standard continues to the present day as focus group interviewee "Audrey Rae" echoed this same sentiment. Audrey Rae is a twenty-eight-year-old, lower-middle-class, religiously eclectic graduate student who claims a "fluid or bi-sexual" identity. Her family desired a committed marital relationship for her and intimated that she needed to exercise sexual restraint until that relationship was established. She was taught, "I am always the one who was in control of other people's sexual desires around me. My boobs, my hips, my behind: I needed to control my body so that I don't cause anybody else to fall." This gendered message, that women are to control themselves or be controlled by others, fits well in a patriarchal hierarchy of secular and religious society, but it is also the modern day re-incarnation of the Mammy stereotype whereby black women are expected to control their desires to the point of asexuality. Indeed every one of my focus group interviewees reported being similarly warned and instructed that sex was permissible only in marriage and that it was the woman's duty to ensure this.

Both black and white evangelical sexuality literature teaches that God created men and women to enjoy themselves sexually in the sanctity of marriage, and this logic is marketed in both Christian media and churches.[20]

Simultaneously black evangelicals are bombarded with messages about the unavailability of marriage partners. The social ethicist Robert M. Franklin summarizes the vast literature on black families, finding that after emancipation, although African Americans initially embraced marriage, the number of black marriages has decreased significantly since the 1950s, which can be attributed to declining job prospects, female independence, increased education leading to delays in marriage, and changing social, cultural, and moral codes.[21] Franklin concludes that the black church should take up the challenge to encourage black marriage, but this privileging of marriage can be read as isolating the already marginalized singles population or as encouraging men to join the marriage ranks. While Franklin's charge is for the black church at large, he is really sending a gendered message from men to other men. The women following faith-based sexuality ministries do not need to be convinced of the value of marriage; they are not a skeptical audience. They believe that marriage is God's best plan for their lives, and they are actively pursuing that goal. Women in my focus groups and followers of these ministries seemed universally to adopt the messages restricting their sexuality to marital relationships, and it was almost heresy to challenge the basis of this assumption. Despite mentally accepting a life of sexual restraint, almost every woman I interviewed had transgressed this agreement. The conundrum of wrestling with the expectation of no sex until marriage while having no foreseeable marriage partner is at the heart of this book. I also foreground the fact that all of these faith-based sexuality ministries share the "No marriage, no sex" assumption as a God-ordained fact. One of my contributions is to muddy those waters and dare to question what seems to be an inviolate assumption.

As Foucault posited, public silencing surrounding sexuality ultimately had the opposite effect because the subject that was deemed taboo was also the topic of public concern. While my focus group participants may not have received the specific information and counsel they were seeking regarding how to exercise their sexuality, there are a vast number of faith-based sexuality ministries that complicate a trope of sexual silence. These ministries operate in a way that influences black female sexual agency; thus my examination of faith-based sexuality ministries reflects my ongoing scholarly and communal commitments to moral decision making and my quest to fill a gap in the research on black women's sexuality. As much as this is a book that brings academic discussion to faith-based sexuality ministries, it is also a womanist envisioning of a sexual ethics for contemporary times.[22] The content analysis of these ministries is essential to investigating their impact on black churchwomen's everyday lives. In fact a womanist sexual ethics is a crucial contextual and methodological framework to interpret black churchwomen's spiritual and sexual concerns.

A primary concern of this womanist sexual ethics is how women become sexual agents through various experiences. On a basic level, sexual agency expresses how women make sexual decisions; this includes the decision not to engage in sexual relations. Yet contemporary womanist sexual agency ties these expressions and choices to an understanding of sexual rights. The notion of sexual rights is part of the human rights discourse that encourages women to demand the right to sexual pleasure, self-expression, intimacy, and freedom from sexual abuse.[23] Advocating for sexual rights must be a part of a womanist sexual ethics because these rights assure that these women's sexual decisions occur in a respectful environment. Thus womanist sexual agency does not determine which responsible actions a person should be allowed to participate in, nor does it foreclose participating in any sexual activities as long as parties are able to give consent. Sexual agency merely states that there is liberty to take any action one chooses with an understanding that this action may ultimately be harmful to one's psyche or body. However, the intent of a contemporary womanist sexual ethics is to equip women in such a way that their choices are made within a guiding frame that advocates for their own sexual rights.

Womanist analysis of sexuality has tended to stay at the descriptive level, pointing to sexual abuse and unhealthy relationships at the expense of a normative analysis of sexual agency. This book instead utilizes womanist ethnography as its main methodology to analyze the impact of religious media on black churchwomen's sexual agency, demanding an interrogation of sexual politics that occur outside of traditional "black church" settings. The women participating in these ministries do so as negotiated readers who take what is useful for their understanding of faith and sexuality and jettison anything contradictory to their moral agency.

Methodology

I expected an analysis of faith-based sexuality ministries to reveal women with complicated sexual realities living out Matthew 26:41, whose "spirit is willing, but the flesh is weak." This was certainly the case with the main leaders who promoted the ministries, so why should the consumers be any different from their models? Thus the book begins with an analysis of Prophetess Juanita Bynum's ministry as an example of the black Christian sexuality genre that provides messages to black single women. I followed Bynum's ministry first as a consumer and true believer in her message of celibacy and waiting for God's man to arrive in God's time. Then I followed Bynum as a participant observer and academic studying her ministry, going to her conferences and buying hundreds of dollars' worth of her materials. Bynum is the progenitor of a movement that disseminates Christian messages of abstinence to single black women, but she is just one in a long line of such messengers. This analysis of her ministry sets the tone for interpreting her successors. But my interest in the movement Bynum built was exceeded only by my interest in how these messages were received by scores of black women participating in these ministries.

To gain insight into these experiences, I solicited qualitative responses from single black Christian women ages twenty-one to eighty-five. I broadly targeted women over twenty-one because adult women's decisions tend to reflect how religion has influenced their sexual decision making and how they adhere to these religious messages; that is, they are not just following their parents' rules. I included a specific emphasis on black women over the age of fifty because this demographic is experiencing a sharp increase in HIV infections, with AIDS being the fourth leading cause of death for black women in that age group. I was particularly interested in their narratives because they reframe faith-based sexuality ministries' discussions on celibacy until marriage given that they tend to seek companionship rather than marriage.

My primary methodology was womanist ethnography, with the goal of studying black women as subjects, not objects, of inquiry. Womanist ethnography involves talking with people and using their voices as sources for research. A particular gift of this technique is that it privileges the thick description of a few black women without seeking to universalize their stories or homogenize their voices. The womanist anthropologist Linda Thomas asserts that womanist ethnography involves entering the communities of black women and learning from and living among them to utilize their life experiences as primary sources, with the task of reflecting their polyvalent stories.[24] Just like womanists who use biomythographies, autobiographies, or historiographies, my emphasis is on creating space for the validity of black women's religious experiences.

In my ethnographic analysis I primarily conducted focus group interviews with semistructured and open-ended questions to solicit participants' involvement in these ministries, their understanding of religious messages on sexuality, and their experiences as a single person. In total I interviewed thirty women over the course of thirteen months.[25] Despite soliciting a larger age range, my data came from focus group conversations with single black Christian women ranging in age from twenty-two to seventy-three. I conducted focus group interviews across the South, as well as two lengthy phone interviews with a participant in Atlanta and one in Chicago.[26] As a product of the South, I was perhaps oblivious in my interviews to the ways that living in the Bible Belt promulgates certain messages about black Christian sexuality. For instance, while being interviewed for a book on single women, the former MSNBC host and political scientist Melissa Harris-Perry stated that in her experience "marriage is an expectation and a desire of young adulthood for both men and women in the South."[27] She likened marriage to a sign of achieving adulthood, and in terms of black Christian sexuality it is certainly a sign of a mature Christian who wants to complete God's plan for her life. In an environment where blacks are expected to join a church, there is certainly pressure to participate in the norms of Bible Belt Christianity, which the sociologist Bernadette Barton classifies as the type of Christianity that permeates beyond religious institutions and is an influence on secular environments.[28] My interviewees reiterated that while growing up in churches in the South they were constantly told not to engage in premarital sex because it was displeasing to God. "Josephine" stated that in the South women are taught to "love your sons and raise your daughters," signaling different gender expectations for chastity. Simultaneously she thought Bible Belt dogma "thrives on people finding out that you did something" because there are numerous stated and unstated rules of propriety that women (especially) are expected to follow. Although the southern woman is culturally framed as a white woman, she is known by her dress, demeanor, language, and submissiveness to her parents, husband, spiritual authority, and God. [29] Research suggests that the standard of what an upright southern woman is expected to do is shared by whites and blacks.

All of the faith-based sexuality ministries I followed were technically international in focus despite being geographically southern. They were also nondenominational. As parachurch organizations, these ministries downplayed denominational distinctions, choosing to emphasize "simple theology that they claim all true Christians hold."[30] Generally they were more apt to discuss broad Christian topics like salvation, evangelizing, or spiritual warfare than to deliberate on denominational theologies. Choosing the broad frame of Christianity and purposely running nondenominational ministries provide mass appeal because the overarching message of crafting a black Christian sexuality can be achieved without a specific denominational viewpoint. The interviewees who participated in these ministries tended to be Baptist, but this reflects my method of reaching out to participants more than it does the overall constituencies of these ministries.

After requesting the pastors' permission to advertise my study, I recruited focus group members from my two family Baptist churches (one in Chatham, Virginia, and the other in Nashville). I repeated the process of seeking pastors' permission and participants by expanding my recruitment to other Baptist congregations in the South. Overwhelmingly participants reported being lifelong members of the same Baptist congregation, middle class, and college educated, and some had graduate degrees. These initial interviews included participants diverse in age, educational background, and marital status. For instance, these women were more likely to have been married and had children at some point in their lives. All of these women were now single (either never having married or divorced), with the exception of two who had been widowed. Though I was pleased with the initial interviews, my focus group interviews indicated these respondents were nominal believers in faith-based sexuality ministries: they were familiar with the ministries, and they had bought some of the materials, but they were not the hard-core adherents I was expecting. Faith-based sexuality ministries were only one source of religious messages these women were holding in tension; others were reality TV shows with a religious focus (such as *Preachers of LA*, which had a story about Dietrich Haddon being an unmarried minister and singer who was living with the mother of his child) and secular shows dealing with sexuality that had a religious influence, like *Iyanla Fix My Life*.[31]

Because my first focus groups did not yield participants who were heavy consumers of any one particular faith-based sexuality ministry, I expanded my data set to target women who were self-proclaimed followers of one of the female evangelists. This focus group also brought a younger, more educated population of interviewees than my previous focus groups. They tended not to have married and in general had a lower number of children (zero to two, the majority having no children). I solicited these participants from Facebook and through snowball sampling of faith-based sexuality ministry group members. I gained access to this subset through my research connections as a participant observer for three years in the online communities of the Pinky Promise Movement.[32] I also gained interviews after having been a participant observer in the Wives in Waiting group for two years.[33] As a participant observer I attended their national conferences and local group meetings and interacted in their online communities by commenting on posts and posting my own discussion feeds. This aided my ability to get to know the women and solicit focus group interviews. It also greatly expanded my understanding of the language and cultural references of these two ministries.

Participating online was at times more difficult than my in-person observation with the groups. In a survey of white evangelical sexuality websites, the sociologist Kelsy Burke notes that digital resources are constantly being rewritten by ordinary believers, all the while shaping the idea of what Christian sex should be.[34] This constant and often anonymous updating makes the task of documenting and being in the field daunting. While I did not always have to travel to maintain my connection to the ministries' community members, my in-person group members got to know me and to trust my research intent. I was never sure I conveyed that to the online communities because of their great variety during any given post. For this reason I put in more time to make my Pinky Promise page representative of my research interests and my personality so that anyone who went to my page would feel welcomed.[35] Yet sometimes circumstances forced me out of the welcoming space I had created.

For instance, while reading through a forum denouncing women who wanted to leave their marriage, I was struck by the founder's seeming acceptance of marital abuse. (She recommended that if a woman was getting abused by her husband she should seek couples counseling but not a divorce since God can "heal a broken, battered, marriage.") Within the forum several women assented to this logic, including a woman who admitted that she had been planning to serve her husband with separation papers that morning because she could no longer stand his physical abuse. As a result of the forum's conversation this woman was now "convicted" and was not going to send her husband the separation papers. I hesitated for several hours trying to decide what to do. No one in the group was suggesting that she leave her abusive husband, yet I felt desperately that she was in danger given what she had posted about his prior physical abuse of her. I knew that if I recommended divorce I would "out" myself as not being a true believer in the community chat room. Unless they had been to my Pinky Promise page it would not be evident to participants that I was in the chat room as a researcher because my rhetoric and responses to the group postings were typically similar to the other women's responses. Ultimately I decided that as a womanist ethicist I could not stand by and be silent while a woman's life was in danger, all to protect my "cover." Using the language of the group I submitted that it surely could not be God's plan that she be abused and that God did not need her husband to physically harm her in order to lead her. Though I followed the blog post for several additional weeks, no one else suggested that separation was necessary for her safety. There was no noticeable pushback to my response from group members, but I continued to walk a thin line between my role as a researcher and the perception that I was a community member.[36]

While situating myself as a former adherent to faith-based sexuality ministries, my identity as a womanist sexual ethicist spurred my decision to intervene while observing these communities online. Womanism was also prevalent in the types of questions I asked the focus group participants. I chose a qualitative approach to reflect on the group's experiences and interpretations of the variety of sexual messages that affected their sexual decision making.[37] Yet when I began coding their responses I discovered that my expectations of faith-based ministry adherents were largely biased by my own participation in these movements. I could speak the language of the various groups because once I too had found solace in sermons, books, and conferences as I struggled with my own celibacy path as a young, heterosexual black woman with deep faith commitments. This bias meant that the questions I selected for the focus group interviews were based on a preconceived understanding of how these women viewed sexuality (based on both historical stereotypes and Christian conservative tropes).

My deliberate use of womanist sexual ethics was in response to traditionally white feminist theological ethics, from which black women's experiences are often excluded, and black feminist cultural theory, in which black women's religious lives seem to be undervalued.[38] Since Christianity is so central to the culture of the black women I was studying, a discussion of their sexual agency required taking seriously their spiritual concerns.

Overview of the Book

This book begins with Prophetess Bynum as a model of a larger cultural phenomenon. I offer one of the first detailed discussions of her imprint on faith-based sexuality ministries and the creation of a black Christian sexuality. While the book is ultimately concerned with the impact of black religious broadcasting on black churchwomen's sexuality, the marginalization of black female televangelism and religious media in scholarly literature is also emphasized. This text breaks new ground in crafting a womanist cultural analysis because it provides the first attempt to address religion, race, and sexuality with specific attention to black female sexual agency.

Chapter 1, "Sexual Purity as PR," describes the theological tenets of black Christian sexuality, providing a particular focus on how these concepts are gendered for evangelical women. I interrogate the theological foundation of many faith-based sexuality ministries by investigating the themes of sin, sexual restraint, submission, holiness, sanctified living, and evangelical purity culture. The chapter concludes by highlighting the allure of sexual redemption or sexual awakening testimonies for black Christian sexuality, positing Bynum as the forerunner in the genre.

Chapter 2, "Reading 'Our' Bynum as Text," deconstructs Prophetess Bynum as a cultural text and representative of a black Christian sexual identity focused on females. I offer a close reading of Bynum's "No More Sheets" sermon because this moment births a genre of black faith-based sexuality ministries. Through womanist ethnography I present the experiences of black Christian women who admit to being as frustrated at Bynum as they try to live their single lives before God, all the while experiencing sexual desire. The focus groups revealed these audiences are negotiated readers of Bynum's messages, persons who choose to follow some but not all of her directives. In my analysis of Bynum as text, her messages are deemed descriptive and prescriptive, ultimately not affirming for a diversity of expressions for black women's sexual agency.

Despite this assessment of her messages for black women cultural readers, Bynum maintains a position of importance for those bequeathed her legacy of black Christian sexuality. The third chapter, "Beyond Bynum," examines why Bynum's movement matters by investigating the various models that followed her. Despite the diversity of media, there remains a similar message of submissiveness and celibacy. The contemporary faith-based sexuality ministries are tech-savvy and move far beyond the medium of television to disseminate their messages. I investigate four faith-based sexuality ministries, namely, the Wives in Waiting group, the Pinky Promise Movement, Michelle McKinney Hammond's Heartwing Ministries, and the *Soul Mate* documentary, by highlighting how these messages have expanded beyond Bynum's neo-Pentecostal beginnings. I interpret celibacy messages that are crafted for black women by black women, ultimately positing the need for a womanist model of celibacy that nuances celibacy as a sexual choice.

The fourth chapter, "'Why I Gotta Be Gay?,'" discusses same-sex-desiring single black women who participate in faith-based sexuality ministries while maintaining allegiance to the category of black Christian sexuality that demands their celibacy and participation in heterosexuality. By interrogating what celibacy means for a woman who believes that her same-sex desire is contrary to God's will, I deconstruct messages from a popular black female e-vangelist, Ty Adams, who shares a sexual redemption story that includes her overcoming same-sex attraction. The chapter provides a womanist sexual ethics intervention in the form of sexual hospitality that accepts a full range of sexual expressions and identities as a push against passing as heterosexual in religious communities.

Chapter 5, "The Lord Still Has Work for Me to Do," analyzes the participation of senior women in faith-based sexuality ministries by investigating what it means to be sexual agents as older black women. This chapter focuses on the ethical dilemma placed before elderly women whose church standing might be questioned if it were known that they were engaging in sexual activity, especially after being widowed or divorced. Using data from focus groups, I concentrate on single Christian women who are seeking nonmarital companionship or engaging in sexual activity, which conflicts with the black Christian sexuality tropes of celibacy and marriage. Elderly churchwomen as gatekeepers of sexual silence is a function of the performance of this black Christian sexual identity. Womanist sexual ethics provides the concept of sexual generosity as a corrective to these discussions of celibacy until marriage, instead offering respect for the multiple types of relationships that senior black churchwomen can experience.

"Horny and Holy," the sixth chapter, begins the constructive task of ferreting out discussions of black female sexual desire and pleasure from faith-based sexuality ministries. Part of the mass appeal of these ministries is the candid discussions of black churchwomen's sexual urges. For those participating in the values of black Christian sexuality, there is profound interest in sexual pleasure within proper constraints. Even though these women agree that sexual pleasure is best achieved in marriage, there is still a great deal of negotiating that takes place around masturbation and other sexual taboos. Explorations of women who are passionately pursuing pleasure is a contribution of this work, as is the crafting of a womanist erotic justice that celebrates the black female body, discusses oral and anal sex, and responds to hook-up culture or nonmonogamous, nonmarital sexual activity by emphasizing pleasure and responsibility as equal moral goods to monogamy.

The book's conclusion, "Living Sexually before God," provides the benefits of a constructive womanist sexual ethics for contemporary times by calling for black churchwomen to experience life-enhancing sex. Highlighting valuable lessons from faith-based sexuality ministries such as accountability, applicability, and accessibility, this womanist sexual ethics responds to the complicated realities that many black women experience by offering concrete tools for embracing sexual agency, pleasure, and healthy relationships. Throughout this text black women are sexual agents who negotiate their sexuality within myriad messages and decisions. This dynamic sheds light on a constructive womanist sexual ethics that encourages sexual intimacy with oneself and responsible intimacy with others. This book provides a means for black women to examine their own sexual values and truths and to give themselves concrete tools to live sexually and morally free.

1 · SEXUAL PURITY AS PR
Tracing the Impact of Religious Media

18 Flee from sexual immorality. All other sins a person commits are outside the body, but whoever sins sexually, sins against their own body. **19** Do you not know that your bodies are temples of the Holy Spirit, who is in you, whom you have received from God? You are not your own; **20** you were bought at a price. Therefore honor God with your bodies. —1 CORINTHIANS 6:18–20 (NIV)

It's OK for a girl who gets pregnant out of wedlock to say "OK, I'm pregnant" and we celebrate the baby. But it's not OK to say "Hey, I'm a virgin. . . ." My story is really to push and encourage others. A lot of people aren't virgins and missed that mark, that doesn't mean God doesn't love them; that doesn't mean that He's going to condemn them. It means they can start a new life, start over and be healed from soul ties, unforgiveness, bitterness, and all that stuff. —BRELYN BOWMAN, "Viral Virgin Brelyn Bowman on Christian Backlash over Virginity Certificate," *Christianity Post*, March 8, 2016

In October 2015 an Instagram photo of a daughter's gift to her father on her wedding day caused quite a stir. Brelyn Freeman-Bowman presented her pastor father with a certificate confirming her virginity, signed by her gynecologist, who verified that her hymen was intact. Brelyn had already signed a commitment contract with her father, promising to abstain from fornication and illegal substances (which included drugs, alcohol, and cigarettes) and to flee from all temptations. Her marriage to a rising gospel music artist, Timothy Bowman Jr., merged two powerful black evangelical families. Yet it was not their union that caused notoriety but her Instagram post offering her father a framed copy of her commitment contract and purity certificate. While some praised her, others found her post an extreme display of purity culture. Undaunted by the negativity, the former singles ministry director wrote a book, *No Ring No Ting*, and she and her husband have an online clothing store to promote celibacy and purity for young evangelicals.[1]

Brelyn's private decision made public is part of a growing purity culture that offers advice and admonitions to singles in Christ. While Brelyn is smiling in the photo presenting the certificate and is seemingly not concerned with those considering her decision patriarchal, one must understand the logic and theological framework of her evangelical world in order to understand her pride in her decision. Her conduct is indicative of evangelical ministries that offer advice to single women regarding their sexuality. Faith-based sexuality ministries are generationally related to preceding evangelical sex manuals. They are part of the growing purity culture that has now gone digital. Yet there are some shared theological tenets or a shared language about God and sex presented in evangelical circles.[2] This chapter provides the theological context of contemporary faith-based sexuality ministries by interrogating the themes of sin, sexual restraint, submission, and holiness. Of particular interest is how definitions of these concepts are gendered with emphasis on evangelical female leaders and participants. Presenting Prophetess Juanita Bynum as a quintessential evangelical leader discussing sexuality, the chapter concludes with an exploration of how Bynum participated in the modern invention of black evangelical sexuality discourses, namely, the singles genre.

Evangelical Sin and Sexual Purity

There is great diversity within American evangelicalism. I am tracking specific black evangelical discussions of sexuality, but these conversations are not exhaustive of the numerous ways evangelicals approach the topic. It is outside the scope of this chapter (and even this text) to fully explore the nuances of white and black evangelicals' theological tenets and those specifically regarding sexuality. Yet the overarching evangelical subculture's emphasis on purity and holiness shares a common language that is gendered in specific ways.

Evangelicals commonly categorize as sexual sin masturbation, premarital sex, adultery, and same-sex desire and acts; however, there are some expansions of this list that are discussed by specific faith-based sexuality ministries.[3] Sin can manifest in a variety of ways that would serve to block the participant from experiencing sexuality as God truly intended. One concept that is universally embraced in evangelical worldviews on sexual sin is that of soul ties. Soul ties are a popular teaching tactic in discussions explaining why premarital sex is outside of God's plan.[4] In evangelical rhetoric lust and attraction to nonmarital partners are soul ties, characteristic of sexual sin; evidence for this is found in 1 Corinthians 6:16–20, which warns believers against uniting with a prostitute or those who dishonors their body and their relationship with God. Evangelicals teach that sexual intercourse with someone other than your marital spouse may feel good, but it intertwines two souls, allowing you to take on the thoughts and will of the other person.[5] Even after the relationship has ended, a sexual connection remains between the two persons that inhibits them from living lives fully controlled by Christ. Only by completely denying these sexual urges and living a life of sexual purity can one sever the soul tie and thus be freed from sexual sin.

Overall, evangelical sexual rhetoric provides Christians with a program of what sexuality should be like if performed as God intended, that is, as marital heterosexual intercourse.[6] While persons are waiting to achieve this goal and even after marriage, this logic extends to living a life devoted to pleasing God in all actions, including sexual activity. Amy DeRogatis describes evangelical purity culture generally as a "lifestyle that requires scrutinizing all one's innermost thoughts and feelings and working tirelessly to guard oneself from any evidence of improper sexual desires or actions." In her extensive study of black and white evangelical sex manuals she observes that one of the goals of the manuals is to reiterate that one is to honor God with one's body and mind. Following this logic, honoring God makes some acts permissible and others impermissible. DeRogatis contends that for evangelicals sexual sins or actions made unlawful by God impact everyone, such that a person's sexual misdeed has individual and communal consequences.[7] This is why evangelical sex is seen as a lifestyle commitment: it is not one lax woman going astray; instead it puts in jeopardy her salvation, the salvation of her future children, and all those looking at the fallen Christian's example.

Sexual purity is generally defined as avoiding sexual intimacy outside of heterosexual marriage, but the meaning behind sexual purity varies based on race. The American religious historian Sarah Moslener views white evangelical purity as not just a response to the sexual revolution of the 1960s but as a way to connect sexual immorality with national insecurity, a declining white middle class, and an impending apocalypse.[8] According to the historian Victoria Wolcott, black sexual purity was largely a response to racialized stereotypes regarding black hypersexuality as well as representative of Christian believers' morality.[9] Within black evangelical spaces there has been greater scrutiny on women's adherence to purity doctrine. Marla Frederick notes that the most "strikingly rigid and influential were Pentecostal expectations for personal purity."[10] Pentecostal piety was based on biblical instructions, which often accepted some gendered restrictions while jettisoning other scriptures. For example, typically women alone bear the sexual stigma of bringing unwed mothers before the church to be publicly chastised and made to repent. Members see this punishment as a means of restoring them to a right relation with the church, and they justify it scripturally by citing James 5:16 and Galatians 6:1. Yet despite this emphasis on scriptural adherence, as in my introductory vignette male offenders are not usually summoned before the church. This gendered dynamic is also present in the accountability expected of female and male clergy. This was especially the case for their participation in the cult of purity demanded by the Church of God in Christ (COGIC), the largest Pentecostal body in America.[11]

Holiness and Sanctification

While on the surface the demand for purity and for chaste dress is an example of the social policing of black women's bodies in churches, the religious historian Anthea Butler suggests that one look deeper at this narrative to see that women called into the sanctified life were not just fulfilling patriarchal expectations in the cult of domesticity and purity but believed they were aligning themselves with the Holy Spirit.[12] Their desire to "live holy" required them to be "in the world, and not of it."[13] This doctrine was best achieved through sanctification of the black female body.

Sanctification is discussed in a variety of evangelical communities. Its meaning is largely taken from the eighteenth-century Englishman John Wesley, who taught that God's grace frees believers from the inclination to sin. The doctrine teaches that a mature Christian is ever striving to live holy to reconcile herself to a God that is completely holy; over time sanctification became a process that a believer goes through to achieve holiness. As described biblically, sanctification is achieved with the help of the Holy Spirit and involves maturing in faith to do God's will in the world.[14] Denominations vary on their interpretation of a person's ability to live out this commitment to holiness, but traditions recognizable to the black women targeted by faith-based sexuality ministries share the concept of the necessity of sanctification and living a pure life for God.[15]

Women who are trained to live a sanctified life are given many prescriptions in behavior and appearance. Since the Holy Spirit was thought to dwell only in pure vessels, those who were inappropriately adorned could not receive this spiritual gift. Purity of dress and behavior indicated a person's capacity to subordinate herself to God's will. This sanctified, complicated female black body was the cause of much discussion because it served as both a representational and a signifying practice. Modest clothing was the means of representation; that is, clothing stood for something much larger than acceptance in white society. It served as a code in a master language of participation in the COGIC community. For example, church mothers and churchwomen strictly enforced these standards so that women who had just converted were encouraged to sew up the splits in their skirts or use modesty cloths (cloths placed across the lap of a woman wearing a skirt deemed to short). Such standard attire deliberately avoided any focus on feminine curves, which were believed to entice men, and thus helped to control the sexual urges of the COGIC community, in addition to preventing women from being vain (and hence less focused on God).

Modesty and Sexual Restraint

Adherents believed that by pure living one could diminish a woman's sexual appeal, thus giving her more credibility as she continued teaching and preaching. COGIC church doctrine encouraged women to avoid the seductive clothing of the "street women" or Jezebels of their day and to be chaste and remember their call to follow God's commandments. In this sense their modified clothing acted as a symbol of sanctification as well as a source of protection.[16] Yet their modest living was not just about refusing European models of beauty and society; it was also about being respectable in the sense of pleasing God, not whites.

Dianna Anderson calls this standard "modesty theology" and argues that it typically makes a woman's body public property—open for public comment and public judgment. She contends that through a misreading of 1 Thessalonians 4:3–7 women are told they must be responsible for their body's effect on men, ultimately making women responsible not just for their body but for everyone else.[17] Self-control is not expected or even encouraged from men. In the language of the purity movement, women are instructed not to be stumbling blocks to men's purity by dressing or acting in ways that can be viewed as sexy. For most evangelicals, the Bible contains all they need to know about sex.[18] Thus following the Bible's instructions on sexual purity is evidence of living a sanctified life. Relying on 1 Corinthians 6:18–20, 1 Thessalonians 4:3–8 and 4: 4, Romans 6:19–22 and 12:1–2, evangelicals argue that believers' bodies are sanctified by restraint so the believer can follow God's will. This message of necessary sexual restraint and purity is especially promoted to women seeking holiness.[19]

Evangelicals and Submission

Women are also largely the only group given messages regarding submission as part of living a sanctified and holy life. In universalizing the notion of submission to include all girls and women, not only wives, submission became a universal sign of sanctification. Young women are to wait for their soon-coming prince while practicing purity; mature women are to continue honoring their commitment to purity by complete submission to God; and married spouses are encouraged to make sacrifices in their marriage by submitting to their husband.[20] This doctrine on submission is an important factor in creating properly ordered evangelical sex. Whether the submission advocated is complementarianism or mutual submission, the end result is a woman who has learned to submit to God and scripture.[21]

One could argue that the submission model is never without negotiation, regardless of the racial demographic. Chapter 3 extends the discussion on submission and how it is regulated within black evangelical faith-based sexuality ministries. However, in R. Marie Griffith's seminal study of the Women's Aglow Fellowship, the largest women's evangelical organization during the 1990s, she describes its doctrine of submission as a strategy that is simultaneously freeing and transformative. Griffith asks readers to trust women's interpretations of what is going on, realizing that the ideology of submission has multiple applications and expressions.[22] Whereas the doctrine of wifely submission was widely discussed in white evangelical manuals, black evangelicals were latecomers to the evangelical sex manuals market. By the time they took on the genre, even the white evangelical view of wifely submission had been modified to something more in line with mutual submission.

Sexual Redemption or Awakening

When looking at the markers of popularized black evangelical sexuality there are numerous benchmarks, some adapted and greatly modified from larger white evangelical discussions of sexuality, such as soul ties, sexual purity, sanctification, holiness, and submission. Yet there is distinctiveness in the creation and mass production of black evangelical sexuality, namely its reliance on sexual awakening or sexual redemption. Frederick defines sexual redemption as the narrative sexual testimony that reveals God's power to heal a person from sexual sin. She highlights the gospel of sexual redemption as applicable to the televangelists Joyce Meyer, Paula White, and Juanita Bynum; however, only Bynum's testimony is built on her acknowledging having a licentious sexuality before God's restoration.[23] Whereas Meyer's and White's testimony includes childhood sexual abuse, which led to poor sexual and marital choices, Bynum's promiscuity identifies her with the historical stereotype of Jezebel, who had a hard life but was not a blameless victim. In Bynum's sextifying, or sexual testifying, she admitted what few others dared to, that as an unmarried Christian woman she missed sexual pleasure.

Kelsy Burke calls this Bynum's sexual awakening story, which is like evangelical salvation stories but follows the narrative of discussing a time of sexual sin that has been overcome by believing in God, who has the power to transform the believer's sexual life.[24] These stories rely on female pleasure as women try to make sense of this pleasure in light of their Christian beliefs. Bynum is key in this discussion for black evangelical singles; however, her testimony is made possible by pioneers in the evangelical sexuality industry like Marabel Morgan. When Morgan first published her Christian sex advice book, *The Total Woman*, she had a defined focus and goal: to teach women to please their husband sexually. However, her book spurred a religious response to the secular sex manuals that were best sellers at the time and that did not advocate sex solely within marriage. It also spawned Total Woman workshops and conferences, which expanded the reach of the resources, specifically the manual. Morgan's fame came from encouraging women to play into their husband's sexual fantasies, but another effect of her workshops was the emphasis on orgasm in marital sex. Arguably Morgan began the successful marketing of evangelical sex manuals (even though most of these primarily catered to married couples). White and black evangelical manuals began to focus on single adults or "born-again virgins" and posited that "evangelical Christians had the best sex."[25] However, this reiteration always referred to sex within marriage and was very focused on pleasing men sexually. To make matters worse, these manuals tend to discuss sexuality as something only for married persons.

Thus Bynum inherited the legacy of white evangelical sex manuals, which she modified for her predominantly black audiences. Her niche is the contemporary result of a convergence of other influences and types of spectacle. Bynum is a hybrid of the effects of African American culture on televangelism. She is the progenitor of the black Christian sexuality category that takes shape after her discourse on singles sexuality begins.

When Bynum entered the scene in the late 1990s, her take on singles sexuality was a welcome change. It was similar to the singles discussions that had been going on in churches, but with a twist: she began by acknowledging her own sexual desire and her daily struggle to remain celibate, something no one else had admitted. Prior to Bynum the Christian singles market focused on spiritual topics like living in God's will, but rarely on bodily needs. To be clear, while she still advocated for sex within marriage, she did not act as if sex was something that should not be thought of until marriage. Thus her ministry opened the doors for numerous others to follow in her footsteps. The next chapter further interrogates Bynum's message and how black women read it.

2 · READING "OUR" BYNUM AS TEXT

For a Black Woman by a Black Woman

I was more concerned for my image, what I would project and what others were going to "read it" to be. —JUANITA BYNUM, *Matters of the Heart*

Never allow people to tell you what they think about you. You tell them what they should think about you. —JUANITA BYNUM, quoted in Kenya Byrd, "Juanita Bynum: I Will Never Allow Anyone to Misrepresent My Name," *Essence.com*, December 2009

The history of Prophetess Juanita Bynum, born in Chicago and reared in the Church of God in Christ, is extremely relevant to her image production. As demonstrated in the epigraphs to this chapter, Bynum has remained conscious of how she is marketed, as even before her marital abuse and scandal in 2007, she was one of the most recognized female televangelists in America. Currently calling herself Bishop Bynum, she has ministered to hundreds of thousands across the globe. Her narrative has much more humble beginnings. In her conflicting autobiography, she describes both being born in the "ghetto" and being reared in a suburban neighborhood in Chicago. After her divorce she was anorexic, and she was an overeater. She was on welfare with nothing to eat and nowhere to turn, and she was surrounded by family and church members who cared for her. She tells of moving east of Detroit with her husband at twenty-two, and relates that by that time her marriage was already over or she fled to Michigan to start anew. However, one detail of Bynum's narrative that has not changed is that in 1981 she married for sex but not whom God wanted for her, and this marriage ultimately unraveled. As a result of the stress of this failed relationship, she led a life of sexual sin, having premarital sex with numerous men. At her New York church home, New Greater Bethel Ministries, she began speaking to small groups of women, and in 1996 she met the televangelist Bishop T. D. Jakes, who invited her to a singles conference where she later preached her infamous "No More Sheets" sermon. Thus her contemporary notoriety could be foretold by examining her past, which requires paying attention to how the prophetess was produced and to what ends she owes her success. While most of her viewing public learned about her from her "No More Sheets" message, the catalyst for contemporary faith-based sexuality ministries that target single black Christian women, there has been little scholarly attention given to her and to the circumstances leading up to her success.

Analyzing the rhetorical content of the "No More Sheets" sermon requires looking at the sermon and the video recording of that sermon and the books that resulted from the sermon. While my book is a form of womanist cultural criticism, this chapter is particularly concerned with unveiling Bynum and interrogating the creation of a black Christian sexual identity focused on black single females. This analysis provides a rationale for the negotiated reading of how black churchwomen utilize her message. Deciphering her sexual messages and scripts reveals that her message is evocative and strict and ultimately unaffirming of the numerous ways black churchwomen assert sexual agency. Yet Bynum's sermon is a shift from itinerant messages to institution building. Thus to understand Bynum's ministry is to understand the empire of faith-based sexuality ministries that succeed her.

Bynum's Biography

The facts in Bynum's biography are provisional at best, but most sources agree that she was born in 1959 in Chicago to Elder Thomas Bynum Sr. and Katherine Bynum. Her family attended St. Luke Church of God in Christ in Chicago. She also attended Saints High, a COGIC boarding school, in Lexington, Mississippi, where she started preaching and graduated second in her class. These facts may be the only consistent and verifiable information in her biography. However, contradictory data should not be quickly dismissed for televangelists are very careful and intentional about crafting their public image, and differing statements can offer insight into their narratives. Bynum remains concerned for her image, so her complicated narrative also teaches her viewers about her interpretation of history and what she chooses to erase or include.[1]

Bynum built her early career telling the story of her failed 1981 marriage. Her No More Sheets singles ministry and her modeling of chastity until marriage culminated in her televised million-dollar wedding to Bishop Thomas Weeks in 2003. She and Weeks extended her singles ministry by launching a relationship ministry called Teach Me How to Love You soon after their wedding. Three years later she and Weeks cofounded Global Destiny Church in Duluth, Georgia. Her marriage to Weeks publicly unraveled in August 2007 after Weeks assaulted her in an Atlanta hotel parking lot, and they divorced the next year. Thanks to her strong personal appeal, she has been on popular radio morning shows, on BET, and even on the nationally syndicated *Good Morning America* speaking of her marital strife. Declaring herself a survivor of domestic abuse, she marketed a new message to black women, namely that God sent her this suffering so that she could lead a new domestic violence ministry. In 2009, to commemorate her fiftieth birthday, she appeared in her wedding gown wielding a large sword and renamed herself Juanita Bynum II to remind people to "make the decision to redefine your self."[2]

Bynum's self-titling reflects her conscious effort to tell people what to think about her as she journeys from Prophetess to Doctor to Ambassador and most recently to Bishop Bynum. While it is not atypical for a woman from the Church of God in Christ to be without ordination and titles provided by ecclesial hierarchy, Bynum's ministry has been successful without this sanctioning because of her ability to name herself and have this name certified by others. Her honorary doctorate in theology comes from an equally noncredentialed male pastor; in fact none of her credentialing is from traditional sources. This reflects a growing trend in televangelism of enhancing titles to secure prominence and establish authority.[3] Bynum seems to prefer to publish as Dr. Juanita Bynum, but in her marketing materials she is Bishop-elect Bynum of the Global United Fellowship. While there was much fanfare regarding the title "prophetess," she now changes titles without a detailed explanation. She tends to use the title she feels is appropriate for her audience.[4] As a result her image as Prophetess Bynum is a relic of past testimony. By providing a thick description of her testimonial sermon "No More Sheets" this chapter reflects on the cultural impact Bynum had on the larger genre of faith-based sexuality ministries that target black Christian women.

A Womanist Cultural Analysis of Juanita Bynum

The cultural theorist John Fiske hypothesized that cultural studies' development showed two distinct methodological strategies, one derived from ethnography and the other from structuralist textual analysis.[5] The ethnographic method encouraged the study of meanings that the audience created by listening to them, reading with them, and observing them. For my project, this would involve conversations with black churchwomen about Bynum, singles ministries, and sexuality, a clearly womanist process. Yet Fiske rightfully acknowledges that this method alone is not enough. He partners ethnography with close readings of the text itself, acknowledging that every text allows for polysemic readings, ranging from discussions on the structure of the text to its connection to the audience. This step suggests that when looking at Bynum and subsequent faith-based sexuality ministries, we realize that meanings lie not just in the prophetess but also in the ideologies that made her appealing. Combining these two methods and disciplines provides both the requisite ethnography and semiotic analysis. Most important, a womanist cultural analysis does the work of analysis without jettisoning these women's articulated spirituality. This method allows room for rigorous religious and cultural criticism while simultaneously highlighting these women's faith experiences as sources of moral agency. I begin this process by deconstructing Bynum's participation and her reception in the larger televangelism world.

The Spectacle of Religious Broadcasting

Black religious broadcasting dates back to the 1920s, but COGIC members did not begin embracing these radio broadcasts until the 1940s.[6] Some of the more popular radio evangelists and audiences were leaders of Holiness or Pentecostal churches, which appealed to both white and black audiences. This interest in and demand for radio personalities are cultural shifts away from participation in a local church and even a larger denomination to being part of a national Christianity.

FIGURE 2.1. Juanita Bynum preaching "No More Sheets" sermon. Source: Screen capture from Bynum, *No More Sheets* DVD.

Religious broadcasting is "religious activity produced and viewed by people who share common symbols, values, and a 'moral culture' they celebrate" and includes televangelism, which was and is dominated by white culture.[7] Popular televangelists tended to reflect Pentecostal worship because the glitzy spectacles they produced of people praying, speaking in tongues, and healing the sick made for more riveting television than Protestant worship services. Thus, a successful televangelism ministry required that black evangelists had to be both media-savvy to market themselves and their messages, and project a certain charisma. The charisma turned out to be particularly important. The historian Gregor Goethals writes that the "charisma of the preacher is critical to effecting a change of heart"; "his 'presence' and words seem as 'real'—perhaps more real—to the viewer at home than to the person in the pew."[8] Through her performance the televangelist is able to lead listeners away from their problems to an arena that she is preparing. In this sense words possess a dominant reading encoded by the preacher to participate in her larger goal: selling the spectacle of her ministry.

This spectacle culminated in Prophetess Bynum's recorded sermon "No More Sheets." Although frank discussions on sex and self-respect were standard in her sermons, this one preached for Bishop Jakes's singles conference in 1997 catapulted her to a new status as an expert in the field. The conference was held in a packed Dallas Convention Center; attendance estimates range from 17,000 to 36,000.[9] A visual scan of the massive crowd gives credence to Jakes's power to draw an audience across generations, races, and income classes. The crowd is overwhelmingly female and predominantly black, although the cameras tend to focus on the whites, Hispanics, Latinos, and men.

When Bynum appears on the stage, she brings a Bible and a binder to the podium, although she rarely opens either. Instead, to focus their attention, she directs the audience to be seated and instructs them that she has an awesome task and responsibility to make sure that "there is no flesh" presented to them, just the words of God.[10] Her attire also reflects this desire to remove from the audience the sight of her flesh. We, the spectators, look with the camera, which looks at Bynum, who looks at her audience. Thus there is an innate interest in what Bynum looks like, what she says, and ultimately what she is perceived to be doing. In this instance of analyzing her appearance, one must remember that meaning goes beyond the visual. As partially shown in figure 2.1 she is dressed in a pink suit with a long skirt and a loose top covering her hips, buttocks, and thighs. She is completely covered from her head to her ankles; she even wears a white scarf to cover her neck. She goes to great lengths to draw as little attention to her body as she can. However, her clothing serves as more than just rhetorical support or tactical function for her sermon. It also reflects her COGIC background as well as proper pulpit etiquette for women speakers at that time.

For example, when Bynum expounds on her clothing in *No More Sheets: The Truth about Sex*, the book-length version of the sermon, she writes that women "dress to attract the attention of a man, so he has to see an appearance of where we're going," not where we have been.[11] In this sense clothing should model your new relationship with God. It should provide evidence of your sanctification, as was expected of women in COGIC years before. As Bynum said in an interview years after the sermon, during that time the "Lord wouldn't permit me to wear makeup and pants . . . because my Spirit wasn't ready to look like that. I wasn't to be trusted to know that if I were to look like that and I were to be approached by a man and I wasn't married, would I have the strength not to fail God."[12] Thus her clothes serve as double signs, constructing meaning and carrying particular messages. She wants the audience to perceive her as a representative of holiness, which her modest attire attests. These assumptions and messages are carried out through an even larger sign system: her body.

On first examination, Bynum's desire to "kill the flesh" is also a desire to disguise her feminine form.[13] Yet her refusal to accentuate it does not remove her body from sight. In fact although she makes proclamations about the dangers of the body, she uses her whole body in preaching. From the start of the sermon until its close, she waves her arms, touches her body, walks around, and bends over to emphasize her points. Her testimony ends in retrieving her misused, sexualized body; even as she preaches to redeem it, she remains tied to the wounds inflicted on it. This is to be expected; as the womanist scholar Linda Thomas argues, what the mind forgets, the body remembers.[14] Bynum has a body in motion despite her desire to project an absent body.

Deciphering the codes inscribed on Bynum's body is a task of great import because this conflicted body serves as a model for many black women.[15] When she wraps three bed sheets around her body, they create a form-fitting costume that eroticizes and enlarges the shape of her buttocks. She enacts a modern-day Hottentot Venus as she parades around the stage wearing the sheets, which symbolize her baggage. Draped in the sheets, Bynum moves her body in exaggerated motions across the stage. When she begins removing the sheets, it is in a manner reminiscent of a striptease that the entire audience gets to participate in. This is further magnified when she closes the sermon by running through the auditorium waving a sheet as a flag. Her sanctified body bounces before the Lord. Yet this same body urges restraint, modest attire, and both physical and spiritual covering, which present the audience with multiple meanings.

Bynum's Testimony

The success of her sermon is also the result of the compelling language she uses, which is an equal component in creating a desired effect among the audience. Bynum uses a trope of honesty to direct her message. She believes God has called her to be vulnerable and naked before the audience so that they may be set free from whatever struggles they are experiencing.

She also uses straightforward, plain speech that speaks directly to her audience, who are starved for this type of communication. Her message has a "sister friend" feel as she weeps at the camera, suggesting that she is merely telling you something for your own good, as opposed to giving you a mandate on celibacy. Bynum preaches that if you've been a virgin, she's been there; if you've been divorced, she's been there; if you have nonmarital sex, she's done that too. She reiterates to the crowd that she has been where they all are. This is one of the key characteristics of televangelism: as the cultural critic Quentin Schultze explains, the televangelist must appear to tell the truth, all the while hiding the real truth, which is that he or she has no relationship with the viewer.[16] Yet Bynum is able to be so effective because she presents her testimony to the audience packaged in a language that is easy to relate to and similar to many of their own stories.

Her sexual redemption narrative is peppered with sexualized verbs, a mechanism that perhaps diffuses the tension of discussing the pleasures of sex in a religious setting. For instance, she begins the sermon by "mounting" the stage, vulnerably telling her story so that God can use her narrative to bless or encourage others. She then questions why God would "do" her like that, that is, expose her sexual nakedness before such a vast audience. She concludes that the audience is to treat God as their man, and they must vow not to go home to this man dirty. In her attempt to be "real" with the women gathered, her language goads them to become sexually aware.[17]

This awareness sets the scene for her discussion about the pleasures of sex and how she longs for sexual intimacy even though she is single. She repeatedly tells the audience not to marry for sheets, that is, just to have sex. Although she does reminisce with the audience about the pleasures of sexual touch, noting that if church leaders "indulge in back-rubs from their mate, they can't fathom my longing to be touched," her framework for understanding sexuality is spiritualized.[18] For her, sex is ordained only by marriage, but she advocates that women (especially) must realize that marriage is not just sex. Marriage is a ministry. In a long section of the sermon, she tells those cheering her on that if they are not prepared to minister to a man of God, then they should leave him alone.[19] Bynum chastises women who claim they want to be married (ultimately so they can return to having good sex) but who do not want to be a helper to their mate. In her traditional view women are not suitable spouses until they can cook, clean, and perform a long list of tasks that minister to their husband. They are also unsuitable mates if they are in debt or seeking a man to get them off welfare or to buy them things. Instead Bynum encourages them to "buy [their] own furniture, flowers, TV, VCR, and car" so they can decide for themselves if a man is marriage material or just able to provide for them materially.[20]

Encoded Messages

While delivering these statements, Bynum looks seriously at the camera, Jakes, and the audience. Her cadence changes, as does her vocal pitch. These changes are dramatized because she wants the audience to buy into the concept of marriage as a necessity. This is the first step to accepting her dominant messages of marrying and achieving the middle-class American dream. Marriage is seen for many, including Bynum, as a means of social uplift. Marriage is supposed to guarantee financial mobility so that those like her, who are living in poverty, can marry and ultimately have wealth and prosperity. This notion is intertwined with her capitalistic principles that underline the "No More Sheets" sermon and much of her later ministry.

Schultze rightly connects the emergence of televangelism in America to the capitalistic yearnings of the American dream. Televangelists tailored their messages to the audience as efficiently as advertisers, creating an American religion with the imprint of the capitalist ideology of the country. This perfect adaptation results in messages like "No More Sheets," which reach a niche audience and have an easily acceptable model. Even the way her message is marketed follows the capitalist model, as her sermon is produced, distributed, and then reproduced for future audiences. Yet there is more here than televangelists preaching purely what they think audiences want to hear.

The encoded message also has to support the televangelist's goals. Bynum began evangelizing as a teenager with a series entitled "Lessons in Submission," and this message carried over to her sermon during Jakes's conference. After she married, she preached a sermon based on Proverbs 31 entitled "Giving Sex but Not Romance," in which she encouraged women to serve and service their men, "making them feel like a wonder, when you know he ain't!"[21] She later expanded her lessons on submission, as it was not enough for her to teach women to be submissive to their husbands; she also wanted to teach them to submit to their spiritual authorities, and this allowed Bynum to produce (and sell) more materials.

These notions are embodied in her sermons just as much as her messages of heteronormativity and sexual purity, but they must be reproduced. She has to constantly reiterate these messages so that she continues to be of interest to consumers. Thus a sermon such as "No More Sheets" is more than words and performance. Sermons are texts; even Bynum is a text because she is offering a message, even if it is a polysemous one.

Bynum as Text

Fiske considers the three levels of texts in his criticism: the primary text that is produced by or for the culture fully encoded with the dominant ideology; the secondary or sublevel of text that is also produced by or for the culture but represents different parts than the dominant ideology; and the third level that explains the texts that viewers produce themselves.[22] Analysis at the primary level defines Prophetess Bynum in terms of the capitalistic influences of American televangelism. She can also be read through the lens of Neo-Pentecostalism and gender, although her dominant message refers to fulfilling the goals of capitalism, which she promotes through marriage. At the secondary level one sees the various marketing forces that reinforce the image of Prophetess Bynum. These include Jakes's marketing of her sermon and the television producers on the various networks on which her presentations are aired. This work and that of others who critique Bynum's ministry are also part of her secondary meaning; she *is* because we are interested. Analysis at the third level of textuality reveals her revamped image as she responds to audience members who are unable to dress as holy or act as holy as she demands. Much as the cultural shift in COGIC women's dress in the 1950s was a response to the changing cultural climate, Bynum's new image is partly created by her viewers. She has gone from matronly modest to girlishly glamorous. Her short hair is gone, replaced by a long hair weave, makeup, and glittering jewelry. Bynum stated that when she realized there were "younger women who were being blessed by the ministry" she decided to convey the image that you do not have to dress "so religious" to follow God.[23]

When interrogating this particular text it is useful to look at omissions in her performance as well. For instance, men are largely absent from the audience for "No More Sheets," so that it seems she is directing the entire message to women. However, men are prominently positioned in her discourse, for example, in how to get a man and how to keep a man. Although chapter 12 in her *No More Sheets* book is entitled "The Other Side of the Gender," it is clear that her target audience is female and her messages are better received by women. Even in this framing, men are still the objects of discourse in a sermon that is supposedly about setting women free.

Although men are largely absent in her audience, Bynum does not lack male acceptance or mentorship. She spends a great deal of the "No More Sheets" sermon preaching directly to Bishop Jakes, and she openly admits in interviews that she is without female spiritual mentors. It should not be surprising, then, that her preaching style and ministries follow more traditionally male models. She always acknowledges the guidance of Pastors Terrell Nichols and John Boyd, who provided her with her first opportunities for leadership, alongside Bishop Jakes and Pastor John Hagee for providing her with national exposure. None of these men claims ties to a particular denomination or credentialing body. This is sadly representative of many in the televangelist world. Schultze points out that televangelists now possess technology, so they need "no degree, no denominational credentials, no years of waiting, and [only a] small amount of training."[24]

Paying attention to what is missing in her narrative is helpful because if, as Bynum says, "one of the most powerful tools that anybody can use is his testimony," then this testimony needs to be completely analyzed.[25] Womanists have lauded the importance of black women telling their stories, but these stories must be available for critique in order to be useful. This is especially the case given how often Bynum's message was reproduced. After giving the sermon she wrote the book and a journal devotional accessory and then led several conferences under the same name. Her ability to market herself as a spiritual leader for women brought her fame and wealth. In fact it placed her squarely within the ranks of other televangelists.

"Our" Bynum: For a Woman, by a Woman

The ethicist Jonathan Walton reads black male televangelists as part of the dominant televangelism culture while also retaining remnants of black religiosity. He portrays these televangelists as "both uniquely 'ours' and 'theirs.'"[26] Bynum can be read through the same lens. She has emulated the best of capitalist televangelism (perfected by white televangelists), and she portrays the sensibilities of black religiosity. However, she must also be read through the lens of her gender, making her part upholder of dominant ideology, part expounder of black religion, and part black female. This is an important distinction because although she is usually read as emulating Bishop Jakes or imitating the stage presence of the televangelist Kathryn Kuhlman, there is something uniquely "ours," something unique to black femaleness, in Bynum's rhetoric and movements.

During my focus group interview with "Natasha" she remarked that part of what drew her to Bynum was that she knew Bynum's message was for her community specifically. She read Bynum's rhetoric as very black church, which for her meant black Christian women. Even Bynum's black female body cues black women who face the legacy of denigrated black female forms. These women choose to forgo the pains felt in their physical body to embrace the joys present in the spirit. Thus black women embrace Bynum's call for holy living because it indicates that the Holy Spirit can overcome the body, giving women the authority to flee temptation. Bynum's being a black female minister often tests this recognition of authority, but if she can succeed, her audience can as well. Ultimately she has an outsider-insider relationship with her audience, which allows her to say and do things that are not possible with other televangelists. For example, when Bynum addresses issues related to women, she can critique women in a way that would be uncomfortable if the message came from a man. She can tell them to get themselves together and be convincing rather than condescending because she is one of them. In this light, being a black female televangelist connects her to audiences and holds her accountable to those audiences in ways that others are not required to be.

This sense of connection has led Bynum to attest that her story is representative of all black women's stories. Yet this representation must be interrogated because even though she looks like other black women, this does not allow her to speak for them without being challenged. She has helped institute a black Christian sexuality that hails black churchwomen particularly, but this representation comes at a price because it is intertwined with the spectacle of televangelism. Her participation in televangelism initiates her into spectacle because she is usually seen before she is heard. Thus her black female body must be dealt with. She is of interest potentially because of these factors, but those who participate in such spectacle run the risk of being only publicity dupes who are used by the same media that makes them of interest. In these cases the representative story loses its ability to advocate for the masses of black culture because they are just figureheads for the media. For Bynum, this means she loses her ability to offer redemption for black women because she is tied to the capitalist market interests that push her to preach messages that connect to the masses' purses, and not just her passions.

Reproducing the Spectacle

Thus the very thing that makes Bynum uniquely "ours" is also the trait that makes her more marketable and hence corruptible. In the first chapter of *No More Sheets* she writes that after she preached the sermon, pastors, friends, and colleagues insisted that she write the book version because she would be handsomely paid for it.[27] She denounces this saying that she is not about the market but about following a God-given mandate. It is interesting to read her publicized view given the fact that shortly after the book sold hundreds of thousands of copies, she followed the market's interest in her topic and presentation. For instance, an interviewer noted that when Bynum preached "No More Sheets," she tapped into two of the hottest topics for black women—God and sex—and in return women bought over a million copies of her video.[28] Her mandate and market were quite profitable, and she began spinning her notoriety into more money. At first she used her fame to publish other books unrelated to the topic of her famous sermon; when these were not as successful, she returned to the message that had brought her crowds and began preaching at women's conferences and singles conferences across the country, advocating that women leave their premarital and extramarital sexual relationships. She ended up in a legal quarrel with Bishop Jakes over royalties, and Jakes reportedly responded by blacklisting her from preaching venues.[29] Prevented from preaching in large venues and conferences, Bynum eventually apologized to Jakes so that she could be restored to her prior glory. Even this apology was spiritually strategic as she publicly apologized on her knees to Jakes saying that God had blocked her opportunities to preach to rid her of her pride and that she was returning as a prodigal daughter to be rebuked for not following Jakes's spiritual authority.[30]

Before this public restoration, Jakes's blacklisting had forced Bynum to reinvent herself again and take her expanded message to other markets, namely white churches. This was the beginning of the mogulization of Bynum. Exposed to the wide world of televangelism, she stripped her sermons of the remnants of black religiosity, evidenced in her black vernacular and use of call-and-response, relying instead on her femininity and "spiritual" preaching to draw crowds. This was a highly successful move, making her message of sexual purity marketable to all races. She was able to reach much larger audiences while at the same time giving a diverse yet dominant message. This allowed her to become an industry.

The theologian Priscilla Pope-Levinson's work on women evangelists in the Progressive Era comments on how female evangelists shifted from merely preaching the good news to building institutions to teach others how to preach the good news.[31] Their institutions changed the landscape of American religion during that period. Likewise Bynum's popularity centered on sexuality and faith and changed the landscape for female evangelists, allowing them to be more open about their own sexual histories. Her candid sermon heralding a black Christian sexuality that was unashamed, offered grace for black women in similar situations.

Admiration for her empire building does not equate to lack of criticism of Bynum's ministry. She preaches that women should obey scripture completely, submitting to the teachings of the church and male leadership while they wait on *God's man* to arrive in God's time. In Bynum's teachings, God grants husbands only to women who have purified themselves, a process that includes reclaiming a traditional understanding of femininity.[32] Bynum instructs women to prepare to be men's helpmeet, referring to the Genesis description of Eve as Adam's helper. In her traditional view, women are not suitable spouses until they can fulfill domestic responsibilities. This is problematic because the types of relationships Bynum is encouraging women to seek are based not in equality but in complementarity.

Additionally problematic is the sermon's connection of one's purpose in God to one's finding a heterosexual partner. This reaffirms heteronormativity by privileging heterosexual marriage as a divine good. By her own admission she endured abuse from the man God had prepared for her because she was obedient, yet her messages have resulted in physical and emotional ramifications on her body as well as on her worldwide audiences.

Bynum can also be criticized for not repudiating the double standard that punishes women for being sexually active while overlooking male sexual activity. Marla Frederick notes that Bynum's phenomenal rise can be linked to her ability to share her struggles with sexual indulgence, which accounts for her missing the mark of purity, thus validating this mark as legitimate.[33] Male ministers seldom hold themselves to the same mark, so the restrictive nature of purity culture remains unchallenged. Expecting women to remain sexually pure makes Bynum's rhetoric popular and opens up space for contemporary ministries to reproduce the same message.

Though Bynum eventually expanded her marketing and production opportunities, she never ventured far from her legacy of "No More Sheets." Her contemporary endeavors include her music label Flow Records, a book-publishing house, and a live web stream called JBTV. These industries bring in lots of revenue; Bynum's sophomore CD, *A Piece of My Passion*, went gold in fifty-nine days, and her books *The Threshing Floor* and *Matters of the Heart* were *New York Times* best sellers, the latter selling over 600,000 copies.[34] Thanks to her growing popularity, she now convenes her own megaconferences, focusing on prayer, empowerment, and living your best life, topics distant from the controversial sermons on singles sexuality. While these recent ventures have left the genre for which she first became notorious, she always acknowledges where she got her start, uncovering sheets for millions of women.[35]

Bynum's Consumers

Despite Bynum's flawed ministry and perhaps flawed character, she can claim fame for proliferating a genre of faith-based sexuality ministries that target single black Christian women. Bynum speaks to a new generation of unmarried Christians boldly discussing sexuality outside the confines of marriage. This was appropriate for her time. The cultural milieu for black women during the late 1990s was one of perpetual singleness. This lament inspired Terry McMillan's *Waiting to Exhale*, Pearl Cleage's *What Seems Like Crazy on an Ordinary Day*, and dozens of articles in *Ebony* and *Essence* that reiterated the dire statistic that nearly a fifth of all black women in the late 1990s had never been married.[36] Bynum's context rehearsed the mantra "All the good men are taken" and that black women were too independent for marriage. Thus when she preached about her struggles with singleness in a room full of black women, she was sure to have a large number of listeners whose life experiences would resonate with her message. And when she said she was telling "our" story, some women trusted that she had found a solution. Bynum problematically reiterated that black women are "needy" and not yet ready for marriage, which is why their relationships are purely sexual.[37] However, she did not leave them hopeless: the first step to redemption was to commit to having "no more sheets."

These women bought into her solution because they shared her problem, a history of being considered sexually loose. But Bynum offered them a way to be freed from sexual sin! Those who accepted Bynum's solution were offered redemption, and those who rejected the message were doomed to remain in sexual sin. The number of women running through the aisles during the "No More Sheets" sermon, shouting and crying, seems to indicate that Bynum had many converts.

I interviewed one such convert, who reported on the allure of Bynum for audience members. "Biansay" responded that during the heyday of "No More Sheets" she found Bynum's ministry "necessary and powerful." Biansay is a thirty-three-year-old single, heterosexual, middle-class black woman with graduate degrees, who recalled owning copies of the video and the book because "for years what Juanita Bynum said to me was gospel and I tried to follow it to the letter of the law. And when she got married, I was like 'This could really work. You too can get a husband if you do all these things correctly.' I felt like when I didn't know any better she was the hallmark of what effective ministry was." Another interviewee shared this opinion. Natasha, a thirty-four-year-old single, heterosexual, middle-class black woman with a graduate degree recounted Bynum's popularity as the "gospel of the time for single, celibate women." Key to Bynum's attraction for Natasha, Biansay, and other interviewees was that her message of controlling their sexuality was reiterated in their church homes. While the message is not new, the freedom to talk about their struggles achieving this goal was indeed new and appealing.

These converts are instrumental in gaining Bynum other converts as they take the message back to their communities. Bynum is able to sell over a million copies of the video because these women believe they received something worth spending their money on. In this sense Bynum is successful on two levels because she is able to connect with her immediate audience in such a way that they become her advertisers for a larger audience. As a result of their perceived solidarity with Bynum, they are able to share in her solution as they take this message to others. They transform from being ashamed and ignored singles to being empowered and committed singles. Although all Bynum offers them are steps to celibacy, as a group they grow to being saved and satisfied.

Negotiated Cultural Readers

This solidarity does not indicate passive acceptance of everything that Bynum has preached or of the foundational tenets of a black Christian sexuality. On the contrary, viewers rarely accept everything that a televangelist says or portray all of the characteristics of an identity group. Instead they pick and choose, just as they typically pick and choose what to follow from the Bible. In the case of televangelism, viewers "bring their own perceptions and understandings of conservative Christianity to their viewing," as they make their "own independent judgments about what is presented, evaluating the message in light of their own faith or opinions."[38] This selectivity is known in cultural studies as *performing a negotiated reading.*

Some of Bynum's supporters are negotiated readers because they accept the dominant ideology but must make it work for their particular social location. This adaptation may include resistance to certain tropes from the dominant group, but it does not question that group's ultimate dominance. Bynum's viewers may reject some of her message, but they do not question her pursuit of marriage as an ultimate end. In her discussions of sexuality, they accept the dominance of heterosexuality, gender norms within traditional marriage, and marriage as a means to achieve the American dream. Several of my interviewees had been married and divorced multiple times, yet they still pursued marriage as a goal. "Diavante," a fifty-four-year-old member of my Chatham Baptist church, said, "I've been married three times, and I love the institution of marriage. I'm not rationalizing anything. I didn't really listen to people who were telling me things or warning signs. I just wanted to be married." Equally telling were the occasions of negotiation within marriages, as interviewees shared stories of fighting for their marriages through significant circumstances. Josephine, a forty-year-old attendee of a local Baptist congregation, expressed her frustration at having been the "good girl" who happened to marry a man who did not like to have sexual intercourse. Expressing her frustration she exclaimed, "This is some bullshit! I waited and I did what my momma said . . . and I marry him and I ain't getting nothing. . . . I wasn't going to embarrass my husband. I stayed faithful. I just masturbated a whole lot." The decision to masturbate instead of divorcing her sexually incompatible spouse is one such negotiation that is expected from someone who has been taught to place supreme value in traditional marriage.

As a middle-class divorcée with a graduate degree and a child, Josephine was also an example of negotiations of faith and sexuality because she was one of a few participants who expressed a fluid sexual identity. She described herself as "hetero-bi-curious," her views reflecting an equally diverse understanding of the Divine and sexuality. For her, sexuality was valuable and sacred, but there is a catch:"[When we] get to this ecstatic experience in sexuality we take God and say 'Oh No! this is nasty and dirty and we're not supposed to be doing it.' We take the value and ecstasy from that unless you're married or in a certain spiritual type of relationship." Josephine was familiar with Bynum's teachings and the church's religious message that sex is ordained only in marriage, but she readily admitted that she likes having sex and talking about sex even outside of those set parameters. She said it took a process of learning to value her body as sacred because she had experienced sexual abuse at a young age, which distorted how she views and appreciates men. Despite this distortion, she works hard to reorient her values by meditating and attending therapy with a Christian pastoral counselor.

"Heroshema" was another divorcée and a member of the Nashville focus group whose negotiations of faith and sexuality often countered her reality. She believed that sexuality was sacred only if "established under the spiritualness and oneness of God's command," despite admitting sexual contact outside of this rubric. Heroshema is a heterosexual mother of one who attended the local Baptist congregation for most of her life. As a thirty-seven-year-old, middle-class black woman with a graduate degree, she admitted that her previous marriage was not a spiritual marriage. She denied that sexuality in its physical form is sacred; instead she posited that allowing our carnal flesh to enjoy and feel connected to others is just another example of Satan's influence in our lives. Heroshema talked with the group about her previous sexual choices; at one time she always said yes to sex and was sexually available even if the person or relationship was not God's best for her, but now she is saying no to sex without the right relationship. She thought that churches should teach children and adults that just because we enjoy sex does not mean it comes from the spirit of God. In her framing, sexuality has a proper God-ordained order, and choosing to live outside of that has consequences. Although her rhetoric maps perfectly onto the logic of Bynum and other faith-based sexuality ministries, even with this adherence to religious restrictions she still acknowledged the need to have conversations with youth and adults because she did not presume everyone would follow the "right way."

Negotiations also include managing others' interpretations of singleness and faith. For example, "Kelli" is a middle-class, heterosexual, thirty-two-year-old mother of one who attends singles conferences and purchases various books and CDs to bolster her Christian walk. She was actively celibate and discussed her negotiations with various men around her celibacy. She told the group she found dating difficult because she was abstinent and would share that up front with her potential partner. She did not want to "lead anyone on," so she did not flirt or act in ways that would make her seem available for sexual activity. In one relationship with a man in whom she was interested, they ultimately chose to break up because she was explicit about being sexually unavailable without a marriage commitment. They could not navigate her abstinence in the relationship, so they chose not to have a relationship. She attends a singles Sunday school class in her nondenominational church that emphasizes being whole in her relationship with God whether or not she ever marries, but she admits that she enjoyed her singleness more before she began practicing celibacy. At age thirty-two she feels pressure from her family and society in general to be in a relationship, but she has not been able to find a way to be in a relationship that respects her commitment to abstinence. She told the focus group that after she cut her hair her grandmother told her that a man wouldn't want her now that her hair was short. She commented on how much societal value is placed on being in a relationship, and especially that "people put so much pressure on single women, and that's a difference between single men and women." She believes men are not pressured in the same way as women. Despite the pressures, she stated that she was "okay" where she is as a single person and that if she gets married "that's awesome," but "if that's not what God has for me, then that's okay."

Biansay responded vehemently to hearing her colleague being "okay" with being single, as this is one of her many negotiations with her faith and sexuality. She rejects the notion of singleness as a normative value to which God is calling her for this season of her life. In fact she told the group, "I'm over being single." She enjoys dating but also has a desire for a relationship, one that is "committed, substantive, long-standing." She boldly announced that, at thirty-three, she was not ready to say that if she didn't get married she would be okay with that. In a reflective and communal moment she added, "This is not to say that the other women may [not] feel that way, but I also think that the church teaches us that 'I'm okay with singleness' is supposed to be our response." Even those ready to reject many of the church's restrictions and engage in premarital sex interpret these sexual relationships as a poor substitute for the marital, committed bliss promised to them.

While all of these negotiations seem to collude with Bynum's logic of marriage as a worthy pursuit, many black churchwomen do not passively accept all Bynum's views. Instead they make their own meanings by rejecting her earlier ascetic appearance and her exorbitant pleas for money. Some even reject her logic of submission or negotiate it in specific ways. "Ms. Joyce," a sixty-nine-year-old Baptist churchgoer, shared with me how for years she couldn't even read the passage on submission without getting upset, but she had learned to read the passage and understand it as meaning that the husband and wife mutually submit to each other. These negotiations can be experienced in singleness or in marriage, but they often share the same text or sexual message of sexual restraint provided by Bynum and her successors.

Womanist Cultural Readers

Learning to interpret cultural readers is a task that benefits from both womanist and cultural studies. Womanist ethnography insists that black women must be taken seriously as cultural readers and that their attempts to navigate their own meanings are to be commended and upheld. Black women reading Bynum are wrestling with the diverging messages provided; they accept her emphasis on marriage because it resonates with their desires, while they simultaneously resist certain expectations she enumerates. Bynum's model has little space for such loopholes; she affirms only one type of sexual agency. A womanist analysis reveals women who recognize that Bynum and their own church call for complete celibacy before marriage but who themselves exercise a type of restraint that allows for exceptions.

This circumvention of sexual regulation is an example of how women find meaning not just in Bynum but also in the context of forming a black Christian sexuality. Bynum's viewers do not take her message without reflection. These women wrestle with her advice and struggle with their competing religious frames of reference: a church that advocates only abstinence but does not tell them what to do with their sexual urges, and

Bynum, who advocates abstinence but offers repentance if they fall into sexual sin. It is not as simple as Bynum telling them what to do; instead they struggle and negotiate with her as text.

Unfortunately this struggle is one that women face alone because they leave Bynum's conferences or turn off her video and on their own must choose to act in their own best interests. Bynum's open discussion breaks the silence, but still she offers only celibacy as a long-term solution for handling their sexual frustrations. While celibacy is a valid option for black women, it is not the only option. Rather than dealing just with the pain of unfulfilled sexual urges, Bynum and other televangelists must also deal with the emotional shame of those who succumb to their urges. While Bynum admits her own "slide into the sheets" after choosing celibacy, she offers the mantra "No more sheets" as a means of recalibrating one's life. Those for whom the shame leads to unhealthy sexual decisions need more than a mantra. However, it is not only televangelists but also Christian ethicists who are implicated in this failure, for both groups are engaged in public religion, and both share responsibility and accountability. It is not enough just to reject what does not work when messages are being sent that restrict one's sexual health.

This chapter has set the scene for demanding a new sexual ethics so that black women cultural readers can find a healthier sexual message. Bynum's popularity demonstrates that her audiences are as likely as secular black women (if not more likely) to follow her advice about their sexual frustrations, but the work of ferreting out what is beneficial from Bynum should not be left for them to do alone when womanists and cultural critics can be of assistance. The next chapter examines the empire Bynum built by interrogating several faith-based sexuality ministries that promise black churchwomen responsibility and accountability.

3 · BEYOND BYNUM
Analyzing Contemporary Faith-Based Sexuality Ministries

Add your church not supporting you as a single and treating you like a second class citizen while the married people are ministered to and celebrated and it's enough to make the average person feel pretty naked, vulnerable, and overlooked. —MICHELLE MCKINNEY HAMMOND, "Life as a Family of One," *Gospel Today*, May/June 2006

Celibacy should be infused with the deep spirituality, not the façade, of the religion you may claim. —DONNA MARIE WILLIAMS, *Sensual Celibacy*

Ruth patiently waited for her mate Boaz. While you are waiting on your Boaz, don't settle for any of his relatives: Broke-az, Po-az, Lyin-az, Cheating-az, Dumb-az, Drunk-az, Cheap-az, Lockedup-az, Goodfornothing-az, Lazy-az, and especially his third cousin Beatinyo-az. . . . Wait on your Boaz and make sure he respects Yo-az. —PASTOR JENTZEN FRANKLIN, *The Boaz Family Tree*

A recurring message to single black Christian women is that they are single because God is still preparing them for their spouse. In this logic God is also preparing their Boaz,[1] and the celestial matchmaker will join this properly prepared couple. I heard references to Boaz in almost every singles event I attended, and the quote from Pastor Franklin circulated in all of the groups I participated in, along with the accompanying video. There was a simple recipe for success" celibacy in singleness yields a God-fearing husband in God's own time. Also being conveyed to the masses of single black Christian women hearing and trying to adhere to this message was that they needed to be prepared and that some seasons of preparation last longer than others.

For example, at the national conferences of the Pinky Promise group the founder, Heather Lindsey, and her husband admonished the single women gathered that they not use the group as a social club but as a means of seeking out their purpose in the Lord. During the 2015 national conference Lindsey preached that single women are to prepare for their final marriage in heaven to their heavenly husband. This preparation requires women to pursue God fully, to suffer no distraction from the calling to win souls for Christ. The founder reminded the audience that Pinky Promise was about obedience to God; rather than using the group to commiserate about being single they should use it as a catalyst to change the world for Christ. The message was that kingdom building makes one too busy to stress over being single. The women were constantly reminded that the time was nigh to win lost souls for Christ, to encourage people to have a personal relationship with Jesus. They were encouraged to start with the women who were lost right there in the city of Atlanta.

At the close of that conference I exited the hotel lobby and returned to my car, which was parked across from one of Atlanta gentlemen's clubs.[2] I was surprised to see a small delegation of twenty or so women from the conference gather around the entryway to the gentlemen's club and begin to pray. The command to win souls for Christ motivated some women to take immediate action out of respect for the presumed purpose of their singleness. While I paid for my parking I observed women preventing dancers from entering the establishment by offering to pray for their release from sin's bondage. In an almost surreal exchange the dancers ignored the women's offers of prayer and the bouncer eventually asked the women to move their protest to the public sidewalk and off the private property of the establishment.

While trying to make sense of what had just occurred I was confronted with the ethical decisions that single black Christian women make when navigating their singleness and faith. They can respond in frustration to their single status, or they can choose to use their season of preparation to better themselves and God's kingdom. Prophetess Bynum initially offered black single women suggestions for addressing the sexuality and spirituality, but there are many others hearing the call to serve. These new media models—Christian televangelists, the Wives in Waiting group, the Pinky Promise Movement, and other e-vangelism groups—are parachurch opportunities that symbiotically support black church messages on sexuality. Women following these contemporary faith-based sexuality ministries express a black Christian sexuality that is focused on their needs as single black women. These ministries' messages transmit well through televangelistic media because the words and images are texts with a dominant meaning encoded by the preacher. While this meaning speaks first and foremost to marginalized Christian singles, it speaks more widely to black women because the black woman preaching to them seems to share their struggles.

This message to concerned single black women was amplified in the twenty-first century. Bynum had opened up a niche market, and a plethora of new producers arrived to offer their wares. The faith-based sexuality ministry genre first experienced a proliferation in book sales as various women and men offered their expertise. Heeding Bynum's exhortation that we should hear from folks who are actually experiencing singlehood, single religious leaders emerged from the shadows. Not all of them utilized Bynum's model of television. Some gained acclaim through their countless hours counseling women, providing the one-on-one attention that televangelists could not provide. Yet their ability to host conferences and gain attention was completely contingent upon Bynum opening up religious spaces where women could discuss their sexual frustrations.

Another important distinction in these newer faith-based singles ministries is that their messages are not restricted by their denominations or by a particular doctrine. Bynum was clearly operating under the influence of her Pentecostal background, but the more recent singles ministries leaders emphasized scripture and their personal experience with singleness. While Bynum relied heavily on Pentecostal tropes in her message, evidenced through ecstatic worship, those who entered the market after Bynum have expanded it and made the message accessible to married black evangelical women for whom this rhetoric would also be useful. In fact this represents a trend within the black evangelical movement whereby denominational affiliation is not considered as important as emphasizing salvation, a conservative agenda, and Bible-based preaching.[3]

While these new ministries seem to disregard denominational preference, they are inheritors of Bynum's frank discussions of the struggles of celibacy. Like other successful parachurch ministries they are built around a single personality who, in Bynum's case, draws followers with her accessibility and willingness to engage in conversations that other religious spaces restrict. In this chapter I analyze several of the more prominent ministries' messages while providing a brief genealogy of celibacy, noting how specific rhetoric, symbols, and media construct our twenty-first-century understanding of celibacy, making sure to delineate how celibacy has been gendered and racialized. After analyzing specific ministries created for and by black women, I offer a womanist model of celibacy that represents the sexually agential choices of scores of single black Christian women today.

The Genealogy of Celibacy

Unlike in Catholicism, in the Protestant Christian tradition there has been no substantive, definitive, or clearly articulated discussion on how to achieve consecrated singleness. Historically evangelical culture distinguished only loosely between abstinence, celibacy, and purity, and that remained the case until President George W. Bush's administration forced those seeking federal funding for their abstinence programs to follow a more streamlined definition. From that point on abstinence was "voluntarily choosing not to engage in sexual activity until marriage [and] sexual activity refers to any type of genital contact or sexual stimulation between two persons including but not limited to, sexual intercourse."[4] Because Protestantism generally has numerous ecclesial leaders instead of one centralized leadership source, this streamlined narrative had traction only with those faith-based sexuality ministries that were applying for federal funds. Those outside of these funding streams ceded abstinence language to those participating in federal models by adopting purity language that included chastity as well as celibacy. These terms became interchangeable and were used to describe a person seeking a pure life who was concerned about more than just sexual activity. Chaste living surely involved sexual restraint but it also involved monitoring one's thoughts, companions, and other lifestyle choices to make sure that they were pleasing to God.[5]

How, then, are we to think about women who actively call themselves celibate and choose this as an identity construct? They are participating in the larger purity narrative popular among evangelical sexuality discussions, but they are also stating something specific about their understanding of the concept, notably that "celibacy starts in the mind" and chastity is lived out in the genitals.[6] Tracing a genealogy of the various interpretations of celibacy helps ferret out women who find community among celibate persons who are likewise called to serve the Lord.

Benjamin Kahan, a women's and gender studies scholar, discusses celibacy in the twentieth century as a sexuality in its own right, a synonym and expectation for the unmarried, a choice or performative vow, a political self-identification, a resistance to compulsory sexuality, and a period in between sexual activity. He begins with celibacy as a sexual orientation of its own that is distinct from asexuality or homosexuality; however, the typical black single Christian women being studied do not view their celibacy as a sexual orientation.[7] They instead adopt his framework of celibacy as a synonym for the unmarried. Using biblical interpretation (especially Paul's writings in 1 Corinthians 7) as a mandate for celibacy, contemporary single black Christian women are operating in a religiocultural world that emphasizes that the appropriate behavior for unmarried women is to choose celibacy. This expectation can be frustrating for women, particularly those who have already experienced sexual activity either prior to marriage or within a marriage. Typically, religious conversations about unmarried women include celibacy, and while this may be the presumed expectation, there are interesting nuances in the meaning and purpose of celibacy for a twenty-first-century audience.

Kahan's category of celibacy as a choice is at the heart of women's participation in a variety of faith-based sexuality ministries. For Kahan, persons interested in celibacy's history must look at how certain groups were constrained from the choice of celibacy and others were coerced into the choice of marriage.[8] While he cautions people not to avoid celibacy for a "better" choice of sexual intercourse, for some single black Christian women, celibacy is a conscious choice to pursue righteous living, a choice to flee from temptation. They want that choice validated and normalized.

Christine Gardner, a communications professor, examined the rhetoric of white evangelical abstinence campaigns that emphasize that teenagers are choice-making agents who have the power to control their own body.[9] While her study focuses on teenagers, many of her conclusions are relevant to adults participating in faith-based sexuality ministries. Gardner presents the evangelical model of purity as a positive choice that is emboldened by the power of testimonies from others who make a similar choice. This is definitely present in faith-based sexuality ministries that target black women, as those ministries are almost entirely focused on testimony and transparency as means of offering hope and reassurance that celibacy in singleness and submission in marriage is the right path.

This rhetoric and use of media and symbols is appealing because choosing celibacy is never just a personal decision. Personal commitment must be bolstered by external proof of the decision. Choosing a life of celibacy ultimately means choosing to participate in a large-scale lifestyle modification. This can be manifested by wearing a purity ring, taking vows and getting married to Christ, actively avoiding sexual activity, or sharing testimony of struggles and victories in singleness, all the while providing a rationale that includes a decision to honor God by honoring one's body. Each outward act is a reiteration of the internalized commitment. For many single black women, their black Christian sexuality extends beyond mere respite between relationships to encompass a whole system of living.

Given the history of slavery that prohibited both marriage and the expectation that a black woman would be in control of her sexual decision making, the choice of celibacy was fought for but was not necessarily an easy identity to maintain. The hardship of getting the outside white world to acknowledge the possibility of black chastity led to a legacy of black female sexual restraint for long periods in American history. This restraint led to the policing of black female bodies and sexualities through codes of silence and public shaming within the black community, as I described in the introduction. Choosing to pursue celibacy can be read in the same way as attempts to sexually silence community members.

Those advocating for a celibate identity argue that their personal choice is about conforming to the expectations of God, but their choice is not solely personal because it does have communal and societal effects. This is one of the reasons that testimony and accountability in the faith-based sexuality ministries are so valued. Sisters are encouraged to hold each other accountable for living a pure life because achieving this goal depends on the entire community. Not since Father Divine's Peace Mission has there been such a standard of black communal celibacy. Those participating in faith-based sexuality ministries are part of a noteworthy legacy.

Michelle McKinney Hammond

A leading voice in the faith-based sexuality movement is Michelle McKinney Hammond, a black female author, relationship expert, and life empowerment coach. She is evidence that the singles ministry has expanded beyond its stronghold in evangelical and Pentecostal communities. She was reared as an Episcopalian; served at the nondenominational, multiracial Park Community Church in Chicago; and founded the Relevance movement, a nondenominational group based in Ghana. As a woman of West Indian and Ghanaian descent, she does not share the same cultural heritage as Bynum, and her singles ministry is deliberately interfaith and multiethnic, although her books cater to black single Christian women.[10] Part of her success comes from her "God-given assignment" to help women "live purposefully and to live life as if [they] will never get married."[11] McKinney Hammond founded Heartwing Ministries with the goal of focusing on relationships. She has written more than forty books and sold over two million copies; titles include *How to Avoid the 10 Mistakes Single Women Make; Sassy, Single, and Satisfied; How to Be Found by the Man You've Been Looking For;* and *What to Do until Love Finds You.*

While she eventually became a regular on the Trinity Broadcast Network and other Christian broadcasting sites, many of her fans found her earlier, through her writings. She notes in her autobiographical sketch that she found her calling in writing books for single women because she believed at the time that nobody was being real in their writing: "So I began writing books I wished someone had written for me."[12] McKinney Hammond is not a preacher; her television appearances are the result of her writing, public speaking, and singing ability. She has been praised for her plainspoken, truth-telling style and is particularly revered for her ability to connect with audience members. Most of her events include an extensive question-and-answer period with audience members, a particularly compelling feature because it provides the women with specific insight that they know is truly directed toward them. McKinney Hammond says she noticed that when she started writing and doing singles conferences many Christian singles books were "spiritual" but not practical and made her feel "like a backslidden Christian because [she] had these basic needs nobody ever addressed."[13] Her desire to be practical has resulted in her ability to impress her audience and encourage new participants.

Practicality has now become a primary feature of faith-based sexuality ministries. While the ministries' messages on sexuality may not vary much, the amount of attention paid to sexual frustration has decreased. These contemporary ministries acknowledge sexual ecstasy and do not downplay sexual pleasure (when it is appropriately experienced in marital sex). But they mainly focus on how to live beyond one's sexual frustration by using psychological rather than theological reasoning.[14] McKinney Hammond does not focus exclusively on sexuality or even solely on theological interpretations of how women are to behave in the world. She expands the discourse by encouraging black churchwomen to focus on career advancement, personal well-being, and, of course, a closer connection to God. She argues that completion is not found in relationships with men; it is found only with God. She utilizes the more traditional medium of print and couples it with an emerging web presence to reach her desired audience. While the adaptation of Bynum's messages to the web happened slowly, McKinney Hammond very early on recognized the vast potential of the Internet. Perhaps because she was not a minister, her opportunities on television were more limited, so she knew she needed to find other avenues to market herself. By cross-branding her books with the web, then eventually TV shows and films, McKinney Hammond was able to spread her message of single self-sufficiency across the globe.

Despite her modern approach to celibacy as more than sexual deprivation, her writings and speeches reiterate traditional feminine and gender roles. She is not an advocate of women looking for a mate as she believes it is the man's role to pursue the woman. In one of her many messages on the power of femininity, she tells women that by becoming more assertive they have switched roles with men; she claims, "As long as we are in the wrong position our relationships cannot work. . . . When we switch roles we don't win, we lose."[15] Because of her belief that Jesus is every Christian woman's husband and only soul mate, she asserts the importance of learning female submission to the male. This, she insists, is particularly significant for black women and she presents the following rationale for how black women should interact with black men: "When we buy into the black superwoman image, we destroy our men. God created men with the need to be needed. We have to allow our men to be men and learn to enjoy being a woman. God never saw women as weak; feminine does not equate to weakness. It actually takes strength to be feminine—allowing your mate to be stronger. . . . It'll take lots of prayer and then, taking that fearful step of submission, whether or not she thinks that he desires to be in authority."[16] The Superwoman image is often interchangeable with the Sapphire image that portrays black women as usurping their traditional feminine roles, and this is what McKinney Hammond alludes to in this quotation. Yet, these messages do not vary much from Bynum's discourse. Noteworthy here is that despite the message remaining virtually the same, there are enough interesting nuances to make consumers believe that she is a needed voice for them. Her presentation of a model of a "purpose-driven life" for singles focuses almost entirely on the woman occupying her time with things of God, but this does not mean a life that is solely sacrificial or as a second-class citizens as women are encouraged to fully live life beyond religious restrictions and she provides a how-to guide for managing one's weight, finances, relationships, and overall self-fulfillment. This written guide was soon duplicated in television shows and even in a documentary on single black women's struggle through singleness.

McKinney Hammond's rhetoric of Jesus as the ultimate spouse was soon adopted and marketed through most of the ministries addressing single black Christian women. She teaches that singles are not really single because they are all engaged to Jesus. Responding to those who find her claim of a divine spouse suspicious, she says, "I've heard the 'Jesus-is-your-husband' lectures and probably cringed as much as you have. . . . I'd say, Yeah, well, he's not here to take me to the movies, but it's because I didn't really have a revelation of what a husband is supposed to be. . . . When we get a revelation of what God expects from our husband, then we see that Jesus really is the perfect husband. He's faithful, He's tender, compassion-ate, warm, loving, consistent, generous, a good listener, and a wonderful friend."[17] This type of theological underpinning that allows women to focus completely on their spiritual self and their union with Christ is noteworthy because instead of seeing Jesus only as savior, Jesus here takes on the role of spouse.

This logic is prominent in *Soul Mate*, a 2006 film that listens to the pain, frustration, and joys of single women. The filmmaker Andrea Wiley publicizes the film as a message of encouragement for single women who are waiting to become wives. In the film and in her marketing materials she showcases examples of several successful, heterosexual women who are beautiful and powerful. Their definition of a healthy relationship is one that leads to marriage. One of the women featured in the film is Mi-chelle McKinney Hammond, who discourages extensive dating, contend-ing that men put women into the "friendship, freak, or forever file. Within two dates." [18] Since marriage is the goal, dating must have a purpose. The dominant message in the film is that marriage is the only acceptable rela-

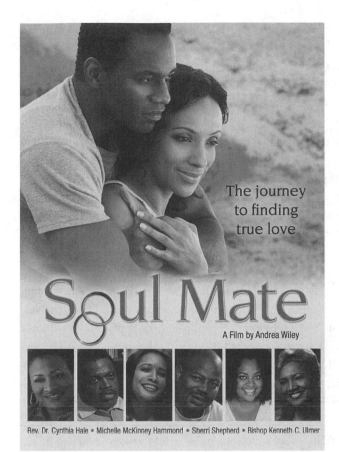

FIGURE 3.1. Poster for *Soul Mate* DVD. Source: Media kit from *Soul Mate* DVD website.

tionship and all others are poor substitutes. Such thinking does not model the variety of healthy relationships that are possible, nor does it allow these women to think of a meaningful relationship outside of marriage. The film shows single black Christian women that they are part of a larger community that desires long-term commitment. Much like the video watch parties associated with Bynum's "No More Sheets" sermon, the documentary *Soul Mate* was also circulated among churchgoing women as a tool to help them in their journey.[19]

Wiley chooses to open the film with the statistic that as many as 70 percent of black women are not married and 42.3 percent have never been married. From the outset, prolonged singleness is depicted as a problem, especially for the Christian woman. Wiley states that God moved her out of her career as a television executive producer because God wanted her to tell the story of her single girlfriends so that others will be inspired to move beyond the traps that singleness sometimes creates to find an intimate relationship with God.[20] She does include a quotation in the film from Bishop Kenneth Ulmer, who said that not everyone marries, but despite this truthful caveat, the stories brush aside that reality. Her film website is captioned "Soul Mate: We All Have One," and her marketing materials are captioned "Still Looking for Your Soul Mate? He's Closer Than You Think." Wiley chooses to end the film with interviews of women who married when they were over forty because she wants to give older viewers hope that they too will get married. Her dominant message of heteronormative marriage remains unchallenged specifically because its fits into the larger genre of faith-based sexuality ministries marketed to single women.

It is important to examine how Wiley's film is discussed and embraced by media as well as consumers. Among the media outlets that interviewed her were *Precious Times: The Magazine* for *Today's Black Christian Woman, Gospel Today Magazine, The 700 Club* on the Christian Broadcasting Network, and the Total Living Network. Combine these appearances with her attendance at singles conferences and savvy marketing distribution, and Wiley fits perfectly into the world of other successors to Bynum in discussions of single black Christian women and sexuality. This symbiotic endorsement is not just found in Christian media. In November 2007 the *NBC Nightly News with Brian Williams* broadcast Rehema Ellis's report on redefining black families, in which she interviewed women who had found relief from watching *Soul Mate*. They appreciated the practical advice in the film about loneliness, facing one's biological clock, and finding an intimate relationship with God. By gaining exposure on a national secular TV show, Wiley was able to expand from her smaller population of Christian female viewers, and she in turn responded to the secular attention by broadening her message to include men. Wiley states that the film is for men as well because she wants everyone to take away the message of the necessity of an intimate relationship with God.[21] Whether Wiley was targeting single black women or men, her success relied on heterosexual marriage being seen as a necessary and God-ordained step.

Concomitantly, submission in marriage is also expected and explicitly reiterated as one of Wiley's core messages. Marriage is the brass ring of faith-based sexuality ministries, but not just any marriage: a properly ordered marriage that requires a male head to which the female submits.

While this does not differ from the dominant message of submission provided in faith-based sexuality ministries that are popular among white women, the more successful ministries that followed Bynum explicitly explored the theme of submission as a characteristic that was not innate to black Christian women. Because of the gendered and racialized discourse present in these ministries, one must interrogate why these leaders felt it necessary to be so explicit.

In Wiley's publicity tour for the film, she did an interview with *Beliefnet* about what black Christian women could do to help their relationships. She provides testimony from her own marriages as solutions for unmarried black women. In a section titled "Who Is the Head of the Household?" she details a problem with Type A women who are highly educated and high achievers. She states that because these women tend to be the boss at work, they have a hard time turning that off when in a relationship. She contends that black women in particular need to look at how they treat their men, and she insists, "You can still have your career, run your company, and have your business, but there should be a shift in the dynamic at home. Men are wired to lead and to be respected, and [women] are wired to be loved."[22] In a subsequent interview with the African American radio talk show host Audrey Adams, Wiley reiterates this message, stating that black women make the mistake of considering themselves self-sufficient, which grieves God because God gives them everything and leaves men feeling like they do not belong.[23] She argues that this mentality of self-sufficiency thwarts God's order and leaves black women in relationships where God is not at the center. Wiley's film is meant to target just this population of successful, single, saved black women. She offers statistics indicating that the more education and higher income a black woman receives, the greater her chances of being unmarried, and suggests this is why success and submission must go hand in hand if black women are to marry. It is ironic that in the discussion of submission it does not matter if one has economic and social accomplishments; the solution called for is the same. This ideology is important to track because it means that the message is universally effective, creating further demand for these particular types of faith-based sexuality ministries.

Part of what makes the submission narrative effective is that women are told they must practice their submission in the same way that they practice purity: by being the bride of Christ. One person who interpreted this as more than just a metaphor was a *Soul Mate* participant named Vanessa, a forty-year-old president and CEO of a celebrity makeup artist company. She celebrated that it has been "just me and God literally since 1996."[24] She sees her union with Christ as more important than any physical relationship she could form. Her model of manhood is God, and if a man does not live up to the attributes of God, she does not deem him worthy of her body. Of course no man can meet those expectations. Jesus as replacement spouse denies women the opportunity to experience tangible, physical relationships with men. Another woman in the documentary, Valerie, reports that when she decided after seven years of celibacy to be intimate with a man, God stepped in and spoke to the man, telling him not to touch her. This way of belonging to God usually comes out of a patriarchal, heterosexist understanding of God.[25]

Wives in Waiting

Though it has a long historical tradition, most recently the concept of being the spouse of God took off thanks to marketing in the late 2000s and has reached an impressive segment of the black Christian singles market. An example is the faith-based sexuality ministry Wives in Waiting. According to its website, Wives in Waiting is a movement based on Isaiah 54:5: "For your maker is your husband—the Lord Almighty is his name." The founder, Rev. Chante Truscott, started this faith-based sexuality ministry in November 2012, teaching that women should be prepared to be a wife in the spiritual realm before they get married in the physical realm. In her biography she states she felt God called her to a be a Titus 2 woman who pours into other women a particular message, and her message is submission to God with one's whole heart. Her first step in this calling was the creation of the Wives in Waiting movement.[26]

While this is a relatively new ministry still gaining in popularity, it is worth highlighting for two reasons. First, Reverend Truscott's ministry is geared toward black Christian women with her rhetoric teaching women to respect the marriage they have with God by honoring God with their whole lives. For its members, Wives in Waiting is a means of establishing and nurturing a relationship with God, which sets the tone for everything they do in life. As an organization leader, "Nic," explained to me, the group helps women create a connection with Christ, and celibacy could be a byproduct of that deeper relationship.[27] Despite the possibility that women may not find celibacy a necessary result of their walk with Christ, great attention is given to sexual purity on the group's Facebook page and in Twitter feeds and Google chats. Typical of faith-based sexuality ministries focused on single black women, Wives in Waiting is a sex-positive space—as long as sexuality is properly ordered through marriage. During the group's January 30, 2015, Date Night the conversation was "Let's Talk about Sex," and Truscott made a point of interjecting that there is nothing as freeing as married sex because it comes without God's condemnation. Yet she acknowledged that there is a process to realizing this. In a moment of transparency she shared with group members that she had freely engaged in some sexual acts with men she was not married to, but once she was married she considered those same acts forbidden. She noted that some sexual acts we call "nasty" are acceptable if practiced with one's husband because the marriage bed is not defiled by it.[28] This frank discussion is typical of ministries geared toward black women. What makes her Wives in Waiting ministry unique is that she emphasizes God as the celestial husband and black women as brides of Christ.

Truscott does not publicize statistics on the ministry, so it is hard to determine the popularity of Wives in Waiting as a faith-based sexuality ministry. She operates as CEO and business manager and relies on the Sister Circles in various cities across the globe as accountability groups for participants to supplement the messages received from the founder.[29] When I conducted my interview with two Wives in Waiting leaders who were members since the organization was founded, we talked about the function of Sister Circles. Both women told me they found authentic female friendships and sisterhood within the group. Nic, a thirty-three year-old, middle-class, unmarried, heterosexual black woman from outside of the South, stated that in addition to providing sisterhood, her Sister Circle provided believers with something to do on the weekends, when Christian social activities are sometimes limited. She said one of her goals as a leader was to make sure that women got together for more than just girl talk; she wanted "kingdom entrepreneurship," where women are busy at their divine appointments. Being the bride of Christ is a means of preparing a woman to live for Christ her entire life, not just when dealing with the emotions of singleness.

Part of the appeal of the group is its ability to offer information and help on a vast area of topics, which is bolstered by the founder's focus on one-on-one mentoring, bimonthly interactive webinars, bimonthly early-morning prayer services, and personal development or life coaching. In addition to these interactions, Truscott makes sure her message is available on multiple platforms. One of the trademarks of an effective faith-based ministry is its accessibility and media utility. Wives in Waiting has an Instagram page, a Facebook page, a Twitter feed, a website, an online store for merchandise, a YouTube channel, and a Google Hangout chat room, and the founder makes her rounds to Christian singles conferences. The group is constantly in communication with its members. This is not just savvy marketing; it responds to a deeply held belief that one must actively flee fornication and attest that one is practicing purity. For example, in a group testimonial one member testified, "Wives in Waiting has given me the strength to hold on to my vow of celibacy because it's not a commitment to man but a commitment to God. On some of my lowest and darkest days, those text messages of daily encouragement came through right on time."[30] By participating in these various media, women keep their time occupied and are fulfilled through the community.

This ministry is also worth investigating because of its particular analysis of black women and submission. Wives in Waiting understands being celibate as a period in which a single woman learns the importance of submission. Participating in the movement requires taking vows that reiterate this notion. New members are encouraged with sobriety and discernment to take the following vow: "I, _____, take you Jesus to be my Heavenly Husband, placing no one, no thing, or no situation above you, to have and to hold from this day forward, for better or for worse, for richer, for poorer, in sickness and in health, to love and to cherish; forsaking all others; from this day forward until death reunites us."[31]

The website, new members' welcome packet, and Sister Circle meetings help women take these vows seriously. During a Wives in Waiting Facebook exchange on March 29, 2015, a group member asked whether the ministry teaches that God promises black women a husband (a particularly poignant and risky question given the census data on the low marriage rates of black women). The organization responded with a resounding "Yes" and "Amen," followed by scripture passages in support.[32] However, there is a caveat: before getting a husband, one must learn how to become a true bride of Christ, and this requires submission.

Vows to Christ:

I, _____ , take you Jesus to be my Heavenly Husband, placing no one, no thing, or no situation above you, to have and to hold from this day forward, for better or for worse, for richer, for poorer, in sickness and in health, to love and to cherish; forsaking all others; from this day forward until death reunites us.

Date: _____

FIGURE 3.2. Wives in Waiting vow. Source: Wives in Waiting membership welcome packet.

Evangelical women who subscribe to the doctrine of wifely submission are welcome participants in such faith-based ministries. Because these ministries tend to be biblically based they draw women who adhere to more traditional and conservative biblical interpretations. These ministries appeal to these women because they require participants who believe they can know God intimately and that God can directly intervene in their lives. While some women who join the movement are already part of the purity culture, having joined a chastity club or worn a purity ring as a teenager, others have not fled far enough from fornication and are deeply desirous to live a righteously pious life. For this second group, even if they do not come to the ministries as biblical literalists, they so desire a change that they are amenable to trying submission too. Wives in Waiting promises to groom a woman into someone who keeps her covenant with God and thus keeps her covenant with her husband. Following this logic, when God sends a natural husband she will be able to recognize him after devoting her time to Wives in Waiting.[33]

A womanist analysis of such participants reads them through a lens of sexual agency: they choose to submit to God, they choose to remain abstinent, and then they choose to submit to their husband. They express their sexual agency by "owning up to [their] responsibility to make decisions and . . . being willing to accept the consequences of [their] choices."[34] Nic expressed this agency as freedom in Christ. She was reared in a Pentecostal environment but now is nondenominational and feels that the black church can be experienced as oppressive because of its legalism and prohibitions. She suggested that seldom do people talk about the freedom to choose because celibacy is not about restrictions for her: "I have the freedom to choose not to have sex. There are guys that I would love to have sex with, but I choose not to. That's freedom, and I don't feel bound or upset about it. Sex is not what I want to do to honor God, so that's not what I'm going to do!" Her experiences had taught her that having sex outside of marriage was typically the symptom of a void in one's life or simply not trusting God to fill certain areas of one's life. In her personal walk with God she has found that God provides for her spiritually so that she has no voids for others to fill.

Similarly "VirtueLove" a forty-four-year-old, divorced, heterosexual, black Sister Circle leader living in the South told me that in typical church discussions on sexuality women are given the false information that there is something wrong if you want to have sex. They are told only about the prohibitions without the freedom of knowing the parameters of sex. VirtueLove said that celibacy is erroneously framed as God saying no, when women should be taught that God created sex: "Just because the world has taken it and perverted it doesn't mean its intent is not still beautiful and of God." Having been divorced for several years she is practicing abstinence but sees forgoing sex as the evidence of her relationship with Christ, not a reflection of what her Baptist church or parents taught her. For Wives in Waiting members the relationship with Christ offers abundant freedom and not a life of restriction because living for Christ according to biblical principles, mandates how one should live.

The Pinky Promise Movement has expectations similar to those of Wives in Waiting. Both require taking vows to honor God with one's life and body, and both advocate submission in marriage and submission to God (even going so far as to encourage "date nights" between members and God). The Pinky Promise is a promise to "honor God with your body and

FIGURE 3.3. Sign at Pinky Promise Movement Conference, July 2014. Photo by author.

your life. To refuse to give your body to anyone that hasn't paid the price for you called marriage. It's a promise to stay pure before God in EVERY single way. It's a promise that says, I won't test the boundaries in my relationship to see how far I can push it sexually—but instead—I want God to have my heart. It's a promise to God that you will honor your marriage covenant. It is saying that I promise not to step outside of my marriage, cheat on my spouse, and I'll work through every issue"[35] (figure 3.3). Heather Lindsey founded Pinky Promise for single and married women in January 2012.[36] As an evangelical ministry focused on women and organized by a black woman, it follows some of the same markers of other faith-based sexuality ministries. Pinky Promise is presented on multiple platforms and has three websites, a Twitter feed, Facebook and Instagram pages, a YouTube channel, and four books written by the founder. The founder preaches globally at singles, women's, and marriage conferences, and she also organizes her own Pinky Promise Movement Conference, held each summer in Atlanta. As is typical in faith-based sexuality ministries, the founder is charismatic and seems to be readily available to group members. Lindsey speaks to her audiences with straight talk, lovingly chastising them for falling away from God's plan of celibacy for singles. Reminiscent of Bynum's popularity, Lindsey uses all facets of religious media to gain a platform to attract masses of single women to her ministry.

The ways she does this are distinct from the Wives in Waiting organization. First, Pinky Promise is quintessentially an international women's celibacy support group. The group began when Lindsey designed and sold a few bracelets that would remind the women who wore them of their divine worth. From this initial interest she realized how important it was to get more people involved, at least to foster accountability for keeping their promises and vows to God.[37] While both organizations are a sisterhood of believers, Lindsey particularly encourages her women to promote the organization and its values through virtual means. She has created a virtual community that rivals the electronic church empire built by televangelists like Bynum. Pinky Promise's local groups organize events at least twice a month, and Lindsey does an online study on her YouTube channel that has an interactive message board where members talk to each other during the live-streamed study. She sends tweets and Instagram quotes and photos daily and offers chat rooms, forums, and ways to "friend" members and send messages throughout the network.

These communication tools are ways to feel an intimate connection within the larger structure that Pinky Promise has become. According to the Pinky Promise website, there are over 33,000 members of the organization, and while this number may be grossly overstated, it is evident from the live-stream events that thousands of people are participating in the community.[38] Lindsey imagines this online community as a modern-day reenactment of Acts 2:42–47, in which believers come together to help each other and surrender completely to God. Her imagined virtual community is what the communications scholar Heidi Campbell refers to as making the Internet a spiritual or sacramental space.[39] While the founder's intent is to replicate the early church's sense of community and obedience to God, she wants to do so without the drama that she experienced in other women's organizations or the doctrinal differences that hamper parachurch organizations. Her solution is to encourage her members to be extremely transparent with each other, which is promoted in the steps

FIGURE 3.4. Participants at Pinky Promise Movement Conference, July 2014. Photo by author.

in Pinky Promise membership. Her own testimony of her sexual mistakes before marriage and struggles within her first year of marriage reveal her attempts to be transparent in the group. Group members are encouraged to be honest in the nightly or weekly "bed checks" about who is in their bed (the right answer is no one but you and the Lord) and "gate checks" to make sure that they are guarding their heart.[40] These checks are virtual or media-based and are sent via text message, group chat, or in an online forum on the Pinky Promise website. By participating in this personal transparency, members are holding each other accountable for living pure lives.

Campbell lists several key attributes of a strong online religious community: relationship, care, value, connection, and intimate communication.[41] The Pinky Promise Movement and its accountability measures highlight all of these features. The community in Campbell's study was an email-based community; Pinky Promise members have the ability to hear and see each other in video and phone calls, creating more personal opportunities for fellowship. During these encounters, group members share intimate details with each other, including their sexual shame, angst for a husband, struggles in their marriage, feelings of purposelessness, and overall problems pursuing a pure life. Instead of harsh castigation members are lovingly corrected and encouraged back into God's perfect plan for their lives. The local in-person Pinky Promise groups reiterate the shared value of honoring God and one's body and are a natural next step after getting to know a sister through chat rooms and text messages. In this way Pinky Promise represents the evolution of faith-based sexuality ministries. Though it takes its cues from Bynum, Michelle McKinney Hammond, and others, it pushes aspects of their ministries forward into the twenty-first century, particularly with the use of media.

In one sense this is to be expected given consumer demand, but these changes are also a response to the ease and cost-effectiveness of the Internet and social media. Lindsey can most accurately be described as an "intervangelist," or someone who emphasizes the Internet as her primary means of communication, maximizes the interactivity of this medium, integrates several media platforms for her ministry's message, and manages to have an international reach because of the accessibility of the web.[42] Yet the intervangelist does not stray too far from the tools of earlier televangelism because success is only realized when a community is built. What Victor Turner termed *communitas* is reproduced in the Pinky Promise Movement as participants supplement their individual religious practice with a particular online community.

Pinky Promise remains a distinctive community because of its media use, advantageous accountability structure, and emphasis on living a fabulous celibate life or having a satisfying marriage. Similar to other faith-based sexuality ministries, Pinky Promise encourages single and sexually frustrated women to consider dating or marrying Jesus. In Lindsey's first book, *Pink Lips and Empty Hearts* (see figure 3.4), she describes her date nights with Jesus and invites members to do the same. At Pinky Promise's annual conference in July 2014 she brought out a fully dressed bride and groom as a sermon prop and encouraged women to run to God, their heavenly husband, and not return to old soul ties and sexual bondage. At the close of the sermon she recounted her own decision to marry Christ and asked women to come down the red-carpeted aisle (symbolizing the redeeming blood of Jesus) to take Christ as their husband and choose to submit to God as practice for how to submit to their eventual husband. I witnessed approximately 1,500 women come down the aisle to make this choice known. As a participant observer I wondered how many women went forward because of peer pressure and how many were actual believers, and I got an anecdotal answer on the closing night of the conference. While in the hotel lobby I witnessed an exchange between a conference attendee and a male hotel guest. He asked her if he could take her out to lunch, and she responded boldly, "Get behind me, Satan. I am married to Jesus," to which the sisters around her nodded in affirmation. What are we to make of such a declaration? Has her decision to marry Jesus closed doors for her to meet a potential earthly spouse?

This concern is emphasized in Sophia Nelson's chapter "Jesus Is Your Savior, Not Your Man" in *Black Woman Redefined*. She poignantly suggests, "We need to question the motives of spiritual leaders who encourage single black women to take the vow of celibacy outside of marriage one step further and live lifelong monastic experiences. We were made for love, warmth, touch, companionship, sexuality, and intimacy. Anyone who is preaching anything contrary to this message from the pulpit, sisters, is not preaching the gospel of truth."[43] Churches and faith-based ministries that preach and teach that celibacy is the only option for single women must realize that what they are demanding may be achievable only with great sacrifice. As a corrective to this one-sided approach, I offer a womanist model of celibacy that is in tune with the sacrificial experiences of single black Christian women.

A Womanist Model of Celibacy

This womanist intervention interrogates the notion that black Christian sexuality is equivalent to celibacy by viewing the experiences of unmarried black Christian women holistically. I offer a response to what is going on spiritually and physically with these women as they negotiate their sexuality. Alice Walker's definition of a womanist provides an example of how to do this. She defines a womanist as a responsible, grown, black woman who is sometimes a lover of individual men, sexually and/or nonsexually, is sometimes a separatist, but is always a lover of the Spirit.[44] In this paraphrased definition, there is space to explore the sexual and spiritual lives of single black Christian women. For instance, women who choose seasons of prolonged celibacy are consciously choosing for their own spiritual and physical health to separate from men they may love (or from men with whom they love having sex). They feel called to love and serve God with their entire mind, body, and soul. For some this decision causes frustration and for others contentment. This womanist model of celibacy demands conscious awareness of both the frustration and happiness involved in making such a choice, and it ultimately promotes celibacy only for those who feel that its benefits outweigh its consequences.

I noticed several themes when surveying the literature and conducting my interviews with single black Christian women. Those who had voluntarily experienced a season of celibacy due to their faith convictions typically had strong emotions underlying their decision. I expected that those who were able to remain celibate would also have feelings of piety, satisfaction, and pride. I hypothesized that those with a religious belief that they should remain celibate would experience guilt and shame if they were unable to meet this goal. These hypotheses were true of some of my interviewees, but I also was able to chart additional conflicting opinions that I had not considered.

For instance, those who were celibate expressed concern that they were judgmental toward others who had not made a similar decision. Their pride and satisfaction seemed to push them toward a public piety that distanced them from other single Christian women. During my interview with Natasha, she remarked that she had a wide-ranging religious upbringing and had followed Bynum's teachings on celibacy until marriage because she agreed that this was expected of Christians. She considered the height of her season of celibacy to be the years from 2004 to 2010, when she believed that celibacy would lead to marriage and prosperous blessings. It also led her to become very pious: "[That] meant for me as a person to outshine others, to be pure, to say, 'Look at me.'" This look-at-me model may have presented her as an exemplar, but she noted that her celibacy limited her ability to talk with her friends, and, because they were scared she would judge them for enjoying premarital sex, they were not willing to discuss their lives with her.

Being celibate led to similar results for Biansay. She said that her decision to become celibate meant she didn't engage in any of the activities she previously enjoyed. She remembers throwing away all of her R&B compact disks, no longer watching certain TV shows or going to certain places, and not talking to certain friends because they were having sex outside of marriage. In retrospect she exclaimed, "For a good five to six years everything was sinful [to me], and it makes for a very lame life. But it also made me elitist, extremely judgmental in a way." Judging pits women against each other in particularly gendered ways, some women being deemed more celibate and more Christian than others. In Christine Gardner's study of white evangelical purity culture, she found a prevailing sentiment that secondary virgins got to have their cake and eat it too, but that God would more richly bless those who had done things the "right way" from the start.[45]

While there may be palpable resentment toward those who experiment sexually before marriage, I also noticed a trend of frustration in those who were waiting. Nelson considers these women "celibate and bitter," but my research also revealed sincere frustration. In my interviewee with "Jay," a twenty-four-year-old, heterosexual, middle-class Pinky Promise member who had recently moved from Texas to New York City, she responded that in her different seasons of singleness she had felt "miserable, frustrated and hypersaturated" with singleness, so much so that she needed to take a break from everything that reminded her of her single status. As a college-age virgin, she would sometimes see promiscuous people or people who weren't pure get married and leading happy lives, which made her wonder, "God, why am I doing this?" Similarly Natasha, once proud of her pious living, realized that her black Christian friends who were having sex before marriage were getting married and seemed happy, while she was still single. For her this meant that something in the formula she was living was broken.

Diavante shared with me that while she agreed with the teachings on celibacy until marriage she was frustrated about the lack of male companionship that resulted. A middle-class, college-educated divorcée, she had girlfriends and her sisters, but there were times when she yearned for a relationship with a member of the opposite sex. Given that the messages on celibacy tend to become commandments on what type of company one can keep, it is not a surprise that women miss the company of men. Women are told that men's duty is to find wives, which leads to an unrealistic gender segregation where women are left alone, waiting to be "found." This was very frustrating for Winnie, a participant in the documentary Soul Mate, who tearfully admitted that she was not content being single. She wanted desperately to be a wife but wondered how that could happen if she was never around men.

Closely tied to emotions of frustration were stories of feeling guilt. Sandra, another *Soul Mate* participant, shared in the film that feeling lonely is a way of saying that God alone is not enough. Since she can't agree that God isn't enough, she chooses not to be lonely. In an update to the film, Sandra admits having a meltdown because of feeling like a fraud for admitting that she felt so lonely. Feeling guilty because her emotions do not match her Christian witness, in the film she experiences a moment of transparency in which she acknowledges that God is enough but that she still aches for companionship.

Jay also acknowledged loneliness despite having been a member of Pinky Promise since 2012. For her this loneliness in celibacy could turn to gratitude in celibacy when she realized that celibacy was teaching her delayed gratification, granting her spiritual power in her ministry, and showing her how to have deep intimate relationships with people in Christ. These examples of frustration and guilt were from those still walking the celibacy path, but when I interviewed women who had strayed from celibacy, their expressions of guilt were even more stark.

"Zuqueta," a thirty-eight-year-old mother of two, shed tears in our focus group as she reflected on being raised in a Baptist church with relatives who are ministers and preach about doing things the right way, that is, engaging in sexual relations only within marriage. Zuqueta has a graduate degree and is a middle-class, heterosexual black woman who had never been married. Her story resonated strongly with other focus group members and illustrates how deeply felt religious guilt can be.

> I live with my fiancée and we're not married and I'm telling my child one thing and doing something else. I'm not blind to the fact that I know that I'm being a hypocrite to my own child and that I have two kids out of wedlock, but I was the same way. My parents told me that you're supposed to get married first. I have a relative that is a pastor, and I'm getting talks all the time about my living situation. . . . And it's an uncomfortable thing. I know in my heart that I'm wrong, that we should not be living this way, because I was told my entire life that you're supposed to get married and then have children. I did it all backwards. I want my child to do it the right way.
>
> When I teach Vacation Bible School [the kids] ask me questions. I'm telling them one thing, and they are looking at me saying, "You got a kid." What am I supposed to say? I'm honest with them. We all

fall short. We all make mistakes. But I feel like that's a cop-out with them. I just cop out and gave them the answer to make them feel good. But I feel guilty all the time. It bothers me. And I talk about it a lot, how much it bothers me raising a child, and I know my child sees me living this way and I'm trying to correct the situation. We're getting married. But I didn't do it first. The child is not going to remember the fact that I got married later, just what I did first. And I hope I haven't messed up my child because of the choices I made in my life.

In the rhetoric of many of the messages around celibacy is the warning of a generational curse because of sexual sin; thus Zuqueta's actions have potential consequences in her family. In my follow-up interview with her two years later, she was still engaged and living with her fiancée but less troubled by the need to marry to satisfy family and religious concerns. She recognized that she was content in her current status and did not want to become a divorce statistic, but she had to deal with family pressure for being unmarried. The ultimate negotiation for many single black Christian women is rejecting any internalized beliefs from religious and family messages that condemn their sexual choices.

Nelson's study of professional black women revealed that 75 percent of those surveyed were "raised to think that freely expressing my sexuality outside of marriage was bad or in violation of God's commandments."[46] Despite this high number, roughly 56 percent of women had engaged in premarital sex, but only 14 percent reported feeling good about it, although 42 percent said they would do so again. Guilt is a powerful motivation that can be correlated to depression and other mental distress. For example, Biansay talked openly about her many years participating in the chastity league in high school, completing the True Love Waits twelve-week program, and having a wedding ceremony in which she made a vow to God. These notions were reinforced in her family and church; she told the focus group that she learned how to be an "asexual being in the church and at home." The expectation of sexual containment was so extreme that she was encouraged to wear a girdle at age thirteen so that her buttocks would not shake and lure men. Even with all of this indoctrination, she "messed up" and had sex prior to marriage. She remembered being "so overwhelmed with grief that the trajectory of [her] life was going to be horrible" because she did not wait. I had expected to hear about such feelings of grief and guilt when I began this project, but these feelings were often one of many, not the dominant feeling expressed throughout all the narratives.

If celibacy can lead women to be judgmental and feel frustrated, guilty, and depressed, one wonders whether and why we should bother to redeem the practice for single black Christian women. A womanist reframing is necessary to make the choice of celibacy more rewarding for all. Taking seriously Walker's notion that a womanist can separate from community when her health requires it, womanist celibacy is best understood as a situational refraining from sexual activity done not out of fear of divine judgment but in acknowledgment of the divine body with which one is gifted. The free choice to share that body with someone else (and in the case of many of the women I am researching, with one man) is a womanist act of self-determination. The womanist pastor and scholar Renee Hill states that self-determination is a radical act because it is an acceptance of a certain vision of oneself and a rejection of the roles that others would try to impose.[47] In this case, single black Christian women are accepting a new vision of themselves as sexual and spiritual beings and rejecting the notion that God requires them to deny their sexualized flesh.

Womanist celibacy listens to the voices and experiences of single black Christian women. For instance, Frederick notes that Sylvia engaged celibacy on her own terms by conforming "neither to church pressure to remain celibate, nor to social pressure that validates a life of reckless abandonment."[48] Celibacy is part of sexual agency, but others cannot demand it of you. It is helpful if the religious communities of those who choose celibacy can support a woman in that choice, without making this or another choice superior to other choices made by other women. This would require constant negotiation and rejection of messages that do not fit within the womanist framework of accepting body and soul.

An example of this negotiation appears in the film *Soul Mate*, where Rev. Dr. Cynthia Hale states that being single and satisfied is a process. At the time she was fifty-two, had never been married, and had been celibate for eighteen years. As senior pastor of a growing Disciples of Christ megachurch in Decatur, Georgia, she exuded peace about her decision to remain celibate, explaining that she chose celibacy because of her relationship with God, not just in response to commandments from the Bible that seem to require celibacy. In the film she remarked that when she feels physically tempted she remembers that she does not want to "lose [her] anointing and relationship with God" because she "needs God's power to do what

FIGURE 3.5. Clockwise from left: Andrea Wiley, *Soul Mate*'s producer; Michelle McKinney Hammond; and Rev. Dr. Cynthia Hale. Source: Media kit from *Soul Mate* DVD website.

God has called [her] to do."[49] Hale shows up in most of the media resources for the film arguably because of her success as a pastor and because of the length of her celibacy. I was initially unsure if her version of celibacy would fall within the womanist celibacy rubric because so much of her rationale seemed to be co-opted by religious messages demanding female sexual constraint. Wanting to more fully understand Hale's internal logic, I solicited an interview with her to discuss how she currently views her decision to remain celibate. In our 2015 interview, Hale told me that she was now sixty-two and still celibate, having had no breaks in her celibacy. Initially she was celibate for her parents, then for God, and now it seems she is celibate both for her relationship with God and because it is what is best for her. She is engaging in a purposeful celibate lifestyle, which is what a womanist model of celibacy encourages. She teaches that the single life is an abundant life, as one explores one's purpose, but that we are equally expected to "avoid the pitfalls that could be detrimental to [our] spiritual, emotional, physical, and financial health." Similar to the womanist framing of being a separatist for health reasons, Hale presented clear steps for how leading a celibate lifestyle led to her being her best and most productive self.

In Hale's writing on singleness and sexuality she provides concrete steps to maintain celibacy that are useful tools in a womanist celibacy model. First, she encourages women to be absolutely clear about why they are being celibate and what their plans are for their celibacy, such as how they will respond to a dinner date with a fine man. Unlike other faith-based sexuality ministries that do not encourage planning (they assume prayer is enough), Hale notes wisely, "If you fail to plan, you plan to fail."[50] Second, she encourages women to monitor their thoughts and be knowledgeable about their weaknesses and vulnerabilities. Third, she urges women to accept no substitutes for real intimacy, noting that sometimes women have sex when what they really want is an intimate connection. These directions demonstrate an awareness of the connection between our body and our spirit that womanist celibacy proclaims.

Hale acknowledges celibacy as a gift from God but one that women must freely choose. I asked her if she felt pressure to be a shining example of celibacy. She responded that she does not think people are looking for an example, as they are quite content being sexually active. While many people congratulate her on remaining chaste, they do so "while [themselves] screwing everybody." She does not consider her life decision to be a commandment for others. In fact she said, "Even as a Christian, I would not tell someone to live celibate if they did not really have a conviction based on their relationship with God, because that is where it has to come from. They have to make up their minds to do that." While she does believe it is the healthiest lifestyle until marriage, she knows that others feel differently. Because they have to have someone to talk to openly and honestly about their sexuality, she provides a listening ear, not condemnation.

Another advocate of womanist celibacy is Donna Marie Williams, who asserts that celibacy is "making the decision to abstain from sexual intercourse when there is no healthy, loving, monogamous, committed relationship present in your life."[51] Key is how she frames this relationship as being monogamous, not married. Yet celibacy is not to be confused with a sexual dry spell. One is not celibate simply because there is no available partner. Celibacy means making a choice, so that even if a partner is available, one still chooses to abstain from sexual activity.

This choice is desired for many reasons. Williams describes her pursuit of celibacy as being a result of the realization that premarital sex did not work for her because she became too attached to a man after she was sexually active with him.[52] Because she was privileging her emotional health, she was celibate for twenty years. For her, sensual celibacy was not just part of a list of things she was refraining from engaging in but an abstention that she found empowering, nonjudgmental, healing, loving, and fun.[53] Her book *Sensual Celibacy: The Sexy Woman's Guide to Using Abstinence for Recharging Your Spirit, Discovering Your Passion, Achieving Greater Intimacy in Your Next Relationship* provides a ten-step guide to encourage women to make the same celibacy choice. She devised this guide in response to her finding that church mothers and fathers promote chastity without explaining how to matriculate through celibacy.[54] Similar to Hale's directions, Williams gives concrete advice that is more than a list of what women should not do. In fact, at its core, Williams advises women to get a life, and not to assume that celibacy is a passive stage of their lives but instead that it is a call to become more active.

While Williams's book is implicitly written for a Christian audience, her model of maintaining the spiritual and physical connection for women is not as direct as a womanist model of celibacy needs to be. For women who are participating in faith-based sexuality ministries and are active participants in their church, Williams's advice to develop some type of spiritual practice would not be specific enough. She includes practices like focusing on a deep spirituality, walking in nature, and talking to a "soul doctor" that would not resonate with the typical Christian consumer of faith-based sexuality ministries.

In an interview I conducted with Williams in 2015, she admitted that she does not consider herself a traditional Christian. She said she wrote the book for those women "who were falling through the cracks . . . unchurched or not religious leaning at all but [who] needed a way to cope" with celibacy. She was not sure that traditional Christian women would find her book useful, but when she visited churches during her book tours she found them open to her message about celibacy, though less so to her untraditional take on Christianity.[55]

I hypothesized that the tension could come from the fact that Williams allows one to end celibacy without getting married. Williams told me that she had taken step ten and was now sexually active after being celibate for over two decades. She feels as comfortable in this stage as she did in her celibacy because, she explained, in celibacy the only thing that she denied herself was sex. She noted that when she was celibate she had a fuller life and that "celibacy was a gift that God gave her." In fact her contentment in celibacy made me wonder why she took step ten at all! Later in the interview she praised God for sensual celibacy because as a "sensual, sexual, loving, passionate woman [she had] tithed sex and got such a great spiritual journey."[56] Sensual celibacy was her healthy way to refrain from sex until she felt ready to reengage in sexual relationships. Given all that she received through being celibate, when I asked her why she felt the need to end her celibacy, she simply stated that she was ready to give love a try, that her youngest child had gone off to college and she felt strong enough to give love a chance. Sensual celibacy had been necessary so that she could be totally available for her children, but now it had served its purpose.

Part of the beauty of her model is the understanding that when a woman chooses to end her celibate lifestyle she must also be supported and nurtured, not rebuked. Williams recommends ending celibacy with a ritual and contraception. For her, the decision to end celibacy is a "mind-set and an act of faith that says you're ready for a healthy, loving, committed, monogamous relationship that includes sex."[57] Likewise the womanist model of celibacy advocates waiting to end celibacy until a healthy relationship is available. However, there must be communal support for women who choose this option, in the same way that celibate women must be supported in their decision. In this sense those who act on their sexual desires in healthy relationships are still participating in the sacred act of sexuality.

This chapter has investigated specific faith-based sexuality ministries as by-products of Bynum's niche marketing. Each ministry has revealed a unique engagement with sustaining a black Christian sexuality that the subsequent chapters examine further as *Passionate and Pious* interrogates the varied experiences of singleness as it relates to same-gender attraction, senior sexuality, and pleasure and desire.

4 · "WHY I GOTTA BE GAY?"
Approaches to Womanist Sexual Hospitality

We must prioritize knowing each other deeper than what our eyes can see because celebrating community that is truly diverse requires a new way of seeing and a new way of being. The Scripture implies that we can celebrate one another in some new and powerful way in Christian community—some way that both accepts who each of us is in a human sense and transcends our humanity, allowing us to see each other as God sees us. —BISHOP YVETTE FLUNDER, *Where the Edge Gathers*

In my introduction I stipulated that this book would focus primarily on single black heterosexual women and their participation in faith-based sexuality ministries. This remains the emphasis, but while participating in the Pinky Promise Movement I interacted with a young woman named "Jane" who admitted to struggling with her sexual orientation and same-sex desires. Intrigued but not surprised, I decided to explore black church-women with prior same-sex desire who were participating in heterosexual faith-based sexuality ministries.

I have participated in various faith-based sexuality ministries over the past two decades, and in my experience typically all participants express desire for a heterosexual marriage. This was the case with Jane, whom I first met online as a Pinky Promise local chapter member. Yet, in our in-person meeting I was fascinated to hear about her personal struggles to remain sexually pure as these related to banishing her same-sex desires. Jane is a young twenty-something college student. She is a zealous member of a nondenominational Christian church who pours her time into practicing purity. Despite Jane's best efforts, she was still having same-sex attraction and had even been approached by women on campus for romantic encounters, which indicated to her that they could not sense her redemption. In the language of the movement, when you are truly pure and practicing holiness, unsaved people do not show interest in you because you will draw to yourself only those who are likewise serving the Lord by following biblical instructions. Even if her collegiate companions' radar was off and they approached her without knowing that she no longer desired relationships with women, she was still stuck with the memories of her same-sex relationships and with her present same-sex attraction. Her mental anguish was even further amplified as she desperately awaited a husband. Her story was similar to a typical ex-gay narrative wherein the person is converted through Jesus and then denies same-sex attraction as she tries to live a heterosexual lifestyle. In this trope, expertly described by Tanya Erzen in *Straight to Jesus*, participants struggle with desires they consider contrary to God's will and typically enter a perpetual phase of being ex-gay—not quite heterosexual but no longer gay or lesbian. Jane recognized that she could no longer identify as a lesbian, but she also seemed to take issue with being ex-gay. Her desire was to be completely heterosexual, and she fasted, prayed, and utilized the resources of the Pinky Promise network to help her achieve this goal.

Intrigued by same-sex desire within the Pinky Promise group, I searched through chat rooms to see if and how same-sex desire was mentioned. The topic came up more often than I expected so I contacted several women within the group to ask for interviews. One zealous interviewee, "Symone," shared her testimony of being delivered from homosexuality as she was engaged to marry a man.[1] Like Jane, she was a twenty-two-year-old, working-class college student who was an earnest Christian and member of a nondenominational church. Symone actively participated in Pinky Promise, using the group for accountability as she tried to live according to God's commandments. While Jane still struggled with same-sex attraction but desired to be viewed as heterosexual, Symone considered herself an "ex-lesbian [who] completely and fully believes in the biblical definition of marriage." Symone's narrative of deliverance is particularly persuasive given her testimony of having "homosexual desires in elementary school"; she was never interested in boys, never wanted a boyfriend. Her first kiss was with a girl, and despite growing up in a religious home with a close relative who was a pastor, she dated the same girl from tenth grade through college. She considered her past life sexual sin because she was not celibate when she was with her girlfriend and was "not dying to her flesh."

Symone testified that while in high school she had encouraged girls to "be themselves" and to come out of the closet to be as open as she was with her sexuality. Yet, now she was in a social media group with perhaps the opposite message. As she recounted her deliverance from the "homosexual spirit" or demonic influence, she had a new vision of her sexual self that she was freely embracing. Her new narrative would be read as a success story within the Pinky Promise Movement because not only had she turned her heart away from same-sex desire, but she also practiced celibacy, pursued a godly courtship, and married a God-fearing man. However, outsiders to the movement could label Symone bisexual or even passing as heterosexual. While Jane's and Symone's examples may be anecdotal, such narratives are emphasized in the testimony and ministry of a web evangelist named Ty Adams.

In this chapter I discuss women participating in faith-based sexuality ministries who are experiencing same-sex attraction. They are trying to maintain a black Christian sexual identity despite this category's hetero-normative standards, a strategy that they also maintain in black church settings. Ultimately, those who choose celibacy and a black Christian sexuality over fulfilling their same-sex desires can be helped by a womanist sexual ethics intervention that addresses the pervasive sense that compulsory heterosexuality is the only option. Instead, womanists can offer the concept of sexual hospitality and welcome to a full range of sexual expressions and identities.

All of these narratives stress the importance of celibacy until one is in a heterosexual marriage. However, in the case of Jane and Symone, it was never clear to me what celibacy truly meant to them. The definition of sexual abstinence found in most of the manuals and ministries focuses on the avoidance of penetrative vaginal-penile intercourse, but Jane and Symone had previously only been with women. Without a history of penile penetration, were they still virgins and hence sexually pure? Given their belief that same-sex desire was a sin, they could claim abstinence but not sexual purity. Thus my investigation of their participation in the faith-based sexuality ministry first involved interpreting whether they were receiving and interpreting sexual messages in the same manner as their coparticipants. For instance, can either woman testify truthfully that she has "saved herself" for marriage without telling her intended husband about her lesbian past? Does she have to tell that part of her testimony, or is her struggle for sexual purity enough without giving specific details? These questions could potentially be stumbling blocks, but it is clear that the message of faith-based sexuality ministries is that transparency is necessary. Open and honest dialogue requires a complete acknowledgment of one's sexual struggles so that the group can hold you accountable for living a life of sexual purity.

Faith-Based Sexuality Ministries and Same-Sex Desire

Transparency is an important element in Ty Adams's rise to fame. Adams has been dubbed the "Juanita Bynum of her time" and a successor to Bynum's mantle in the singles' circuit.[2] Like Bynum, she has undergone a rebranding of her message to remain relevant to her audience. She now goes by "Dr. Ty," without clarifying this title, and her once shock-value-laden sermonizing about sexuality has become more neutral. It was Adams's *Single, Saved, and Having Sex?* book that catapulted her to fame. The book was an *Essence* magazine best seller and was listed on Amazon's Top 100 Sellers. Her book was even imported to Uganda to be used as a teaching tool in the fight against HIV/AIDS. While she has not achieved the same celebrity preacher status as Bynum, McKinney Hammond, or even Lindsey, Adams's message has been hugely popular in the same black Christian singles' networks.

Adams is a Detroit-based minister who mostly operates on the Internet. She preaches at singles' conferences and even joined Bynum and Weeks in their Teach Me How to Love You couples retreats. She has expanded on her initial book following by using Twitter, Instagram, and Facebook, and she has her own YouTube channel, where she creates weekly webcasts for her followers. Although her book is autobiographical, she does not boast of any particular spiritual tutelage. Her biographical information does not mention her religious denomination or even her ministerial or academic credentials. What we have of her life narrative is what she has carefully marketed and released, which makes her disclosure of a lesbian past quite intriguing.

Adams is known as a frank minister whose style echoes Bynum's model of sexual testimony. However, Adams is much more graphic in her depictions of her life of what she calls sexual sin, which includes premarital lesbian relationships. She also reiterates that God created sex to be passionate and pleasurable. While she does succeed in getting stagnant Christians to discuss sexuality, she does so using shaming techniques.

This is especially evident in her discussion of sexual sin, in which she describes what she did before becoming saved. For her sexual sin includes homosexuality, pornography, foreplay, masturbation, oral and anal sex, penetration of any kind, and even tongue kissing. She acknowledges the shock effect of her message on anal and oral sex but points out, "There are a lot of undercover Christians literally under the covers." She offers her own sexual past and feelings of shame as an example of how "unlawful" sex "severs your union with the Lord"—leaving her with her panties and her self-respect on the floor.[3] This models for her audiences a sexual honesty that she encourages them to imitate.

Detailing how she overcame her lesbian lifestyle, she declares, "There is no such thing as a gay church or gay minister": "God will use your gifts to bless His people, and you can still bust hell wide open."[4] Her internal conflict is apparent to her audience: even as she denounces her lesbian lovers, she extols the pleasures of lesbian sex. She writes that she was never attracted to women, but for almost a decade she has preached and done interviews about her personal struggle to leave that "lifestyle." While her narrative presents this as spiritual warfare, the sociologist Shayne Lee posits that the "mere utterance of her enduring struggle with same-sex erotic urges and sexual practices validates the erotic experiences of presumably numerous other evangelicals dealing with similar same-sex longings and relationships."[5] She preaches this particular part of her testimony not just because it is sensational but also because it is not unfamiliar to her market demographic. Ministries like Adams's often appeal to such a wide audience because they do not decry natural sexual urges, and specifically not women's sexual pleasure. Nor do they cover up relationships that many Christian communities would deem alternative or even immoral. Instead these ministries offer solutions, which mirror the injunction to remain abstinent until heterosexual marriage that women receive in their church, with the added bonus of telling the stories of those who likewise are struggling to remain celibate.

Adams's decision to discuss lesbian sex as a minister breaks an ultimate taboo. If Barbara Smith is correct and heterosexual privilege is the only privilege that black women have, then there is a legacy of hetero dominance that makes seeing and hearing from lesbians or even ex-lesbians an important task. For instance, Ann Allen Shockley's novel *Say Jesus and Come to Me* details the exploits of Reverend Black, a black lesbian traveling evangelist who finds herself "God's gift to the church and womankind" and who has the ability to lure women into ignoring the true intentions of her magnetism.[6] The novel paints the protagonist as driven by her desires for both women and the Lord.

Despite Shockley's great success with her first novel, *Loving Her*, which depicted a black lesbian protagonist, there was little fanfare associated with the second book, *Say Jesus*. Critics of the work were unhappy with Shockley for entangling the secular and sacred in a way that was predatory, deeming it superficial in its portrayal of black lesbians. Reverend Black hides or denies her same-sex desire in public while actively seeking out erotic encounters in private. While she does eventually publicly identify herself as a lesbian, choosing to do so from the pulpit during a Sunday service, the complexity of her identity throughout the novel is noteworthy precisely because it offers a fictional amplification of a phenomenon actively present in black churches: black lesbians in worship who pose as heterosexuals but occupy a fluid sexual identity ranging from ex-gay to lesbian, bisexual, queer, and heterosexual. Thus when interrogating the reality of the evangelist Ty Adams, one must be careful to discuss her categories, identifications, and depictions while offering critical analysis of the ramifications of her ministry.

To be clear, this is not an evaluation of ex-gay ministries or black women who choose to participate in such endeavors. There are specific beliefs and steps in reparative therapy associated with the ex-gay movement that are not at work in Adams's narrative. She describes a conversation with the Lord and then her partner when she decided that she couldn't choose "that lifestyle" over Jesus. After sleepless nights and emotional turmoil over her decision to leave her partner, she eventually decides to have sex with a man to prove to herself and everyone else that she is no longer gay.[7] The end result of this decision is a pregnancy, but somehow this resolves her struggles with same-sex desires. Reparative therapy or the attempts to "cure" someone of same-sex attraction, is not a quick fix. An ex-gay identity typically entails a lifetime of struggling to be delivered from same-sex desire, so Adams's claim of such freedom would be viewed skeptically from those in the ex-gay movement.

Adams testifies to a life of sexual purity since she gave birth, which for her means celibacy until marriage. This testimony of "lesbian turned mother turned celibate" has given her a larger platform; for example, she has been a guest host on *The 700 Club* and TBN's *Praise the Lord* in addition to hosting her own web-based shows. This narrative is particularly appealing to evangelical audiences and is a marker for those fulfilling black Christian sexuality because it reinforces the traditional role of the woman as mother and chaste Christian who waits to become a submissive spouse. It is replicated in the testimony of Charlene Cothran, a black former lesbian who founded *Venus Magazine*, perhaps the first magazine for black LGBT persons owned and operated by a black lesbian. When Cothran leaves her lesbian identity behind, she replaces it with celibacy; she reports no longer having an urge for anyone other than the Holy Spirit. Just as Adams clings to celibacy as a moral high ground and new identity one can still ponder this decision and whether either of them are actually delivered from homosexuality when what they have actually achieved is celibacy in both heterosexual and same-sex relationships.[8]

Accepting their rhetoric and testimony of deliverance followed by celibacy until heterosexual marriage raises questions of how common this reality is for single black Christian women participating in faith-based sexuality ministries. In many ways this population is hard to determine because women can certainly discuss prior same-sex attraction (and a few did provide details in their testimony), but in doing so they put themselves at risk of receiving homophobic responses from group members. Only two women in my focus group interviews mentioned any previous sexual fluidity that included same-sex desire. The online chat rooms and Facebook pages of the Pinky Promise and Wives in Waiting do not request information about sexual orientation (perhaps because it is assumed everyone participating is heterosexual), although both of the founders routinely send out messages that are judgmental toward gays and lesbians. In her sermon "Runaway Bride" preached at the 2014 Pinky Promise Movement Conference, Lindsey admonished women who were chasing after people but not God. She even preached that women were chasing "Lori" instead of pursuing God. If the audience is presumed to be heterosexual, why bother with a homophobic insult?

Lesbians in Black Religion

Perhaps the comments come because the ministries are aware that there is no sacred or secular space without the presence of black gays and lesbians. There are stereotypes of gay men in black churches as ministers, choir members, choir directors, and musicians, whose presence is acknowledged but not affirmed. What are the prevailing stereotypes of black lesbians in the church? The pastoral theologian Horace Griffin argues that these stereotypes are not numerous because the stereotypical black lesbian was not associated with black religion. Griffin posits that black lesbians historically were associated with bars, nightclubs, prisons, and "street" life, and the rumors about lesbians in black churches relegated them to the choir or education board.[9] While it is ironic to presume the absence of lesbians in a religious space constituted primarily by women, it may be in the voids of stereotypes that one can actually garner a more accurate depiction of black lesbian religious life.

The radical pronouncement of queer identity and religious fervor shouts out from the silence that black lesbians are not invisible but invaluable members of black religious congregations. However, a discussion of "out" black lesbians in religious spaces is outside of the focus of this research project. Instead this is an investigation of the negotiations of "closeted" heterosexual-identifying women in black churches and faith-based sexuality ministries. My primary interest is to make visible and audible the voices of sexually fluid black churchwomen.

The black feminist scientist Evelynn Hammonds notes that the historical narrative about black female sexuality has tended to avoid discussion of the lesbian or queer subject, often deeming her dangerous and potentially even traitorous to the black race.[10] Thus it is not surprising that recovering the historical record of black lesbian churchgoers is a difficult but not impossible task.[11] If in general there is silence around black female sexuality, and if black lesbians represent the outsiders within, what lessons can be learned from women who participate in both heterosexual and same-sex religious worlds?

Hammonds posits that a focus on black lesbian sexuality produces a discourse that disrupts sexual silence and offers a positive affirmation of sexuality.[12] Following true Foucauldian logic, any discourse that seeks to silence ultimately ends up saying a lot. First, this discourse illuminates perceived safe spaces to dare speak of one's same-sex desires. Such safe spaces allow members to be transparent with one another, and thus also speak of same-sex attraction. Yet transparency only opens the door; if one is still actively living as a lesbian, then judgment is sure to follow. For that reason black lesbians in black churches have become experts at hiding in plain sight, historically called being in the "closet." Womanist and queer insights complicate this narrative.

The womanist theologian Karen Baker-Fletcher prefers the term *hush harbor* over *closet* to refer to the experiences of black lesbian churchwomen. She describes the hush harbor as a safe, separatist space that provides empowerment for liberation that naturally counters the closet, which maintains oppression.[13] In this women-centered space, says Baker-Fletcher, black women relate to one another in sexual and spiritual freedom by listening, speaking, and learning from each other. The hush harbor overcomes homophobia by allowing grace and space for women to express their understanding of their sexuality in a way that honors their spiritual background. The hush harbor analogy does not seek to pull people out of the closet but waits for them to claim a specific same-gender-loving identity. This idea has some traction within the faith-based sexuality ministries, as they enthusiastically create a safe space for women to overcome their sexual sins. Yet this is where Baker-Fletcher's model is countered by heterosexism in many of these faith-based sexuality ministries because when one is "saved" one has to turn away from sexual sin, which often means same-sex attraction.

Baker-Fletcher describes a world of black women's contemporary fiction that make a hush harbor possible, but in the actual world homophobia and heterosexism in black religious communities can stifle sexual and spiritual freedom. One response to this oppression is passing. Griffin describes four types of invisibility personally experienced by lesbian Christians: (1) guilty passing, when lesbians feel they are sinful and deserving of the rage imposed by heterosexual church members; (2) angry passing, when lesbians publicly deny or remain silent about their own sexuality while expressing rage toward and condemnation of other gays and lesbians; (3) silent passing, when lesbians publicly deny or remain silent about their sexual attraction; and (4) opportunistic passing, when lesbians have accepted themselves but feel they cannot come out or speak out against homophobia in religious settings.[14]

Passing as a Strategy for Black Lesbian Churchwomen

Passing is deemed necessary when black lesbians and gays are denied full acceptance of their expressions of intimacy and relationships. Griffin contends that some blacks are homo-antagonistic because their theological beliefs of biblical opposition to gays and lesbians are then matched with their cultural beliefs that same-sex desire is not natural or native to black culture.[15] This especially has been amplified in the recent same-sex marriage debates. Given the 2009 Pew research that identifies black women as having the highest level of religious commitment, it is worth observing that black male religious leadership espouses opposition to same-sex marriage not only as a result of biblical and cultural interpretations but also because the men are acquiescing to pressure from their predominantly female congregations. This logic was reiterated by the women Marla Frederick interviewed and who applied the "punitive language of death and damnation, rather than that of disgust or negation, to the context of homosexual relationships."[16] Though Jonathan Walton contends that black women embrace punitive language for gays because they see in gays the loss of a potential mate, there must be more to their opposition since they seem to have an equal disdain for lesbians.

For instance, black lesbians who seek to have their relationships validated by the church face similar (although admittedly more punitive) struggles as single women who seek validation for their sexual partners. In several online forums of faith-based sexuality ministries, many group members reported being called a lesbian because they had chosen celibacy and a life of purity.[17] Because of their vow of chastity, they could not "prove" they were not lesbians, as Adams did by getting pregnant. So they lamented the irony that in fleeing one sexual sin they were accused of participating in another sexual sin. Though their hush harbor was a safe space in which to express their frustration, it ultimately reinforced the belief that same-sex desire is ungodly and problematic. When we discussed this concern in my focus groups, single black women often reiterated Frederick's account, saying their "belief in heterosexual marriage is not about dominating another group, but rather about pleasing their God."[18] Thus in order to belong to the community of believers, many women experiencing same-gender attraction felt the need to pass as heterosexual; most likely they were also thankful that by claiming celibacy they did not have to engage in heterosexual sexual relations.

Yet why pass at all? Why not just leave a community that will not accept your sexual reality? Rev. Irene Monroe offers a significant answer that speaks to the reality of many lesbian women willfully participating in homophobic religious environments. Monroe describes being isolated from the black church as being cut off from the black community, the black family, from the space where one is a child of God, someone with dignity.[19] Women with same-sex attraction participate in these religious communities despite not being eligible for key leadership positions because these communities offer validation even as they offer castigation.

Compulsory Heteronormativity in Black Churches and Faith-Based Sexuality Ministries

Passing serves another purpose. It reifies the logic of compulsory heterosexuality by having black women who are attracted to other women participate in the charade of relationships with men. Not only do they participate as singles dating; they also engage in the same rhetoric and media as those ultimately seeking marriage. This is a tragic irony because as participants in these ministries they see the scores of available single black Christian women actively desiring a husband. If heterosexual women who want a husband find them elusive, what are the chances of same-sex-attracted women, who may be only cursorily interested in men? Professor Mattie Richardson questions the continued investment in heterosexuality, positing that black desire for heterosexual marriage over other types of partnerships is evidence of the need to demonstrate black sexual normalcy.[20] Richardson's perspective holds for ministry participants who are invested in black Christian sexuality, the standard of committed, monogamous relationships.

Ironically marriage is the goal whether women are passing as heterosexuals or participating in black church settings as lesbians. Stretching the LUG (lesbian until graduation) identity, women who experience same-sex desire may find themselves advancing to the LUM (lesbian until marriage) identity. This is a result of the societal expectation of faithful, monogamous relationships that punitively isolates singles in black religious communities. If the traditional God-ordained plan is heterosexual marriage, then anyone not participating in this model is deemed sexually deviant. For this reason many sexual ethicists promote heterosexual and homosexual monogamy, finding sexual promiscuity immoral.[21] For lesbians and ex-lesbians the desire to marry is moralized and made necessary. In this modeling a real Christian or a real black person follows the social mores and accepts a heterosexual structure in some form; hence women participating in faith-based sexuality ministries or black churches know the roles they are supposed to play even if it means they must pass to do so.

Womanist Sexual Hospitality

According to Griffin, those who pass and choose the path of greatest conformity do so at the cost of their own sexual fulfillment. That is why a womanist model of sexual fluidity or sexual hospitality is a necessary corrective. In Walker's definition a womanist is a "woman who loves other women, sexually and/or nonsexually. . . . [She] appreciates and prefers women's culture, women's emotional flexibility . . . and women's strength."[22] This definition has space for women like Jane, who have complicated sexual narratives, women who love women sexually and appreciate women's spaces and flexibility. By calling for a sexual fluidity that is not currently embraced in many black church settings and certainly not in faith-based sexuality ministries that target single black women, this womanist model even offers a challenge to womanist scholarship. It joins Renee Hill in charging womanist and black theologians to change the fact that the "lesbian voice is silenced in Christian womanist theology. Heterosexism and homophobia are nonissues in the Christian womanist paradigm for liberation."[23] Hill argues from a liberation standpoint that womanists have a duty to confront the oppression of gays and lesbians because to fail to do so negates the diversity of black communities.

A womanist model of sexual hospitality requires that dismantling heterosexism be a central tenet since the model is grounded in the idea of sanctioning right relations.[24] This has been a problem in womanist sexual ethics, perhaps because womanists are so tied to the black church, which has opposed the full inclusion of gay and lesbian members. This work provides some creative strategies to lead the way. First, a model of sexual hospitality counters heterosexism by taking seriously the fluidity of sexual expression. On the one hand it is a laudable goal that passing no longer be necessary in any community. Yet sexual freedom is more than merely the choice to live freely as same-gender-loving or heterosexual. Instead the model necessitates a complete breaking of the binary to bring about acceptance of healthy relationships and sexual expressions of any kind. This fluidity is what Bishop Flunder describes in the epigraph to this chapter; it can include celibacy, choosing to be in primary relationship with oneself, choosing to engage in a sexual relationship with any gender, and the flexibility to allow people space to identify across a wider range of sexual identities and sexual expressions. In this model Jane can be a former lesbian who identifies as "eventually" heterosexual; there is not a requirement that she be ex-gay, lesbian, or bisexual or even maintain a stable identity as a heterosexual.

The term *sexual hospitality* refocuses the debate on same-gender-loving people participating in Christianity. Primarily, this is a counter to the inhospitality toward strangers presented in the biblical text about Sodom and Gomorrah. This privileges the interpretation of the sin of Sodom and Gomorrah in Genesis 19 as a message about rude treatment of strangers instead of a pronouncement of God against same-sex sexual acts. Sexual hospitality more broadly construed from a womanist approach remains skeptical of a perspective that does not highlight the particularities of its community members. It recognizes the history of hypersexualization of black bodies and the sexual hierarchy that places black women who love women at one of the lowest access points of power. Womanist sexual hospitality is open to the fullness of sexuality. It accepts Hill's charge that discussions of sexual freedom must move beyond seeing LGBT people as a problem to seeing them as a part of creation deserving of dignity, safety, respect, and liberation.[25]

Hospitality means meeting the stranger and embracing her just as she is, without the need for labeling her or stretching her to fit into a compulsory heterosexual frame. While the women who participate in faith-based sexuality ministries are (perhaps) voluntarily placing themselves in a heterosexual mold to be refashioned, womanist hospitality offers them an alternative choice. Honoring their desire to be in relationship, it rejects the idea that relationships should be the only goal. Appreciating singleness, whether as celibacy or as healthy nonmarital relationships that have a sexual component, is an aim of womanist sexual hospitality.

Another objective of the model is to widen the understanding of fluid sexual categories to recognize nonfixed identities. Perhaps my initial interest in including a chapter on lesbians and gays in a book that is predominantly concerned with heterosexual black churchwomen was the fact that Jane destabilized my categories. Her presence was more than an anomaly that could be excused. When I read through chat rooms and discussion groups in each of the ministries, more and more women who were delivered from their same-sex desire appeared. Yet their deliverance seemed fragile because they still required prayer and accountability to keep them on the heterosexual path. Were they lesbians seeking to pass unobtrusively within these ministries? Or were they truly sexually free?

At the October 2014 Columbia University conference Are the Gods Afraid of Black Sexuality? the religious historian Wallace Best gave a presentation on Langston Hughes and the public's fascination with whether he was gay, on the "DL," or even asexual. Best counters with a suggestion: What if, instead of reading Hughes as being in the closet, we allow ourselves to view him as sexually free, as someone who did not express a particular identity but also did not try to live in a heteronormative way?[26] Viewed in this light one need not come out as any particular identity because sexual freedom comes from having the unmolested space to live one's life just as one chooses. Mapping Best's provocative talk onto the experiences of the women participating in faith-based sexuality ministries and attending black churches while simultaneously acknowledging same-sex desire brings hospitality to this multitude of sexual strangers. Since sexuality is fluid, one may meet the same stranger more than once, in more than one sexual identity. Key to this type of hospitality is not surveillance of women and attempting to pull them out of their respective closets. Instead such hospitality waits patiently and with understanding for a woman to enter the hush harbor and share who one is and wants to be as a sexual subject.

Womanist sexual hospitality honors the womanist, grown, responsible sexual agent who has a choice to radically name herself and who requires no permanency in this naming. It pushes back on the concept of passing and of hiding one's identity. This model accepts the possibility that a person's identity can be in flux or is only a desired goal and not yet an achieved reality. By listening to these complicated narratives, womanists can live up to their definition and respond to the criticisms against them and their blindness toward sexual justice. This scholarship opens up such spaces to hear and ask questions of the stranger.

Strangers like Audrey Rae, a twenty-eight-year-old sexually fluid, bisexual-identifying young woman in my focus group who asked that I make sure the book included conversations "about those of us who don't fit into a heteronormative binary." So I include strangers like Jane, who asked that I pray for her in her journey to heterosexuality. I include strangers like Ty Adams, whose vitriolic responses to gays and lesbians provide them no comfort or welcome. And I include strangers like the fictional Rev. Myrtle Black, who is actualized in the everyday experiences of women clergy struggling with their sexual orientation and the ethical use of their clerical authority. To meet the stranger does not require that the stranger come out as "gay and good." Nor does it invalidate the experiences of same-sex-desiring women who are trying to lead celibate heterosexual lives. Hospitality calls for an acceptance of the murkiness of life, which is present in all stages, as presented in chapter 5's discussion of senior sexuality. A womanist model of sexual hospitality reminds the black church and those ministries targeting its constituents that its best self is presented when it advocates for sexual freedom, but if it cannot offer words of welcome to these strangers, then certainly it can remain silent while people advocate for their own sexual liberty.[27]

5 · "THE LORD STILL HAS WORK FOR ME TO DO"

Analyzing Senior Sexuality and Faith-Based Sexuality Ministries

If old people show the same desires, the same feelings, and the same requirements as the young, the world looks upon them with disgust: in them love and jealousy seem revolting or absurd, sexuality repulsive and violence ludicrous. They are required to be a standing example of all the virtues. —SIMONE DE BEAUVOIR, *The Coming of Age*

9 No widow may be put on the list of widows unless she is over sixty, has been faithful to her husband, 10 and is well known for her good deeds, such as bringing up children, showing hospitality, washing the feet of the Lord's people, helping those in trouble and devoting herself to all kinds of good deeds. 11 As for younger widows, do not put them on such a list. For when their sensual desires overcome their dedication to Christ, they want to marry. 12 Thus they bring judgment on themselves, because they have broken their first pledge. —1 TIMOTHY 5:9–12 (NIV)

A few years ago, while waiting for a prescription to be filled at my local Walgreens, I watched an octogenarian couple struggle in the condoms aisle for nearly a half hour, reading the back of packages and looking in bewilderment at the various types and sizes of condoms available. Finally I mustered enough courage to intrude into these strangers' lives and offer my assistance. I approached the elderly woman first, as I believed she would be more comfortable talking to a woman about her needs. She privately told me that she had been warned that she needed him to "wear one of those things" but that she had never actually purchased one. She shared a pleasant conversation with me as I offered recommendations for brands and sizes. I joked that size does matter in condom purchasing, otherwise she would end up on a gynecological excavation trying to retrieve an oversized condom that slipped off inside her. In a moment of pure comedy she yelled down to her partner that he needed to move away from the gold pack Trojan Magnums after I informed her that those were for men of wider girth and size. I stood with her for a few additional minutes, as I also wanted to give her a lubricant recommendation and some preferences for foreplay massagers and oils that I thought she might need to make her sexual experience pleasurable. She hushed me from talking about her sexual pleasure, and I was reminded of the many barriers black women have to discussing their sexuality. While I felt good about my intervention that night, I still remember the elderly woman's look of shame when I first offered my assistance. I left the store pondering the messages that older black women receive about their sexuality. This chapter looks at another marginalized group, as I discuss a long-avoided topic: senior black Christian women's sexuality.

Investigating how older heterosexual black churchwomen participate in faith-based sexuality ministries involves determining what it means to be sexually agential as an elderly Christian woman. Tracing the sexual discourse of seasoned black churchwomen's participation in social and religious media as well as their participation in the Pinky Promise Movement illuminates how little the message of abstinence and celibacy changes from generation to generation. Some senior black churchwomen function as gatekeepers of sexual silencing, a system that ultimately results in their shame and angst. As sexual agents adhering to black Christian sexuality norms, older black Christian women advocate celibacy as still relevant despite these messages typically being marketed to much younger women. While accepting the freely pursued choice of celibacy for some elderly black churchwomen, I suggest that womanist sexual ethics can provide a corrective to mandated celibacy and marriage expectations by recommending sexual generosity, a concept that embraces the plurality of relationships that can be experienced in seasoned age.

The Erasure of Older Black Women from Scholarly Research

While elderly black women can be found in abundance in black churches, research on their lived experiences is often lacking, especially in relation to their sexuality and faith. Although most of the research on the elderly focuses on those who are sixty-five and older, I chose the AARP's definition of *senior* as age fifty and older. I found that tracking the experiences of women as young as fifty revealed how sexual messages are adapted as women age and enter different stages of religious participation and validation. Women over fifty are also an important age bracket; the data from the Centers for Disease Control and Prevention demonstrate that the number of new HIV infections of women in this age group has been rising at a higher rate than in any other age group.[1] In addition my focus group interviews and primary research indicate that women over fifty are prime consumers of religious culture and are an overlooked population in discussions on aging, sexuality, and faith communities.

The turn to black senior women's sexuality means uncovering topics deemed fairly taboo for researchers in the fields of gerontology and sexuality studies. A clear understanding of the many definitions of sexuality can be a good first step in breaking through that taboo. While senior adults may commit themselves to celibacy because of their religious convictions, they may also do so because they have a narrower understanding of sexuality as penile-vaginal intercourse, and they presume difficulties with this type of sexual expression indicate an end to their sexual life (perhaps sanctioned by God). However, gerontologists and sexologists know very well that sexual activity can include far more than just coital sex, and they can instruct physicians and clinicians on how to help seniors "make love with what they have," providing alternatives like creativity in positions and expression, conversation, fondling, kissing, and manual stimulation, before advising sexual enhancement drugs or other measures.[2] These interventions are in some of the more recent research, but while strides have been made in understanding sexuality among older adults, almost all of the major studies (AARP Sex Survey, the National Social Life, Health, and Aging Project, Masters and Johnson surveys, etc.) included only Caucasian, highly educated, healthy older adults.[3] Only with the increase in sexually transmitted infections among communities of color has there been any measurable shift in research. Yet even with this heightened urgency, the multidisciplinary field of gerontology still lags behind in research on black women's sexuality.

Given the increasing rate of sexually transmitted diseases among elderly black women, one would expect an expanded research portfolio to explore the sexual experiences, risk factors, and prevention measures for this cohort. However, sexuality studies as a discipline has presented nuanced scholarship on the lives of older black gay men while being depressingly silent on the heterosexual and lesbian sexual experiences of elderly black women. While this may partly reflect ageism and sexism through omission it probably also reflects the continuation of stereotypes that lead to the sexual silencing of senior black women.

While sexuality studies in general must deal with the asexualization of the elderly, the myths shared about their sexuality are magnified when considering particular cultural contexts. For example, in American society discussions of sexual activity are generally reserved for able-bodied white youth. The bodies of people of color are incessantly sexualized as performing illicit sex as persons of color are penalized for engaging in sexual relationships outside of the norm of white, heterosexual, youthful sexual activity.[4] Implicit in these messages about whiteness, youth, and ableist constructs is the message that senior citizens, whose bodies may be less flexible and deemed less desirable, should not be having sexual desire or engaging in sexual activity. Laura Carstensen, a psychology of aging professor at Stanford University, asserts that these myths reign supreme in society even though life expectancy increased by thirty years in the past century; society has not crafted new norms about life and family that would contradict such myths and show that new research studies are necessary.[5]

The need for new norms increases exponentially when one recognizes that older black women have been stereotyped as asexual Mammies. The Mammy's fictional creation is a "myth that has taken on reality and then moved on to become a stereotype"; historical records illustrate that there were very few women who fit the stereotype of being an overweight, sexless, religious, nurturing domestic; yet this trope was deemed necessary because it offered an alternative to the evil Jezebel imagery who was driven by her sexual libido.[6] Ignoring this legacy meant that the discipline of sexuality studies also neglected to note the racialized differences in the ways that senior black women's sexuality is discussed and perceived.

This neglect of this sexuality in both aging and sexuality studies is further complicated by the staying power of the caricatures of black women that do not mesh with the cultural association of elderly black women with religious institutions. In one opinion, these women are viewed as de-eroticized domestics, making sexually active older black women not match the asexual, religiously pious image of mature black women. For instance, many black churches have a woman or women whose role is that of the church mother, a position that varies but is typically held by a venerable woman who is considered an exemplar of spiritual maturity and morality.[7] After serving in various religious capacities, these women's moral character is unassailable, making any connection to their sexuality suspect. Despite these stereotypes being rooted in both myth and reality, overcoming the disciplinary obsolescence of older black female sexuality in sexuality and gerontology studies is necessary because the increase in HIV and other sexually transmitted infections in senior black women proves that they are sexually active. Their sexual decision making is misunderstood or unacknowledged, which results in their lack of access to critical information to safeguard their sexual health. It is also valuable to connect these images and disciplines because exploring the sexual lives of older adults may also provide a window into their religious lives as well.

Faith-Based Sexuality Ministries and Older Black Churchwomen

Faith-based sexuality ministries tend to be technology based and older women's participation in them goes against another set of stereotypes about seniors, namely that they are less likely to use and be influenced by technology. Yet according to a 2012 Pew Research Center study, more than 50 percent of survey respondents over sixty-five were Internet users; 77 percent owned cell phones (albeit typically not smartphones); 86 percent used email; and 47 percent used social media sites like Facebook.[8] The increase in technology use reflects a national sample of elderly persons' understanding of technology as a means of gaining increased access to social support from various communities and across generations.

Data tracking of seniors' use of religious media and technology shows that while there is not widespread adoption of new technological advances, there are certain mediums that are more appealing to the elderly. For instance, religious technologies such as phone-calling systems, sermons on CD, DVD, and cassette tape, and streaming religious programming on websites are in greater use by seniors. In the American Congregations 2010 survey, supervised by the religion sociologist Scott Thumma, data pointed to increased use of religious media by congregations as both a marketing tool to attract new members and a means of connecting to current members. The study found that because Facebook pages have a dynamic, inter-active quality, they are great tools for "congregational insiders" to maintain their fellowship; this means of connecting could potentially lure more sea-soned individuals into participation.[9]

To test this national sampling with local black congregations, I conducted an informal interview with eight male and two female pastors of predomi-nantly female black congregations. To questions on media usage, all the pastors noted an increased presence of their senior female congregants on Facebook. One wrote, "FB is now for older people. I have several women who use FB and will share things about me or church." Another shared that his elderly female congregants send him more messages via Facebook than any of his other congregants. Rather than read these experiences with technology as anomalies, the impact of senior women texting, using phone chat rooms for prayer lines, and sending inspirational Facebook messages is noteworthy.

I was surprised to find older women participating in the Pinky Promise Movement, given that the founder is a relatively young woman who mar-kets her ministry to women in their twenties and mid-thirties. The Pinky Promise Movement revolves around "intervangelist" Heather Lindsey, who is primarily active online (although she does do limited speaking events at marriage and singles conferences), so I expected her to have limited expo-sure to aging Christians. I was surprised to find myself seated beside black women who were certainly over the age of fifty at the 2014 and 2015 Pinky Promise Conference. Naively assuming these women were seeking to learn more about submission and fidelity in their marriage, I was shocked to learn that they were there as singles in Christ!

It was only then that I began to notice the numerous messages to aging single women at the conference. For example, in Pastor Cornelius Lind-sey's sermon he instructed the audience that singleness is a woman's time to devote to God; if a woman remains single all her life "that's okay because the Lord still has work for her to do." Heather Lindsey reiterated this notion by stating that we were going to have a marriage ceremony to Christ because this is the first person a woman should be married to, and even if no other relationship came along, this is the one that is most important. The Pinky Promise website allows women to create closed-access discussion groups as well as GroupMe text messaging that allows private group conversations. As a participant observer I joined the "40 Somethings and 50 Somethings Sisters in Christ" discussion group, a space created for women who were committed to purity and holiness and looking to connect with like-minded sisters their age. Within this group women were happy to talk with women who were closer to their own age as many remarked that they were the oldest women in their local group. These spaces are unique for women over fifty to discuss the intimacies of their lives.

Similarly senior women from my focus groups had purchased religious books, tapes, and CDsand DVDs because the "truth" shared by Prophetess Juanita Bynum resonated with them. Why was celibacy still alluring to women who were well beyond the expected marriage age? Why would these women choose to spend their time and resources in audiences younger than they? What could these younger women possibly teach them about chastity and the Christian lifestyle? Perhaps they found that these ministries allowed them a level of anonymity; for example, one can join Pinky Promise with an alias, and religious media can be shipped to the privacy of one's home. Regardless of the lure, these women clearly found something instructive in messages that were most likely crafted with much younger audiences in mind. These ministries also offered a relatively judgment-free space to ask questions and seek solutions in ways that may be shunned in churches.

You've Lost That Loving Feeling? Obstacles to Sexual Activity

Black women who are over fifty are part of the baby boomer generation, so they grew up during a time when sexuality was seldom discussed and sexual silencing was the norm; they also came of age against the backdrop of the Kinsey sexuality studies, the "Summer of Love," the availability of birth control and access to abortion, the civil rights movement, and feminism, which challenged the importance of being a virgin before marriage and the teaching that women should be sexually submissive. And they are the first generation to experience widespread divorce.[10] "Sambo," a Baptist, middle-class participant in a group interview in my hometown, said, "Older women are definitely thinking that when you marry someone it's until death do you part. Back in the day those older women put up with a lot with their spouse—other women, other children by different women. But the older generation didn't talk about it because it wasn't a whole lot they could do." At age fifty-two Sambo was speaking of a generation just prior to hers as she noted the variation of values; she felt her generation was more comfortable with divorce than her mother's. Thus despite the fact that as a whole this cohort is known for its sexual freedom as well as its adherence to religious values, these women are still oriented by a unique set of sexual norms.

One particular challenge in this group is the lack of available monogamous sexual partners, which is particularly worrisome because of the privileged place given to marriage as the "right" context to engage in sexual activity. The senior black population has a greater shortage of men than any other group, with an average of 129 women for every 100 men; by age eighty-five there are 200 women for every 100 men.[11] Finding a marriage partner often takes a backseat to finding any available partner for those in this age range who want to date and be intimate with someone of their own race. My interview with Ms. Joyce, a sixty-nine-year-old heterosexual widow and mother of two adult children, uncovered this lack of availability. Ms. Joyce is a religious leader serving in numerous positions of authority in her church. She is middle class with a graduate degree and is proud of her self-confidence and self-reliance. Her parents had not pressured her to marry, but still she married young. Now that she is a widow, she does not express interest in being married again, but she would like a companion and expects that they should maintain separate homes. In discussing her difficulty finding this companion, she commented, "People in the church expect you to find someone. If I have on something nice people will say I've got a boyfriend. No, I wish! I would really like to have a nice companion. Someone to go places with or someone to talk to, but I haven't been around anyone who is single. The men who seem to be interested in me aren't single, and I can't go that route." She explained that she had widow friends who had bad experiences with men they thought were available but who turned out to be married, and she decided that she was better off single and safe from disappointment. I found Ms. Joyce's narrative of being single because of this partner gap quite similar to the stories shared by women who were much younger. Distinctive to her experience is that she had been married for over twenty-five years and had enjoyed monogamous marital sexual relations. Now that she is open to the idea of dating someone, she is considered single by her own choice, that is, out of respect for her late husband and out of respect for her religious status rather than the fact that no one is available for her to date.[12]

Another challenge facing experienced black women who wish to engage in some form of sexual activity is that there may be physical challenges as a result of menopause that impact their sex lives. Divorce and death put many women back into the dating scene at a time in lives when their bodies must make certain adjustments to make heterosexual intercourse painless.[13] These difficulties may go undiagnosed, as doctors tend not to ask about these changes during a woman's annual visit. Since she is beyond needing contraception, conversations about sexually risky behavior are often avoided. While men have had a boon with the availability of Viagra to treat the fact that elderly men may need more direct stimulation of the penis to maintain an erection and orgasm, aging women have not been the recipients of the same marketing frenzy to make Osphena (an non-estrogen oral medication to increase vaginal secretions) as readily available.[14]

One of my focus group conversations concluded with a discussion of senior sexual agency and advocated for greater conversation in our religious communities about the sexual realities of senior citizens. One interviewee, "Shay," age thirty, is a pharmacy technician; she discussed having senior women clients who come in regularly to get their medicine "to keep their juices going." Some in the group were enlightened that there were medications to help women stay lubricated. One participant, "Ms. Cookie," a sixty-four-year-old divorcee, enthusiastically described the medication as "a wonder in my soul!" The group's reaction displayed both the "dirty old woman" stereotype as well an appreciation of the ways black women were learning to express their sexual needs and have them met.

Negotiating Sexual Agency

An important negotiation that more mature black women expressed both in the literature and in my focus groups was the need to move to a more inclusive understanding of themselves as sexual beings. The sociologist Meika Loe offers an astute framing for a more encompassing discussion of sexuality as she discusses four ways in which older adults experience desire: sexual relationships, nonsexual intimacies, caretaking, and intellectual stimulation.[15] This self-defining includes older women embracing intimacy as an aspect of sexuality that does not involve intercourse. Ms. Cookie recalled her relationship with a longtime male friend who was in love with her but had never seen her naked. This move to value their sexual worth not from a place of lack or diminishing capacity but rather from a new place of wisdom was tied into their religious understandings of themselves. This meant that their negotiations as sexual beings also meant negotiating who they should be in light of their Christian commitments.

For some there was outright angst about how to obey biblical scripts about their sexuality. Several women talked about the biblical expectation that they not fornicate or have sexual relations outside of a marital covenant. There is also a biblical expectation that widows not remarry: 1 Timothy 5:6 encourages older widows (those over sixty) to remain single, since "the widow who lives for pleasure is dead even while she lives." How are women to handle these two conflicting realities when their sexual lives are still a vivid part of their current identity?

Ms. Cookie is a middle-class religious leader in her church. She shared with the focus group that the reason she had been married and divorced three times was because the church promoted sex only within marriage. Her mother also discouraged her from having sex or children before marriage, which confused her:

> I grew up in a Pentecostal church. The people would tell you to get married first, but then you would see some of the church leaders not married with kids. So you begin to wonder if this [abstinence] is just something that people can't do! Because even though it's [nonmarital abstinence is] advocated, you have people doing it [having sex] all the time so you wonder why even tell people this [to abstain]. . . . It [nonmarital abstinence] does have value if you can conform your activities to one person and stay with that person. To me, that's almost like a miracle. I know people who have been married forty to fifty years to the same person, and they do it [remain faithful to their spouse]. I just don't know how people do it.

Her transparency with the group that she knew sex to be fun and pleasurable and yet banned outside of marital relationships indicated that she was very aware of the numerous messages telling her how she should express herself; yet, she didn't know if these expectations were realistic given the lives contemporary Christians lead.

Mother Stella Gets Her Groove Back: Reconceptualizing Sexuality

Seeing oneself as a fully aware, personally responsible, sexual being is often a task that takes a lifetime. Perhaps this is another role that faith-based sexuality ministries can serve as they can help women become more comfortable with the skin they are in. Ministries can help women deal with dreams that never materialize (children, husband, wealth, etc.) and can help them celebrate the life they have created and embrace their new identity markers (widow, divorcée, grandmother, etc.).[16] In these contemplative moments, graying women are gifted with the ability to reconceptualize their sexual self by taking into account their entire life narrative. They know what they like and dislike, what they desired to have more of in previous partnerships, how to make sense of how they are perceived, and whether they care about these perceptions. As a seasoned sexual self they may set different parameters for themselves than they had before. For example, Ms. Cookie stated that she realized she now had a lot of things to consider before sex because "[her] value system over the years has changed": "Sex is just not sex for me. Are you after me because I have a good job? Now the person has to be a person I would accept in the social arena, not just a person I would sneak around with. It's changed for me. . . . When I was young I didn't care, but this has changed for me. Now I want a person who can meet my family, that I can take to church with me. . . . I want a conversation too." Ms. Cookie's revelation mirrors the findings of Katherine Conway-Turner's study of older African American women who reported that while sexual activity was pleasurable, it was not the most necessary component of a good relationship. Instead women found more pleasure in affection, kissing, touching, empathy, and seeing their partner as a true friend.[17] Yet this reprioritization of intimacy as a major aspect of sexuality should not indicate that senior women express little desire for sexual intercourse. They just reframe this desire according to their new realities, where monogamous partners may be harder to find and health concerns may make the pursuit of pleasurable sex a lower priority.

Sexual desire is not often associated with more mature women as people erroneously assume that women are beyond that stage of life. In fact one participant came to my Nashville focus group to talk with women more advanced in years admitting that she wanted to learn at "what age I can expect it to dry up." Data contradicts this notion and points to the modifications that women use so that sexual expression can continue. Diavante rejected the notion that sexual desire "dried up" as women aged:

> Regardless of how you get it [sex], you're still a woman. Things that come with womanhood you don't lose. I talk to women in their sixties and seventies that are still very much sexually active or at least have that desire. It's not like they forget what it is like. . . . You might have some physical, I won't say disabilities or things that may prevent you

from engaging in sexual activity, but I don't think that it's necessarily because you don't want to or don't think about it anymore or don't desire it anymore. I don't think age has anything to do with it as far as that desire and being able to talk about it.

My focus group in Chatham had a larger number of participants over the age of fifty (five out of seven participants, and the remaining two were forty-eight and forty-nine), and there Diavante's view was not in the minority. Most of these women were eager to talk about sexual desire and sexual activity (although most overwhelmingly framed it within marriage).

This perspective was the one I expected, since I had grown up in this community around august women since my grandmother raised me. My grandmother's generation of women were sassy, senior women who were never timid about talking with younger women about waiting for sex and, once they were married, about making sure to sexually please their spouse. In fact, in this congregation I did not grow up with silence around sexuality; there was a lot of sexual talk but most of it contained restrictions. I remember being able to traverse new territory in my congregation as a young woman who had decided to study sexuality in college, and one of my favorite memories is of bringing home dental dams (to be used during oral sex) as show-and-tell for my grandmother, who then insisted that I bring them to the church to show her friends. I had a two-hour conversation with churchwomen over seventy about dental dams, oral sex, and why this protection was necessary. No one stopped the conversation or suggested that the church was not an appropriate place for such a conversation. Indeed they seemed eager to receive new information even if they were not going to act on it. Thus my early experiences verified the 2009 AARP sexuality study finding that sexual frequency and satisfaction were higher among unmarried elderly. Indeed, Mother Stella has good company in getting her groove back.[18]

This research contradicts the image of the sexually conservative religious leader who is disinclined to place her sexual desires above her commitment to her religious community. In my interviews and in the literature there was neither an absence of sexual desire nor complete submission to this desire. Instead there were veiled references to sexual pleasure as a part of seniors' current sexual identity. In a 2008 book entitled *Still Doing It: The Intimate Lives of Women over Sixty*, readers are introduced to Elaine, a deeply spiritual, churchgoing, eighty-year-old African American woman who says, "One of the main reasons my sexuality has remained alive is that I love myself. I love masturbation. Thank God for it." She goes on to share that despite the fact that she and many of her churchgoing black female friends grew up at a time when masturbation was seen as a dirty thing that nice women did not do, somehow she was led to believe differently. She states that although she thinks masturbation is fine, her "friends, oh my goodness, they throw up their hands at it. But I'm sure they've thought about it. Maybe they don't know how to go about it, you know, to pleasure themselves. But I do."[19] Despite the stigmatization of seeing themselves as sexual beings, women like Elaine offer a reframing of the sexually active senior who is not paralyzed by her religious convictions to the point of denying part of her sensual nature.

Conversations with elderly black churchwomen reiterate that while some are comfortable pursuing their own sexual desires; many more are rehearsing an old trope in which to receive the companionship and intimacy they prefer they reluctantly concede to what is pleasurable for their male partner. Earlier I described how I encouraged an older woman in Walgreens to purchase a lubricant to make the sexual act more enjoyable for herself when her partner is ready when she is not. She scoffed at my suggestion, assuming that their discomfort was to be expected or ignored since she had a duty to please their spouse. Like Sarah in Genesis 18:12, some older women wonder, "Shall I have pleasure in my old age?" Despite expecting seasoned church members to make different decisions because of their lifetime of knowledge, the prevalent message continues to be that women should privilege men's needs above their own. All of the senior women I surveyed knew men who were nonmonogamous while women were expected to remain monogamous. Particularly pernicious to the aging black female population is the fact that as a consequence, women engage in higher-risk sexual behaviors (such as sharing partners and not requiring condoms).[20] Negotiating for themselves with their sexual partners is often a low priority simply because so few partners are available.

Negotiating Family and Sexual Agency

While negotiating for their own sexual interests can be difficult for aging black women and their sexual partners, evidence indicates it is even more daunting to negotiate with one's family and religious community. Perhaps because these relationships are deemed of higher priority, there is more hesitancy to burst the bubble of piety and restraint. In Conway-Turner's study of older black women, one of her interviewees illustrated this point; the woman believed that even hinting about sexuality in public or at family events would be improper. Conway-Turner notes that her interviewee found it very important not to appear sexual around her family, believing that her role as mother, grandmother, and great-grandmother was not consistent with sexual expression. Instead her role was to care for those in need and to teach God's word, not to promote a black Christian sexuality.[21] This importance of care for family and purpose in God is echoed in many of the narratives of black women's sexual angst. Though they are consenting adults who are physically capable of sexual relationships, many elder black women feel confined by the double messages they receive from their church and family.

My interview with Ms. Joyce demonstrated this dual dynamic in which she felt that her church expected her to find someone else but her children had trouble accepting the possibility of her seeing someone romantically. Her compromise was to be open to the idea of dating but to be content in her single status, which meant not pursuing a partner. Adult children are significant roadblocks to their mother's sexual conquests, as the children often convey ageist assumptions that find their parent's sexuality perverse or at the very least unsettling. Older black mothers who are concerned about their children's opinions often have to negotiate around their children's expectations, which is a bit ironic given that all parties are fully mature adults.

This negotiation is even more awkward when the church community is included. In Frederick's study of black women in North Carolina, she highlights these very tensions experienced by black churchgoing women as they negotiated their sexual and spiritual selves: "Pregnancy for most is a nonissue, fear of 'what people think' has far less importance, and parental disapproval is a concern that carries far less weight. . . . Today however women hold ideas about sexual activity that are sometimes even more rigid than those of their earlier days. . . . Instead of fearing 'mom,' they revere God."[22] This reverence for God is also an understanding of the influential role that women of their status hold in their religious communities and a fear of being perceived as actively living outside of God's laws. Arguably more so than other Christian women who are living for Christ, senior Christian women are given a double expectation of holiness. This expectation that elderly women are assumed to be mothers of the church, spiritual and moral leaders, or, as Beauvoir says, examples of all the virtues, is also the case for parachurch ministries where older women are positioned as spiritual mentors for younger women. At the Oasis Christian Center in Hollywood, the God's Chicks ministry targets predominantly minority women based on the admonition in Titus 2:4 that challenges older women to be morally upright teachers who model for younger women how to be virtuous and pure.[23] Following the biblical model, spiritually mature women are to be exemplars of purity and holiness, not women who dare admit to sexual desire.

This was also evident in the focus group conversation with the women from my hometown Baptist community. Diavante offered an example of this modeling when she asserted that older women were highly respected, with wisdom they can impart to younger women. She advocated for intergenerational sharing in which elderly women talk with younger women about sexuality, love, and relationships. When I asked whether older women would get a negative reputation for sharing this type of information, Diavante said if the woman was strong she wouldn't care what people said because she would be helping somebody: "Helping the next woman coming along, that's what it is all about. It's about teaching even if you've made mistakes along the way." Diavante's suggestion was encouraging; in her vision, senior women's knowledge is accepted regardless of whether they are living or have lived a life that is considered pure.

Mash-up Religion: Negotiating Sacred and Sexual Spaces

In his book *Mashup Religion* the homiletician John McClure presents theological mash-ups as lived religion wherein new ideas are created by the merging of traditional and novel understandings of faith.[24] This is relevant for interpreting the ways elderly black churchwomen negotiate their sexual and sacred spaces. Their mash-up is how they take the biblical mandates of submission and celibacy and create a code of silence around sexual mores. Simultaneously they participate in singles conferences and other faith-based sexuality ministries, evidence that they are not content to ignore their sexuality. They are actively seeking relationship even if ultimately the messages they are getting are remixed versions of the celibacy message. Nuancing the lived embodiment of their faith shows women who are pursuing more relevant messages for their particular life experiences.

The ingredients in this particular mash-up are a reverence for black Christian sexuality as evidenced in biblical standards of purity, models of marriage, and respectability offered to black women who live a "chaste" life. Simultaneously, a sexual silencing takes place as elderly black women enact a politics of decency that chokes them as well as their daughters. The politics of respectability historically may have been necessary to combat the stereotypes of black women, but the current "climate of decency" sets an impossible standard by which to live.[25] This is perhaps what draws women to participate in faith-based sexuality ministries: they hope for clarity about what to do with the sexual urges they still have. This is also what drew women to participate in my focus groups. Packaged as "new, relevant faith," these ministries offer space in which to talk about their sexual frustrations even if they do so as part of an audience that is significantly younger than they.

New Models for Sexual Discourse with Older Black Women

The preceding chapters followed several faith-based sexuality ministries that offer models for conversation on sexuality. This chapter concludes with two potential faith-based models that offer more helpful strategies to senior black churchwomen who are seeking solutions for their sexual concerns. The first model is an adaptation of a CDC-funded HIV prevention curriculum, Sisters Informing Sisters about Topics on AIDS (SISTA), that was developed for young African American women involved in heterosexual relationships. The researchers adapted the SISTA curriculum to assess women over fifty and conducted the interviews in three black churches in Mecklenburg County, North Carolina.[26] This model is notable because it gathered these women in an environment where they would be most comfortable: black churches. Since the church is a community institution, it was an ideal place in which to conduct a forum on sexuality and HIV/AIDS. A participant remarked that the church was accessible to all people, and since these women draw strength from God the church had a responsibility to teach them "how to live, how to love, and how to protect ourselves from the virus."[27] Though they recognized black churches have been silent on the topic of AIDS, the women participants still felt that the church was the ideal space to broach the topic. Concurring with this sentiment, "Ms. White" in my Nashville focus group suggested that the church should have a class on sexuality and what the Bible teaches about it, despite the topic being taboo. At seventy-three, Ms. White was my oldest participant. She had one child and was an active member of a local Baptist congregation. She said we black Christian women have a responsibility to the entire community to better educate ourselves about sexuality and not just rely on prior generations' messages. Perhaps what Ms. White had in mind was something substantive, like the official statement from the Presbyterian Church (U.S.A.) that speaks against the collective denial of the sexual needs of the elderly and even argues for openness to a range of possibilities beyond the traditional norm of sex only in marriage.[28] This type of generational statement would be a great space to start discussions on the sexual needs of older black Christian women, but there are no such universal statements in black Protestantism.

While acknowledging the promise of a church-centered model that targets senior black women (having participated in one in my own church community), I am still concerned that the model requires pastoral approval and perhaps biblical adherence.[29] My lack of faith in pastors' sensitivity to this reality is the result of my own difficulty gaining wider pastoral support for my request for focus group participants. My personal difficulty is also grounded in a 2006 study on whether black churches could play a role in reducing African American women's risk of STIs and unintended pregnancy. This study also had great difficulty getting pastoral approval for the researchers to speak with congregants. Out of fifty clergy contacted, the researchers were able to gain consent from only four black clergy, three of whom were women. A Congo proverb states, "The foolish woman grows angry because they teach her"; for some black male leaders this alternative female-dominated space could be problematic. Some feel threatened if there is space for black women to discuss their sexual agency. This might explain why women view faith-based sexuality ministries as an option.

Womanist Sexual Generosity

Dissatisfaction with the church-based model leads to a mash-up model of sexual discourse that merges the theological framings of the black church tradition with new approaches from womanist sexual ethics. This model is womanist sexual generosity and fits the needs of an aging demographic of black churchwomen. The framing of sexual generosity comes from the Catholic sexual ethicist John Portmann. In his recent book *The Ethics of Sex and Alzheimer's* Portmann wrestles with how to respond to spouses whose significant others have Alzheimer's disease and who want to remain sexually active. His final chapter is devoted to sexual generosity, which he defines as a subset of emotional generosity in marital concerns.[30] While he is intentionally not concerned with a universal sexual generosity that includes premarital sex this is specifically what womanist sexual generosity develops.

Portmann's profile of a sexually generous person is someone who shares her own body freely and, if circumstances permit, shares the body of her spouse with another so that he may be sexually satisfied.[31] Sexual sharing is done to placate the needs of another, but there are always limits. Clearly a sexually generous person does not have to allow anything and everything; nor is this done out of pity for the partner. Portmann's model is only for how spouses with Alzheimer's might make sexual decisions, but the principle behind his ethic is applicable to elderly black churchwomen.

In both instances there are communal expectations that seemingly prohibit sexual expression. For the married spouse of an Alzheimer's patient, the expectation is that she remain sexually faithful to the spouse "for better or for worse," which seems to doom the non-Alzheimer's spouse to abstinence until her spouse's death. Likewise a pious churchgoing older black woman may be expected to remain celibate because of her religious commitment. Both face a scenario that may not match their actual sexual desires. Portmann's model of sexual generosity offers both groups a means of sexual activity. Yet for seasoned black churchwomen a womanist intervention is also required.

This womanist intervention takes seriously the specific faith experiences of black women. Alice Walker describes womanists as responsible, grown black women who are sometimes lovers of individual men, sexually and/ or nonsexually, but are always a lover of the Spirit.[32] This adapted definition highlights the experiences of senior black churchwomen who express their faith as an ultimate concern but who are also sensual beings who may choose to act on their sexual desire with physical intercourse or simply by seeking intimate relationality.

This emphasis on the womanist as a responsible and grown black woman is the result of the increased HIV infection rate in women over fifty. It would not be ethically sound to advocate a model of sexual discourse that did not make responsibility the first priority. This womanist responsibility is evident in Ms. Cookie's conversation with me about how her views of sexuality have changed over the years. She feels she must now acknowledge how her sexual decisions impact others in her community. Her message to the group was this: "Your bodies are temples of God, and you know this, but on the other hand sex is fun. But you still have to bring it under control. Do you let your selfish desires destroy you and everybody around you? Because we are all connected. I would love to fantasize and have all the sex I wanted to all day, every day, all night long, which is not even possible. Everything you do connects to somebody else. You must have some parameters, some respect for yourself and other people." Her understanding of her ability to be sexually agential came not just with religious convictions but also with an understanding of its communal consequences. Advocating for womanist sexual generosity is not an invitation to promiscuity without responsibility. On the contrary, it requires commitment to one's own body, one's partner, and one's community.

In light of the plight of senior black churchwomen who are being advised to wait until marriage to have sex, a model of womanist sexual generosity offers a rethinking of sexual mores for a population who may desire companionship but not marriage. While the culture of decency demanded sexual purity and potentially decades of sexual restraint, this womanist construct presents matriarchs with a viable responsible choice to engage in sexual relationships with an emphasis on the need to protect their sexual health. Despite the demographic partner gap, senior black women may place more value in monogamous relationships as the safest solution for engaging their sexual desires.

The New Testament scholar Michael Brown notes that the "idea of sex as an expression of generosity rarely arises in African American religious discourse"; thus the introduction of the concept is a mash-up attempt to put new wine into old skins.[33] The concept of sexual generosity should not be associated with the double standard that requires only women to restrain their sexual appetites to monogamous marital relationships. Instead these monogamous relationships need not be marriages. In a society where black women have the lowest marriage rates, it is irresponsible to continue to highlight monogamy as the only norm for sexual activity. It negates the desires of those who seek companionship and not marriage, women like Juanita, an African American seventy-four-year-old devout Christian widow who doesn't want to remarry. She was interviewed for the book *Still Doing It* and said she was unwilling to give up the "gratifying relationship and sex life she has with her long-term boyfriend" even though her church considers it a sin.[34] In a womanist sexual generosity model her relationship has standing and value and can even be celebrated, as she is involved in a responsible sexual relationship that brings her and her partner comfort and pleasure.

For senior women who are open to being sexually generous this recommendation brings out of the shadows their "special" friends or unnamed associates with whom they are sexually involved but not publicly presented to their religious community. This framework is based on the notion that we should customize our sexual ethics to fit our life experiences and situation. Rev. Dr. Susan Newman argues that this new sexual ethic starts when a woman takes up the freedom to choose for herself how she will express herself sexually, and a womanist sexually generous person makes these decisions with her self, her partner, and her community in mind.[35]

This new sexual ethic begins by making visible senior black women's sexuality and highlights their sexual agency. While this chapter discussed the numerous obstacles these women face to negotiate their sexuality, the womanist sexual generosity model reframes faith-based sexuality ministries' discussions of celibacy until marriage to fit an age demographic that may no longer seek marriage but desires continued companionship. This model of sexual generosity is centered around accessing the sexual agency of a community whose right to make sexual choices has typically been prescribed for them. These sexual choices may or may not include marriage. They may include living with a nonmarital partner and never having sexual intercourse. As I explain in the next chapter, these choices may include pursuing relationships solely for sexual pleasure. Such choices exonerate senior women from the false guilt they experience if they are sexually active and leaders in their religious communities. They resanctify as moral choices how these women are living their lives. Concomitantly they reevaluate the logic that sexual purity is required for right relationship with the Divine. This womanist model of sexual generosity is a gift to seniors and hopefully one they will bequeath to subsequent generations.

6 · HORNY AND HOLY

Saved Women Seeking Sexual Pleasure

In this here place, we flesh; flesh that weeps, laughs; flesh that dances on bare feet in grass. Love it. Love it hard. Yonder they do not love your flesh. They despise it. . . . This is flesh I'm talking about here. Flesh that needs to be loved. —TONI MORRISON, *Beloved*

Grant me chastity and continence but not yet. —SAINT AUGUSTINE, *Confessions*

Pleasure is revolutionary for me, as a black woman, prioritizing my desires and putting me first. —#BLACKCHURCHSEX

I can still remember my excitement at the opportunity to present with the womanist legend Dr. Kelly Brown Douglas at the 2012 What Manner of Woman Is This: Womanist Gala and Black Church Summit at Union Theological Seminary in New York City. In my imagination Dr. Brown Douglas would lead the group through a discussion of Platonized sexuality, emphasizing how and why blacks have chosen to distance themselves from more fruitful discussions of sexuality. I would then discuss black women and sexual pleasure. Unfortunate circumstances kept Douglas from attending the workshop, and I facilitated the workshop by myself. I stuck with my original plan, discussing Douglas's argument on the bifurcation of body and sexuality from spirit, but when I made the move to talk about sexual pleasure, someone raised her hand and reminded me that we had not talked about the stumbling blocks associated with black female sexuality, such as trauma, abuse, and stereotypes. Sadly, this took up the remainder of our time together, and I was left wondering why black women never get to talk about our bodily pleasure. This was not my first attempt at public discourse on bodily pleasure; often this move is a conversation stopper. There is space for such discussion, as long as it is theoretical or philosophical and does not actually consider pleasuring black bodies. Yet it is to pleasure that my work keeps returning because there must be more than just disdain for black bodies.

In this chapter I unashamedly explore black female sexual pleasure and desire as a valid topic of interest and ethical decision making. For those participating in the genre of black Christian sexuality there is typically great ease in discussing sexual pleasure, although past pleasures are discounted in favor of marital delight. While not ignoring this sexual legacy, I posit that neglecting one's bodily pleasure because of a politics of respectability that prohibits sexual enjoyment is itself oppression. Womanists can reject this oppression by instead offering acceptance of the pursuit of pleasure and love of the body. Thus, a womanist model of erotic justice is bodily centered and action-oriented toward justice. It focuses on self-pleasuring, oral and anal sex, and nonmonogamous sexuality, asserting that instead of marriage as the ethical criterion of "good and godly sex," an emphasis on erotic pleasure and responsible sexuality should be normative.

Theorizing Black Female Sexual Pleasure

In addressing singles' sexuality, pleasure, or relationality black feminist theorists have tended to focus on the interlocking oppressions and history of sexual shame and pain. Pleasure is seen as an afterthought or is rarely discussed. Evelynn Hammonds comments that contemporary discussions on black female sexuality focus on repression which has naturally elided considerations of the varieties of expressions of desire.[1] The exception to this rule is Audre Lorde and her defiant dialogue on erotic desire, which I explore later in the chapter.

Hammonds articulates how Lorde and other black lesbian writers foreground same-sex desire and agency to fill a gap in scholarship.[2] Yet current research on black heterosexual pleasure from a female perspective is quite sparse. Tricia Rose concurs that while American culture is bombarded with stories on sex and romantic desire, we almost never hear what black women have to say, which is ironic given the stereotype that black women are controlled by insatiable sexual desire.[3]

Unfortunately there is likewise a dearth of research on sexual pleasure and the power of the erotic in black liberation theology. Anthony Pinn notes that even when theological discussions do attend to the erotic, these conversations are limited, because they are awkward and superficial.[4] He posits that the erotic dimension to sexuality in black liberation theology has become fetishized in such a way that it becomes relevant only if it is being discussed in a political context. Given the lack of discussion about the erotic in black theological resources, some black churchwomen go back to feminist theology for help, although they often find that "white feminists must refigure (white) female sexuality so that they are not theoretically dependent upon an absent yet-ever-present pathologized black female sexuality."[5]

Perhaps it is the myth of promiscuity or illegitimate children that keep black heterosexuals from exploring and discussing their sexual pleasures. Or it could be the result of a steady moralizing campaign that shuns the "proper lady" from talking about, let alone acting on black sexual desire. The result of this moratorium is that national sexuality studies indicate that black women are less likely than others to (1) masturbate, (2) initiate intercourse, and (3) enjoy giving and receiving oral sex.[6] Are black women reluctant to confirm their participation in acts that are sexually pleasing? Or is there truly a disconnect between black women and their sexual desire?

Though historically black female bodies have been viewed as unclean and less appealing than the European standard, nowadays there is greater acceptance of a diversity of bodily expression. At the turn of the twentieth century black women reformers were engaging in respectability campaigns considered necessary because of a widespread belief that black women were unclean and immoral.[7] Based in racist ideology accepted by many blacks in gatekeeping positions, the result was a reform of individual manners and morals that the contemporary black community perpetuates. While challenging notions of black bodies as unclean, black mothers also instructed their daughters to fight segregation through the legal system and with soap and water, and this response continues: black women still overwhelmingly encourage their daughters to use douching products, despite its lack of medical necessity.[8] The restraint mandated through respectability politics not only constrained sexual behaviors, it also undermined black women's perception of their bodies. If one believes one's body is unclean, one is unlikely to initiate oral sex or manual stimulation of oneself or a partner. Timidity with one's body yields cautious engagement with bodily pleasure.

Black Christian women face another stumbling block to securing their sexual pleasure: Christianity has long linked pleasure to lust and sin. Saint Augustine believed unchecked sexual passion to be evidence of humanity's exile from the Garden of Eden and so called for sexual restraint and indeed celibacy, or else sexual intimacy only for procreation. The early Christian tradition from Aquinas, John Calvin, and Martin Luther all shared suspicion of sexual pleasure. In her thorough examination of Christianity and sexual pleasure, the pastoral counselor Elizabeth Zagatta concludes that current Christian interpretations of sexual pleasure share this suspicion by regulating specific acts and pleasures.[9] Yet, Christian discussions of sexual pleasure usually emphasize the pleasure of the (largely white) males involved, which is not surprising given that many of the early church leaders, theologians, and ethicists were white men.

As black churches assimilated white supremacist views about blackness and black female bodies, they also accepted European views about sexuality and Christianity. Douglas's work helps to negate the unhealthy manifestations of these beliefs in black churches, but she does not take the next step of suggesting what sexual pleasure could look like in light of this history. She does offer a womanist sexual discourse of resistance that emphasizes the goodness of black bodies and sexuality by providing practical suggestions, such as getting reading groups to focus on novels that engage black sexuality, discussion groups to critically analyze black sexuality in popular culture, and Bible study groups to analyze biblical texts through the lens of black scholars. Yet where in this resistant discourse is there space for pleasure, not just a thorough understanding of the painful past?

Faith-based sexuality ministries do highlight pleasure. Whereas Douglas warns, "Passion must be seen as more than lust or desire for sexual activity," sexuality ministries preach that advice *and* revel in the ecstasy of past lustful experiences.[10] Without any allusion to shame about their past sexual decisions, televangelists and Christian leaders encourage their followers to live transparently, to disclose their full past so they can move forward. These testimonies are often filled with sexual imagery, desire, and deep longing. Similar to Foucault's description of fastidious Catholic confessions, these women's sexual testimonies succeed in bringing pleasure to the forefront.[11] Yet the leaders' treatment of sexual pleasure ultimately is not liberatory for all of their black female followers. Instead they have undervalued desire in heterosexual relationships and overemphasized it in gay and lesbian ones.

For instance, Bynum made herself famous by talking about the pleasures of sex. As a single minister she reminded her audience that even ministers long to be touched and that they also remember their sexual escapades as all-night wonders even when sexual fulfillment lasted only minutes. Using her own life as an example, Bynum implored her audience to wait for the "proper" use of their passions, that is, to wait for marriage. Within marriage they could let their inner sex kitten play! In her "Pride vs. Proverbs 31 Woman" sermon she encourages women to learn how to minister to their husband. She orders them to "put that Bible down and put a negligee on and work it," because if they close their legs to their husband somebody else will open her legs to him.[12] Boasting publicly about her own sexual prowess, she reminds them that their husbands do not want to hear them praying in tongues; they want sex! In this hierarchy women are to shake free from their sexual timidity and be sexually adventurous—within marriage. However, critical attention to her rhetoric still reveals an emphasis on the husband's pleasure and meeting his sexual needs, which tangentially then is expected to satisfy a woman's needs.

Yield Not to Temptation for Yielding Is Sin: Masturbation and Faith-Based Sexuality Ministries

Masturbation or self-pleasuring would situate a woman's needs as primary, and historically this was particularly problematic. In her "No More Sheets" sermon, Bynum became one of the first black female televangelists to publicly discuss taboo topics like masturbation and pornography. She wanted women to be sexually free within their marriages. Her daring to bring the topic into public discourse is laudable. Just asking if it is wrong for Christians to masturbate presented the possibility that it was permissible. Though Bynum concluded that masturbation is not allowable, at least she had the temerity to broach the topic and begin a conversation that other Christian leaders continued.

Bynum considered masturbation worthy of conversation because, as a single person, she had done it. Yet despite the pleasure she experienced from masturbation, she concluded that it is the "bait that Satan uses to become a master of you and send you to hell with the spirit of your mind—a form of death by your own hands."[13] Taking literally 1 Corinthians 6:8, which warns against sexual sin as sins against one's own body, Bynum asserts that a demonic spirit sexually arouses the person. She argues that the act of masturbation derives from thought, and that the thoughts needed to arouse a woman are not God-given and therefore contrary to God's "natural" order. As a form of spiritual perversion, masturbation satisfies the fleshly desire at the expense of soul. She argues that at the point of climax you lose control and give yourself over to a corrupted mind, which can encourage the virgin and secondary virgin to seek illicit sex. In a confusing twist, Bynum also finds masturbation unnecessary, a way of saying "I don't need a man!" She warns women against following this path and asks, "Are you going to meet your own needs, or ask God to send a mate to meet those needs?"[14]

Bynum warns "saved" women not to bring their reprobate sexual fantasies into their new God-ordained relationships. In one of the numerous comical moments in the "No More Sheets" sermon, she sanctions women who enter new relationships chastising their husbands, "Flip me this way, spank me this way, say this to me, etc."[15] She concludes that these women are stuck in their sexual past without any acknowledgment that they may be advocating for their own sexual pleasure.

One of the major problems with Bynum's rationale is that these women have been waiting on God to send them a mate and not all results have been successful. Indirectly women are given the idea that if they follow the steps given by the faith-based leaders they will have the tools to either make their sexual urges dissipate or to be blessed with a husband who fulfills their desires. Much of the logic of faith-based sexuality ministries assumes sexual pleasure and great ecstasy in marriage; thus, it is worth waiting for. Marla Frederick's ethnography recalled Marie, who told her daughter, "Society has put sex on a pedestal that it should not be on. . . . If you REALLY want to have some good sex, wait until you're married . . . and you have all the sex you want! Freely because that's how God made it for you to enjoy."[16] Yet rarely is sex—even sex within marriage—discussed from the female perspective of receiving sexual pleasure, not just being the one responsible for providing it. The female perspective would remind us that sexual positions and actions that promote male orgasm do not always promote female orgasm.

These evangelists typically find reprehensible any occurrences of sexual pleasure outside of marriage. In Ty Adams's discussion of sexual pleasure she considers almost everything pleasurable to be sexual sin, even kissing, because it is pleasurable and a form of foreplay. She posits that kissing serves a fleshly need and is a means of sexual stimulation that can lead to sexual intercourse.[17] She joins those who reserve the first kiss for the wedding day. That being the case, it is no mystery that she considers oral sex to be out of bounds for singles.

Sexual passions are to be avoided at all costs because they are only sanctioned within a marital bond. Adams considers masturbation equally problematic, and just like Bynum she reiterates that masturbation, a form of self-sex, is Satan's way of mastering weak individuals. While Bynum testifies that when she masturbated it made her not want a man, Adams sees female masturbation as the gateway to same-sex desire: "If you are masturbating and you are a woman, then you are having sex with a woman and you invite a lesbian spirit upon you."[18] Even if the woman is a virgin, Adams imagines her in Hell with Satan for participating in masturbation.

The irony of Bynum's and Adams's disclosures of their sexual past is that they use such vivid sexual imagery to describe the behavior from which God has delivered them. They both seem to know what they liked sexually and are choosing to refrain from these activities because they perceive them to be outside of God's law. This type of sexual awareness is one of the hidden messages of faith-based sexuality ministries. Contrary to secular feminist discussions of female sexuality or even white evangelical discourses, these faith-based sexuality ministers are not bashful about talking about what curls one's toes or makes one moan. In fact they are so aware of what is sexually pleasurable that they must restrict all such actions to keep their commitment to sexual chastity. Lorde might have rationalized their sexual avoidance as fear of the yes within; these leaders spiritualize their actions by saying yes to God.[19]

Perhaps since faith-based sexuality ministries promote celibacy in singleness they must also be more attentive to alternative sexual expressions such as masturbation, pornography, and oral and anal sex. Heather Lindsey, founder of the Pinky Promise Movement, gives particular attention to self-pleasuring techniques such as masturbation and watching pornography. In a very popular blog post in July 2013 entitled "Secret Sins: Masturbation and Pornography," Lindsey gave instructions on how to free oneself from these sins. For single women she advises (1) that they guard their hearts by avoiding blog sites that talk about sex or show celebrities naked, (2) that they stop hanging out with people who talk about sex, (3) that they avoid music that discusses sex, and (4) that they spend more daily time with God. In each of these steps she posits that participating in any activity that is sexual or provides sexual images produces the need for masturbation.

At the same time, she advises her followers, "Marriage won't cure the lust that you have and the desire you have to watch sexual movies and masturbate." She instructs women to remember that God created sex for marriage, so if women are masturbating or looking at pornography they are deliberately pushing the Holy Spirit out of their marriage and inviting Satanic spirits in. For Lindsey there are no exceptions to this doctrine, no amount of physical or emotional distance, sickness, or varying schedules that would allow a wife to satisfy her own sexual needs. Particularly telling is her advice to women who are not aroused by their husband: "Ask God to help you to be sexually attracted to him. STOP using the world's tactic [pornography] in your bedroom."[20] Such advice leaves many women without concrete and immediate access to sexual pleasure. The mantra of faith-based sexuality ministries is to lead a life of sexual purity, remain a virgin until you are married, and then reap the blessed sexual desire that comes from your obedience. To instruct women who admit that they are not sexually aroused by their God-given mate to refrain from self-pleasuring exposes a flaw in this system. The choice is stark: act on your desires *or* be godly.

Masturbation and Black Churchwomen

In my focus groups I specifically asked women about sexual pleasure and how they responded to their sexual desires. We covered a list of sexual taboos, including oral sex, anal sex, using sex toys for masturbation, watching pornography, being sexually active without being married, and engaging in sex with multiple partners. Masturbation was a topic of concern because women at different ages and relationship statuses wondered if it was permissible within Christianity. While all the other categories were problematic for Christians (although many respondents admitted to participating in these acts), there were more questions surrounding self-pleasure. In my focus groups I used both the terms *masturbation* and *self-pleasure*, in deference to the sex educator Gwendolyn Goldsby Grant's assertion that masturbation can tend to focus the attention solely on what one does with one's genitalia, whereas self-pleasuring suggests treating sexual pleasure as a whole body experience, not just erogenous areas.[21] In our conversations on sexual pleasure, Pinky Promise and Wives in Waiting members rejected masturbation summarily. Symone, a Pinky Promise member, remarked that when she stopped being in a lesbian relationship she found that it was unacceptable to masturbate because that would have been straddling the fence between fulfilling her fleshly desires and being celibate. Another Pinky Promise member, Jay, also denounced masturbation; for her the feeling of an orgasm is not worth missing out on the spiritual power, what she called the "highest places and greatest amount of anointing" that God has for her. Other focus group members found self-pleasuring a poor substitute for the spousal sexual intimacy they really desired, while some found sex toys a natural addition to their sexual tool kit. Thus there was no consensus in most of my focus groups around self-pleasure.

That the topic of masturbation was typically discussed in my focus groups as an alternative when one is out of a relationship matches the larger data set on masturbation and African American women. I had initial concerns that participants would be unwilling to talk to the group about their self-pleasuring given this highly personal and sometimes stigmatized choice, though a 2009 national sexuality study reported that 54 percent of black female participants reported solo masturbation.[22] Yet despite my concerns, participants in my rural hometown's focus group were not bashful in their responses. Asked one participant almost indignantly, "Well, does the Bible say anything about sex toys?" A lively conversation ensued, with some members arguing that using a sex toy was putting the toy in the place of the husband God was going to send and some feeling that it was perfectly normal and probably not a concern of the Lord since they did not see any explicit reasons in the Bible why they could not seek solo sexual gratification. One woman hesitated to reach a conclusion as she pondered out loud, "What if using them things takes you away from your spouse?" While the national sex survey reported that 28 percent of black women reported partnered masturbation, most of our conversations discussed masturbation as a solitary act. When I posed the question of whether they participated in self-pleasuring with their significant others, many laughed but few responded, and I was left wondering if admitting the need for sexual pleasure outside of one's partner was really the transgressive act, not the particular example of masturbation. A woman who seeks out her own pleasure when she has a spouse who is supposed to meet that need can be seen as a societal aberration. She shatters the fantasy that having actual intercourse with a man satisfies a woman's sexual desires.

Donna Williams, author of *Sensual Celibacy*, also takes a hard stance against masturbation. She urges women to engage their sexual passions, to pursue their goals, and to enjoy their celibacy no matter how long the season. Yet, her text adamantly excludes masturbation for women on the celibate path, explaining, "Masturbation can undermine one of the goals of the Sensual Celibacy program which is learning how to love and live comfortably with erotic feelings. . . . A woman gains strength when she can feel horny and simply enjoy the feeling."[23] During my interviews with women who were bold enough to admit being horny and holy, not a single one described this as a position of strength. Most were hoping and praying that their season of celibacy would be coming to a swift end.

I was able to interview Williams in 2015, fifteen years after the publication of her book. One of my first questions for the woman who had practiced celibacy for twenty years was whether she was still against masturbation. Her views had modified because when she wrote the book she was sure that her mother would read it and her mother still thought masturbation makes you blind and crazy. She camouflaged her own thoughts about masturbation because she did not want her mother to know she had even thought about it! Now fifty-six, she jokingly admitted to me that she thinks it's "almost abnormal not to masturbate [because] it's part of your sexuality." Further, she said she'd included masturbation in the text originally only because she knew some people questioned whether masturbating would mean one is not practicing celibacy; they understood masturbation as being sexually active with oneself. Because her book defines celibacy as no penile penetration, for her a woman could masturbate and still be celibate.

This caution was mentioned in each of my focus groups. Some women expressed uneasiness with their bodies and enacting pleasure in their bodies. This is a tremendous burden that cannot be overcome with the help of faith-based sexuality ministries alone. Some women are cautious about self-pleasure because they are so used to sacrificing their own needs on the altar of their relationships, caregiving, and church that it is hard for them to imagine themselves as a priority. On the other hand, some participants were very sexually self-aware and knowingly demanded the right to sexual pleasure.

For example, my focus group interview with "Stacy" revealed a woman who was at a point in her life where she felt justified in her sexual agency. She is a forty-seven-year-old, twice-divorced mother of one who identifies as heterosexual and comes from a middle-class background. While she followed neither Bynum nor other faith-based sexuality ministries, she was particularly eager to join the conversation on sexuality, women, and faith at our church. As my first volunteer, she jokingly told the group that she wanted to come to hear the senior mothers of the church talk about sex so she could gauge when she would not want sex anymore or would require a whole lot of lubrication and help to have pleasurable sex. Stacy told the group that she was "perfectly okay with masturbation [because] if [she] needed to be pleasured and there is nobody around to do it," she had no problems servicing herself. She and Josephine were at the furthest extreme in terms of being open and unapologetic about their need for masturbation. I wished there were more who would openly agree with them. I expected that by having a conversation about sexual pleasure I might open up a new way for women to understand their sexuality. My not so secret agenda was that women would leave the focus group with the mind-set advocated by Dr. Brittney Cooper, who hopes in her blog, *Single, Saved, and Sexin': The Gospel of Getting Your Freak On*, that many women will have a relationship with a B.O.B. (battery-operated boyfriend) because surely someone else should not have the privilege of touching their clitoris before they had.

Despite such wishes for the women in my focus groups, I respected them enough to hold on to my vision when they articulated views that countered my own. This occurred in my interview with "Arden" when we discussed her thoughts on sexual taboos. Arden is a thirty-seven-year-old heterosexual, unmarried mother of two who has attended the same Virginia Baptist congregation for most of her life. She did briefly move away for college and work pursuits but has lived primarily in my rural community. She is working class and has a demanding work schedule that stretches her time, but she likes taking time out of her day to meditate on the messages she receives from televangelists. She was the first person who volunteered to participate in my study, and she wanted to share her narrative, which included "starting off wrong" with her boyfriend by being sexually active before marriage. She also mentioned the taboos against touching yourself and fantasizing, and when I pushed her a little further she admitted having attended a sex toy party in my hometown. She acknowledged this party as "definitely a no-no!" but admitted that she came away thinking it was just a bunch of hype. She recalled it as "having a party and not inviting anybody else there. . . . It's still boring." In her opinion, masturbation is the equivalent of setting up the food and planning a fabulous party—and being the only guest. She is not interested in this kind of event. I appreciated her analogy but wondered, *What's wrong with a party of one?* She did not explain any further, and I was left imagining her possible rationales: that masturbation is being self-centered or is a gateway to other sexual acts, or that perhaps her response was prompted by anorgasmia, the absence of orgasm.

My interview with Rev. Dr. Cynthia Hale provided more concrete validations for avoiding self-pleasure. Hale has been celibate for almost thirty years and teaches that persons on a celibate path have to learn to control their thoughts before they engage in actions like masturbation. She believes that people should take responsibility for their actions, as some negative and sinful thoughts come from Satan and some come from our own flesh. Reining in these thoughts is necessary; in her own life she found that the more she thought carnal thoughts, the more she acted on these thoughts and let them have free rein in her heart and life. She realized that for her well-being she must control those thoughts and not let them control her. This prescription of avoiding thoughts that lead to other actions is standard in faith-based sexuality ministries. For example, most ministries suggest that followers change their media choices and social environment to prevent temptation. Many of my interviewees reported actions like throwing away their CDs or avoiding certain movies or friends because of perceived sexual innuendos. While logical and a means of helping some women navigate their sexual frustrations, this prescription gives too much power to the idea that sexual pleasure is irresistible. The feminist ethicist Christine Gudorf contends that this logic contradicts evidence that humans are quite adept at resisting, postponing, and forgoing sexual pleasure despite being sexually aroused.[24] Yet, for many "playing with fire" can lead to burning sexual urges that must be squelched.

Oh Taste and See! Oral Sex, Faith-Based Sexuality Ministries, and Black Churchwomen

Other sexual pleasures that my focus groups mentioned avoiding included sexual taboos like oral and anal sex. While there was far less discussion in the ministries and my focus groups of anal sex, I found the attention on oral sex intriguing because it reflected a vocal expression of black women who wanted their sexual needs met and were unable or averse to allow vaginal penetration to be their only option. At least two faith-based sexuality ministries I researched had specific communications with their followers regarding oral sex. Statistically, rates of black women receiving oral sex are higher than rates of black women giving oral sex to their male partners (44 vs. 37 percent), but these data are not typically accompanied by qualitative analysis to suggest why women are less willing to perform oral sex.[25]

My Nashville focus group interview with Stacy indicated that this may be a generational matter. Stacy shared with the group that she had been molested and that this experience left her desiring control of her body. This need for control got her labeled a "freak" by men because she wielded power over her body and the men with whom she engaged in sexual activities. When we started our group conversation on sexual taboos, I expected her experience with molestation to be the reason she might encourage a partner to sexually please her but not be eager to reciprocate with oral sex. Instead she told the group about a conversation she had with her mother regarding oral and anal sex. She described her mother as someone who did not talk to her about sex in general but felt completely free to walk around the house "butt-ass naked," not caring who saw her because she believed the message that her body was completely natural—whereas talking about sex was not. In a particular conversation about oral and anal sex, Stacy's mother indicated she could never do "that" (perform fellatio) to him but that he could do her! While Stacy acknowledged that was a double standard, the group seemed to nod in agreement with her mother.

Perhaps reflecting the same generational disconnect with performing or receiving oral sex, Josephine also shared her conversation with her mother about oral sex. Josephine listed oral sex as one of the most taboo topics in her house; when she asked her mother to describe a "blow job," her mother responded with great emotion but no information. As an adult, Josephine happily advocates giving and receiving oral pleasure and even encouraged her seventy-year-old aunt to learn how to give her uncle oral sex! When her aunt asked if she thought her uncle would like it if she did that, she took a "hands-on" approach by showing her aunt a pornographic video of someone performing oral sex and the ensuing orgasm.

As revealed in Karrine Steffans's *Confessions of a Video Vixen* and branding as "Superhead," there is perhaps more of a motivation to engage in oral sex within the black community than previous generations have allowed. For those advocating for sexual pleasure, the increasing number of women requesting oral sex from their partners is encouraging. But is this done "under the covers," with shame, or are these practices becoming more normalized and discussed within polite Christian communities?

My examination of the discourse surrounding oral sex in faith-based sexuality ministries highlighted Ty Adams who warns against activities involving the tongue, considering them a type of sexual immorality. She equates oral sex to her reading of the sexual sin that destroyed Samson and other Christians; she believes Delilah performed oral sex on Samson to get him to reveal his strength. In this interpretation, illicit sex really does make one go blind! She warns women that a "brother with his lips on your hips" is not the answer; if one goes searching for a climax it may be found but perhaps with disastrous results.[26] In the "Frequently Asked Questions" section of the revised edition of her book she is asked specifically why oral sex is wrong and if it is restricted to married women. Adams's first response reiterates her previous negative stance toward oral sex that considers any type of sex outside a marital union to be wrong and sinful according to the Bible. Yet surprisingly she advocates for oral sex in marriage because, she says, "marriage guards the sacredness of sexual intimacy between a husband and a wife." She even reinterprets Song of Solomon 4 to be a narrative about a husband engaging in oral sex as he describes the taste of his wife.[27] While Song of Solomon never explicitly names marital union, Adams's two starkly different interpretations of oral sex are interesting: one will leave you blind and the other will leave you in bliss!

This message regarding sexual pleasure is common in faith-based sexuality ministries, where women are expected to suddenly engage in activities they have previously been told are wrong. It is no wonder that women are confused about whether or not oral sex is acceptable. Yet the discussion of oral sex in these ministries can be read as a positive sign of women engaging in sexual acts that may offer them more variety and pleasure than the standard missionary position does.

This interpretation stems from witnessing women navigate these complicated messages, where an act is permissible only under certain circumstances. Women participating in the Wives in Waiting Date Night discussions of sexuality demonstrate such a negotiation. In a December 2014 Date Night Google Hangouts discussion, women gathered over the topic "Let's Talk about Sex." Led by five Sister Circle leaders, the conversation covered usually taboo topics like whether oral sex is permissible within marriage. A large part of this questioning stems from the antisex purity culture that forbids every sexual act and the fact that once they are married, women who believe this logic often require great convincing that they can now engage in all of the actions that were previously banned. One of the group participants remarked that the marriage bed should be undefiled, meaning that everything is permissible. As a divorced woman she cautioned that women who were trying to "keep it fresh or fun" for their spouse should not yield to actions with which they were uncomfortable because their feelings matter too.[28]

Such a negotiation meshes well with the growing trend in sex advice for Christian marriages that encourages both sexual pleasure and mutual vulnerability in both partners so that neither feels obliged to engage in sexual activities that make him or her uncomfortable. It is beyond the scope of this book to provide a more in-depth analysis of ministries like Covenant Spice, a website designed to enhance "passion and intimacy in Christian marriages" by providing sex toys like vibrators, penis rings, and aids for oral sex, foreplay, and sexual intimacy.[29] Yet this site as well as that of the American Board of Christian Sex Therapists indicate a massive shift in opinions and behaviors from the views expressed in Marabel Morgan's Christian sex booklets in the 1970s.

Sextifying Singles: Confessions of Nonmonogamous Black Churchwomen

The ministries this book discusses primarily target singles, and perhaps the most avoided sexual taboo in my focus groups is nonmonogamous sexual relations. Overwhelmingly those admitting to engaging in nonmarital sex with multiple partners are seen as promiscuous and are encouraged to repent. Yet given the sexual stigma involved with the presumed licentious nature of black women, the fact that there are so many women willing to sextify, or testify about their sexual escapades, is noteworthy. This fascination is also a marker of my own politics of respectability that in some unconscious way prioritized monogamous sexual encounters as more appropriate than others. Black women sexing multiple partners are especially frowned upon in the Christian tradition, where any and all sex outside of marriage is taboo.

As I coded my focus group interviews, I began to notice that while there was quite a bit of discussion about women having multiple sexual partners, it was never the personal story of any of my participants. Each woman was careful to distance herself from that reality in our public conversations. Similarly in Candi Dugas's book on black women's sexuality and faith exploration, she remarks that two of her participants were careful in their discussions of their sexuality, revealing that they were not engaging in casual sex but *merely* unmarried monogamous sexual activity. She believed they felt the need to justify their encounters to make them acceptable, and pondered how the church's admonishment to abstain until marriage created a strong desire in women to claim any form of monogamy.[30] Dugas's question had a sobering effect on me as I read through my transcripts and realized that my questions implied my disapproval of scenarios that were casual or intended only as a "hook-up." In retrospect, in trying to remove any justification for those who find *all* black women to be sexually immoral and always sexually available, I was implying an implicit belief that nonmonogamous sex is immoral or at the very least a lesser sexual good.

This is certainly a generational inheritance and a consequence of my conservative Christian upbringing. Yet my hang-ups in this area are not necessarily reflected in the younger generation's views. For instance, "Michelle" was the youngest member of my Nashville focus group at age twenty-eight, and as such she expressed some initial hesitation to comment in the group because so many group members knew her mother and grandmother well. In a group where women were divorced or had children, she stood out as a single, heterosexual, nonpartnered young woman. I had personally invited her to join the group because I wanted to diversify the conversation, but I had underestimated how being so much younger might stifle her participation. She remained silent for most of the conversation until we got to the topic of monogamy. Then she told the group, "With the young people this day if you're not in a relationship it doesn't matter how many relationships you have, you're not a ho. You can't be a THOT [that ho over there]! I'm not talking about myself, so let me clear that up. If you don't have, like, a boyfriend or girlfriend, you can sleep with however many you want to. It doesn't make you a ho or a bitch. It doesn't make you whatever. If guys can do it, how come a girl can't do it? To be honest, I don't really disagree with that. I'm not saying I have sex with every guy I talk with—let me clear that up since ya'll know my parents—but that is true. Girls are, like, 'If a guy can sleep with every girl, then I can too.'" To Michelle, Christian women having multiple sexual partners was not problematic because the same behavior was not problematic for single Christian men.[31]

There is a double standard facing women who engage in the same sexual activities as men but bear the brunt of the consequences for such actions. Their reputation is sullied and outsiders challenge their walk with the Lord. In the Nashville focus group, Shay, a thirty-year-old, engaged, mother of two reflected on this dynamic as she recounted a conversation with her teenage daughter regarding sexual standards. Her daughter wondered why young girls were being talked about for doing the same sexual thing as the guys in her high school, yet publicly the guys' actions were never seen negatively. Shay told her daughter that she felt "it was wrong for the men to sleep with a bunch of women and women to sleep with a bunch of men. You get you one person and you fall in love with that person, or a real deep-like, whatever connotation you want to put on it, and you're with that person." Shay's advice to her daughter did not promote sex only within marriage but it did sanction it only within a strong relationship.

When I considered why I resonated with Shay's conversation with her daughter, I recalled my desire as a sexual ethicist to ensure that black women receive the best information possible to make the safest sexual decisions. Most of my education has been informed by a public health perspective in which studies on sexuality are conducted with the goal of minimizing public risk of infection. On a very practical level, monogamy lessens sexual risk, but this advice provides only part of the equation. What I really want to advocate, more than monogamy, is for women to engage in radical sexual honesty and responsibility. In *Black Sexual Politics* Patricia Hill Collins challenges readers to have pleasure and remain safe during an era of HIV by developing honest bodies in which all partners are aware of the rules.[32] Being sexually honest in this case means both partners agree that having sex does not require any other type of relationship. Sexual honesty requires responsibility for one's own actions and responsibility to oneself and one's partner to be safe. This dialogue is missing in most discussions of casual sex; the presumption is that if the person does not know the partner well enough to know his or her name, then the consequences (e.g., disease or heartbreak) are just.

Womanist Erotic Justice

Radical sexual honesty and responsibility are the cornerstones of the womanist erotic justice model, starting with the black churchwoman prioritizing her desires and her body. This prioritization is a womanist act, which takes seriously Walker's definition of womanist as a woman who "loves dance, loves music, loves love and food and roundness."[33] In this framing womanists are women who are inclined to seek out pleasures in life and do so in appreciation of their bodies. Thus womanist erotic justice begins with the black woman's body and what can be done to and through that body to cause ecstasy and joy. This model does not focus on stories of trauma and abuse that are the legacy of black women; instead it focuses on desire, self-pleasure, and bodily goodness. Highlighting bodies that love and experience longing is an attempt to see black women as sexual agents who are in control of their bodies rather than responding to violence enacted on them. Pursuing sexual pleasure is often a taboo topic because it returns the focus to the body, reminding black churchwomen to love their flesh. The body is the site for sensual pleasure and to encourage relationships and sexual expressions to be pleasurable means encouraging bodily awareness.

Thus, this womanist erotic justice model privileges pleasure, but does not create hierarchies for what constitutes pleasure. While it encourages orgasms, this is not the only goal. Ultimately this model advocates that a woman know what brings her pleasure, both physically and emotionally. This requires self-awareness before beginning to seek pleasure in relationships with others. Bynum and the other leaders of faith-based sexuality ministries start with the dichotomous assumption that a body is either pure or impure. The women who participate in these ministries hear that they can choose for their body to be a (pure) temple of God, valued, uniquely created, and precious. Because such ministries offer women a way of seeing their bodies, as valuable and highly desired, the same ministries' emphasis on controlling women's bodies is particular problematic, especially since we are meant by God to experience our bodies as sensuous, not be ashamed of them.

Womanist theo-ethicist Eboni Marshall Turman reiterates this when she implores black women to attend to their "in the flesh" experiences by reminding them of the God within them, without requiring some proof of purity for divine favor. [34] Indeed black churchwomen who participate in a womanist erotic justice model of sexuality must be in touch with their sensuousness, their roundness, their feelings, and their desires and claim what they need to be fulfilled. [35] Sometimes this is an orgasm; sometimes it is sensual touch; sometimes it is a relationship; and sometimes it is the thrill of a hook-up. Producing a womanist ethic that is centered in erotic justice sets new norms that emphasize more than virginity and marriage. This model is a retooling of Christian ethicist Marvin Ellison's concept of erotic justice. Ellison presents a feminist, pro-gay and -lesbian, antiracist text that encourages a model of sexuality that is interpreted through the lens of erotic justice. His sexual ethics promotes the well-being of oneself and others, which necessitates a sex-positive view, an overcoming of compulsory heterosexuality, and the eroticization of equality between persons and between groups. Eroticizing justice means "sex is not doing something *to* someone else, but is rather a mutual process of *being with* and *feeling with* another person."[36] In a liberating sexual ethic, one is allowed to enjoy sex whether or not one is in a marital relationship. In fact a liberating sexual ethic demands a rethinking of marriage as a moral necessity, instead urging as a priority sexual relationships that are just and mutually respectful. Ellison even goes so far as to suggest that sex can occur whether or not one loves the other person, as long as there is respect and consent, a stark contrast from the contemporary Christian view of sex.

Articulating a model for black churchwomen who are often silenced because of their race and gender validates Ellison's notion that erotic justice is sexual justice that fights for the marginalized. In light of the particularity of the black female Christian experience, as was discussed in my focus groups and elsewhere, a womanist erotic justice model must address self-pleasure, nonmonogamous sex, sexual fluidity, monogamous nonmarital relationships, and monogamous marital relationships. This model provides alternatives for black churchwomen participating in church- and faith-based sexuality ministries.

Revaluing the Erotic

This first requires an in-depth discussion of the value of the erotic for black women. This goes hand in hand with the idea of reminding women to appreciate their bodies; yet, it goes a step further. It involves reclaiming the erotic to create space for sacralizing the erotic as a source of power that black women can and should utilize. Many black churchwomen associate the erotic with pornography or something that to them is sexually illicit, which makes redefining the erotic necessary.

One way beyond this stigmatizing view of the erotic is found in Lorde's definition of the erotic as power, a creative energy, a type of sensuality, and a form of wisdom, including being responsible to ourselves.[37] Particularly unique to Lorde's understanding of the erotic is that it does not have to be tied to sexual or genital expression; it is about feelings. While her view does not denigrate the importance of touch, sensations, and sexual pleasure, it places greater emphasis on connection and emotions. This allows the erotic to function as the sharing of joy, not merely the sharing the bodies. She urges women not to fear this type of desire or settle for less.

I expected some bashfulness among my focus group members when I connected the erotic to bodily pleasure, but neither they nor the followers of faith-based sexuality ministries are shy about questions regarding erotic expression. Indeed, I found them eager to learn how to integrate their sexual longing with their Christianity. While I have been most focused on masturbation or self-pleasuring as a means of this integration, the womanist model of erotic justice also highlights the importance of intimate touch. Just as Toni Morrison's character Baby Suggs preached to her hush harbor congregation about the importance of touching themselves and loving themselves, it is necessary for our communities of faith to emphasize that all of humanity craves touch. In Sophia Nelson's research with black women, she concluded that they overwhelmingly crave touch with a purpose or a deeper sense of intimacy than is expressed in typical sexual intercourse.[38] Jay concurred with Nelson's perspective; she described her longing during singleness as the desire for human connection and compared it to Maslow's hierarchy of needs. She believes that deep loneliness comes from a lack of personal connection to others. While I am not suggesting these views pertain to all black women, rather than seek sexual intercourse, some women are more satisfied with an intimate touch that connects them to their bodies, perhaps another person, and their God.

Ellison likewise considers touch to be an important aspect of good sex. He writes of an "ethic of respectful touching" that bolsters the idea of good touch that we teach children.[39] This type of respectful touch is about much more than what one does with one's genitals. It is also about what one does in general to produce the sense of pleasure. Many churches have a symbolic moment of passing the peace or welcoming each other in worship. For some women, this is the only touch they receive during the course of a week. Touch-starved individuals approach the topic of erotic touching from a place of deficit. What a womanist model of erotic justice can offer women is a way to reconnect with their bodily presence and the bodies of others. By emphasizing the sensual nature of touch, the model presents women with an alternative to a body-negative culture that does not embrace bodies.

Embracing one's body means much more than sexual pleasuring. It means being comfortable with one's body, despite whatever we perceive as its limitations or faults. When we hear female breast cancer survivors describe how doctors discovered a lump in their breast during a routine examination, we must wonder when our faith groups will become serious about encouraging women to touch themselves. Women are literally dying from fear of touching themselves. If this model of erotic justice can offer a sense of touch as normative, perhaps it can respond to not just the sexual and spiritual but also the physical needs of women. After all, the womanist affirmation of loving one's roundness means touching those round parts and even caressing them to euphoria. Black churchwomen must retrieve this love both by giving themselves self-love and self-pleasuring and also by daring to demand physical, intimate contact on a regular basis.

Bible on the Nightstand and Condoms in the Drawer: Pursuing Sexual Pleasure

How then can one go about pursuing sexual pleasure, and in what type of scenario: solo, nonmarital, or marital? Regardless of the situation, sexual honesty and responsibility are just as important as sexual pleasure. When Dr. Brittney Cooper hosted a Google Hangout conversation on the topic of being single, saved, and sexin', she opened the conversation by saying that she wanted to promote a theology for "grown black women."[40] This emphasis on grown black women encouraged participants to be "womanish" or grown meaning responsible, as they admitted their desires and made appropriate sexual decisions. Thus having several sexual partners does not necessarily demand restraint so much as responsible conversations and actions that protect one's own body and one's partner. Sexual relations that involve higher risk (e.g., multiple partners, inconsistent condom use, anonymous sex) can certainly be pleasurable, but a womanist model of erotic justice calls for these sexual relations to be responsible as well. For example, all partners should be aware of each other's HIV and STD status, should be aware of and accept the ground rules in the relationship (whether it's just about sex, sex and companionship, sex that is leading toward an exclusive relationship, etc.), and should treat all bodies with respect.

This womanist model of sexual justice is heavily influenced by the practices of Rev. Dr. Susan Newman, a former pastor, chaplain, and HIV/AIDS prevention advocate. Newman's practice is steeped in the lived experiences of black women. Her book *Oh God! A Black Woman's Guide to Sex and Sexuality* does not simply repeat the refrain that women should be abstinent until marriage. While she certainly encourages celibacy and monogamy, she also advocates sexual responsibility. She recounts a counseling class titled Sex and the Single Christian in which she encouraged her participants to engage in honest dialogue with one another about what happens when they love the Lord *and* require physical intimacy from another person. In my focus group in Chatham, Diavante said she was tired of the sexual dishonesty of churchgoers: "You have people in the church that are just so righteous that they have never done anything [wrong] at all, but when you start looking and listening and going back, you realize they too have done some of the same things." Only in a space of honest community could they shed their pretenses about their struggles with faith and their sexuality and actually engage in discussion about responsible sexuality. In this space black women can find a "sexual ethic with which they can peacefully live—one based on truth."[41]

This truth can be unconventional but certainly freeing for the women involved. Josephine told the focus group, "I appreciated having the freedom to choose my partner, and if it is not the same person as the last person, I'm totally okay with that. Praise the Lord! Having that freedom is okay with me because it's a particular agency that I enjoy. Although I may not always use that freedom I'm glad to have it." Thus, monogamy is no longer the brass ring to pursue; it has been replaced by a sexually honest, responsible encounter. Contemporary hook-up culture may not meet this criterion because this model encompasses religion scholar Richard W. McCarty's view that if "hooking up means anonymous sex without actual concern for the total well-being of the other . . . and without establishing play commitments basic to the criteria of sexual justice, then 'hooking up' is morally problematic."[42] Hook-ups are not by nature exploitative, but a womanist model of erotic justice cannot justify as morally good rendezvous that are objectifying. Establishing ground rules for sexual engagements with multiple partners is necessary; if monogamy is not the woman's desired goal, she could instead seek sexual accountability as she pursues the just goal of sexually pleasurable liaisons.

Evaluating Black Churchwomen's Erotic Desire

The focus of this chapter has not been solely heterosexual discussions of sexual pleasure, but it is sadly still necessary to state that conversations about sex for pleasure can occur outside of gay and lesbian relationships. A prevailing evangelical stereotype of gays and lesbians is that they have sex for pleasure, whereas heterosexuals stereotypically have sex to procreate or maintain a marital union. Based on public discussions of sexual pleasure in black communities, one might conjecture that erotic desire is possible only between same-sex persons since it is extremely rare to hear black theorists discuss the pleasure of sex or orgasm. Yet a truly womanist model of erotic justice is attentive—one might say hospitable—to the pursuit of pleasure in same-gender relationships.

Because of my interest in faith-based sexuality ministries and black Christian sexuality, most of the women in my study were invested in heterosexual long-term committed relationships. While the ministries and most black churches identify and promote marriage as the only relationship that is committed, the women's personal narratives depicted a more expansive relationality than simply marriage. Many women are engaging in long-term sexual relationships with men to whom they are not married. For some this is a reason for shame, and for others this is a conscious decision to prioritize their sexual needs. Donna Marie Williams's "Sensual Celibacy" model (discussed in chapter 3) allowed for an end to celibacy when a healthy, monogamous relationship is entered that could include sexual activity. This chapter's womanist model of erotic justice includes support for those who choose the nonmarital monogamous sexual relationship option.

For women who want to be in a long-term sexual relationship, this womanist model of erotic justice suggests setting parameters for these relationships, parameters that contain accountability features similar to those suggested for nonmonogamous sexual relations. In this case, I recommend Dr. Gail Wyatt's measure for healthy relationships. Wyatt, a black psychologist and sex therapist, outlines principles of self-respect so that one can be in relationship with another; of compromise with partners, while not ceding all control to them; of self-protection; and of controlling one's own sexual decisions.[43] When a woman follows these guidelines, she is much more likely to be participating in the type of relational, mutually respectful expression of sexuality that is advocated by a womanist model of erotic justice.

Williams decided to begin a sexual relationship after twenty years of celibacy. She had to determine who put the idea of marriage in her head as an ultimate goal and reevaluate if that is really what she wanted in her life. She determined that she was not sure she wanted to be married, but she was sure she wanted companionship that could include sexual intimacy. Sensual celibacy was her path of making peace with the voice in her head that expected marriage before sexual expression. When she was ready to engage in a sexual relationship her model allowed her a "self-loving, self-accepting, self-forgiving approach" for her noncelibate life.

I interviewed Arden about a month after she got engaged to her long-term partner and the father of her children. She and her fiancé met in 1997, when both worked in the fast-food industry. In our interview she talked about her belief in the validity of abstinence before marriage, even though she had not lived up to this goal. When I pushed her to explain why abstinence should be preferred, she said that even though she felt that it was a strict policy she definitely should have waited because her timing was not right because it was against God's way. She admitted feeling guilty for being sexually active and having to get this straight before God. Yet she believed her story had a happy ending, as they were now engaged after having been together off and on for fifteen years. When I asked her to describe her perspective on monogamy, she indicated that they had gotten their nonmonogamous "crap" out of their system in their years apart. They entered their current relationship with the understanding that exclusivity would be the goal. In Arden's case her decision to be sexual and not be married was a negotiated process. She told me that she was tired of the church double standard, which persecutes single women for their sexual indiscretions but does not demand repentance from married people who commit adultery. However, she still felt that she needed to seek forgiveness for not waiting to have sex and for having children outside of marriage. Despite this disclosure, Arden's closing comment to me was that she wanted women to know that they should "wait for the right person that you know is truly God-sent." Her disclosure did not include the amendment to wait until they married that person.

Ambivalence and Frustration in Sexual Relationships

Such ambivalence about long-term nonmarital sexual relationships was common among the women I interviewed. They were resistant to forgoing sexual pleasure and companionship, but none seemed able to reconcile this with their understanding of their faith. They adopted the view of a participant in Sophia Nelson's research group, who stated, "I know it's wrong to have sex with my boyfriend outside of marriage as a Christian woman.

No argument. But I like sex, and I don't want to deny myself that very important need as an adult woman."[44] Similarly when *Essence* published an article on young Christians forgoing abstinence, Yolanda responded that "she was grown and longing to be touched. . . . I struggle with sin. . . . Just because I have a Bible on my nightstand and condoms in the drawer doesn't mean I love God any less or that He doesn't love me."[45]

This conflicted perspective thankfully did not lead any of the women I interviewed to engage in risky sexual behaviors (at least they didn't admit any). But is living in limbo the answer? An impetus behind a womanist model of erotic justice is to ease the negotiations women experience as they choose to meet their sexual needs as a person of faith. This model eradicates the perspective that sanctions sex only within marriage and instead offers women who engage in nonmarital monogamous sexual relationships the same blessing and sacrality that married women experience.

New Approaches to Erotic Justice

After I drafted this chapter, two separate faith-based conversations about black churchwomen and sexual pleasure started online. The first was a *You-Tube* dialogue on faith and black female sexuality, and the second was a Twitter chat at #BlackChurchSex. Their willingness to dare to do something different was striking. To choose voice over silence suggests to others that black women desire sexual pleasure. Both conversations reminded me that those who engage in these brave conversations are not doing so under the aegis of womanism. It never occurred to me to do this work using other tools, even though I was aware of the overwhelming silence about sexual pleasure in womanist conversations. The womanist theologian Karen Baker-Fletcher explains that womanists have written more about sexuality than others have noted, and she encourages scholars to look at how womanists discuss spirituality, which typically encompasses sexuality.[46] Therefore I hunted for resources and searched for interviews, and I discovered a lively conversation with womanists engaging fiction, literature, art, and more that also addresses sexuality. This is worth celebrating, but what about the lived experiences of black women wrestling with their faith and pursuit of sexual pleasure?

While this book is for the black church and the academy, media like Twitter and *YouTube* are broadcasting to the larger public. Both efforts are holy work, and both have lessons to glean from each other. For example, in the

YouTube dialogue between Candice Benbow and Candace Sampson, Benbow's statement that she believes black churches are stumbling blocks to black women's sexual pleasure because black churches do not want women to be empowered to know what they want was compelling.[47] She contends that this empowerment presents an independence that goes against patriarchal hegemony. She is alluding to tenets presented in this womanist model of erotic justice. The womanist erotic justice I have described discusses sexual pleasure and desire and addresses taboo topics like oral and anal sex and nonmonogamous sexuality. The black church is one space to have these discussions, but the womanist model of erotic justice leaves space for other pathways to liberation. If black women are going to be sexually free to pursue pleasure and uncomplicated sexual realities, we must use all the tools available to us to dismantle the house. We must remain attentive to the needs of women participating in black churches and faith-based sexuality ministries, because for those who are passionate and pious it is past time to move beyond prohibitions to pursue pleasure as paramount even if religious restrictions seem to counter advocating pleasure as a moral good.

LIVING SEXUALLY BEFORE GOD

A Contemporary Womanist Sexual Ethics

The God I believe in believes in sex too, and doesn't hand out rejection slips when you do the heathen thing every once in a while. —ZOEY, in Julia Boyd, *Embracing the Fire*

When the Black church is able to talk honestly about sex, teach about sex, and preach from the pulpit about issues related to sex—then we will begin to see powerful changes in the life of the black community. . . . Our new sexual ethics is based on believing that we have the freedom to choose how to express ourselves sexually. —REV. DR. SUSAN NEWMAN, *Oh God!*

Beyoncé crooned, "If you liked it then you shoulda put a ring on it. Don't be mad once you see that he want it" in her 2008 megahit "Single Ladies." This female anthem was a major topic of conversation when I began conducting interviews with black Christian women for this project on black women's sexual decision making. Participants in the youngest group I interviewed were in their early twenties and members of my local Baptist congregation. We met around the time of Beyoncé's "Single Ladies" fame, and its culturally pervasive lyrics became an entry point for conversation on single women and the pursuit of marriage. The song fit perfectly into a popular and religious culture that promotes marriage as the ideal despite the reality that, as Beyoncé sings, many women will go home as single ladies. For black churchwomen inundated with both religious and secular messages, I expected the song to resonate with their perceived longings for a husband. Instead I was shocked at my focus groups' interpretation of Beyoncé's song. Some respondents heard in the lyrics not just the promotion of marriage but of healthy sexuality, that is, a man should put a ring (a condom) on it before trying to connect with them sexually. They understood the religious restrictions on premarital sex, but they were aware they should be responsible if (and when) they were sexually active. How did they get that message? How were they able to ignore the expectations of celibacy the black church demands of Christian women? Stunned by these disparate views, I needed to investigate more completely the plethora of messages about sexuality complicating black women's lives. I soon discovered that my investigation could not end with an interpretation of biblical prescriptions provided in black churches but would need to interrogate the faith-based sexuality ministries that were symbiotically imprinting black single churchwomen as well.

In this book I have outlined how faith-based sexuality ministries have instructed and inspired black women's sexual decision making. This exploration of faith-based sexuality ministries stems from concerns about what is happening with the women in the pews. Looking around a typical black church on any given Sunday, one sees women who are lesbians, heterosexuals, elderly, young, sexually active, celibate, who are pleasure-seekers (typically deemed promiscuous), and who are affected by HIV/AIDS. Whether considering the women in the pulpit or those in the pews, I have provided a womanist sexual ethics that matches women's lived realities. In this conclusion, using the tools garnered through an examination of faith-based sexuality ministries, I examine healthy sexual relationships, a concrete example of womanist sexual ethics.

An updated model is needed for our contemporary times, and contemporary womanist sexual ethics remains the most relevant theory for interpreting black churchwomen's sexuality. In Alice Walker's womanist definition, a womanist is someone who "loves herself. Regardless."[1] The desire to be responsive to the needs of black churchwomen comes from this space of understanding the need for black women to love themselves regardless. If a womanist loves herself she protects herself; chapters 3, 5, and 6 emphasized the necessity of responsible sexuality for the physical and spiritual well-being of black women. If a womanist loves herself, she is fully herself, no matter how that complicated self presents, as I argue in chapter 4. Finally, if a womanist loves herself, she gives herself what she needs, including sexual pleasure, discussed in chapter 6. A contemporary womanist sexual ethics expands the charge that Kelly Brown Douglas articulated in the question "Does having sex enhance your life possibilities at this moment? [Because] good sex allows you to be all of who you are."[2] A contemporary womanist sexual ethics asks black churchwomen to consider Douglas's question while remembering our contemporary reality in which life-enhancing sex must also be responsible sex.

Remembrance of our contemporary context also requires a womanist sexual ethics model to be as responsive as possible; thus it utilizes techniques from faith-based sexuality ministries. I have discussed faith-based sexuality ministries from a critical standpoint. Any adoption of these methods is careful to avoid duplicating any "theocultural malpractice" embedded within.[3] It rejects the idealization of a black Christian sexuality that fetishizes abstinence and the constraint of female sexuality by acknowledging the double standard that occurs when women's sexual autonomy is hindered while men's sexuality is allowed to flourish.

Despite this tendency, faith-based sexuality ministries do offer some significant and valuable lessons for a womanist sexual ethics, namely, the import of accountability, applicability, and accessibility. One of the major contributions of faith-based sexuality ministries is to display a fully functioning accountability network. While women in those ministries use these skills to adhere to a rigid sexual abstinence code, when the skill set is conveyed in womanist sexual ethics it can add support for diverse sexual expressions and sexual relationships. Primarily support and accountability partners are best suited when they are peers and share common life experiences. Peers who accompany women support them by sharing their real experiences, whether being celibate, being sexually adventurous, or pursuing other forms of healthy relationships.

This emphasis on shared experience does not necessitate that peers be of the same age. In fact when my older focus group participants waxed nostalgic about times long ago, when church mothers were comfortable pulling young women aside for conversations on relationships and sexual restraint, I cringed at memories of the advice I was given but recognized the importance of intergenerational sharing. The pastoral counselor Dr. Hilda Davis-Carroll presents intergenerational stories of health and resilience as one of the key factors in an ethics of resistance amid the damaging public debate about black women's sexuality.[4] She emphasizes the need for elderly women to engage in conversations with younger women because both populations can learn from each other. Womanist sexual ethics should be intergenerational; younger women can help empower and instruct senior women on contemporary sexual lingo, techniques, and safer sex practices, while older women can provide younger women with value systems that encourage them to seek respect and recognize that there are ways to overcome their obstacles.

Accountability partners must also be vulnerable to each other and willing to learn from each other, which presumes that each partner has done her own work or is in the process of doing this work to be sexually free. In her aptly titled chapter "Let's Pray for Sexually Active Daughters," the journalist Cora Daniels encourages mothers to become sexually comfortable because only then can they raise sexually empowered daughters.[5] Daniels prays for her daughter's sexual desires to be met, and she tries to raise her daughter to be a young woman who respects herself and her partner and who demands sexual pleasure. In a womanist example of sexual freedom, she does not fear her daughter's sexuality; instead she tries to equip her daughter to advocate at the appropriate time in her life for her own sexual needs.

While the mother-daughter dyad can serve as one model for accountability, in many black churches accountability partners could be unrelated aging women and younger women who are just beginning their sexual paths. Intergenerational messages enable conversations that are female-driven and often outside of the purview of the typically male leader. A contemporary womanist sexual ethics does not capitulate to conversations of old, where accountability led to chastisement with no assistance. Instead this model promotes straight talk and women consenting to journey to sexual freedom together, holding each other accountable for making responsible, respectful sexual decisions.

Part of what makes accountability groups so successful in faith-based sexuality ministries is that the members are not ashamed to share their real struggles. They disclose everything with confidence in the group members' ability to honor their sharing and keep confidentiality. On one level this helps the group police its members' behaviors. On another level it provides an opportunity for group members to self-evaluate. Self-evaluation is crucial to womanist sexual ethics because the way forward to healthy relationships with others starts with a healthy relationship with oneself. Yet once this personal work has been done, women must feel comfortable sharing their realities with others, and black churches must seek to respond to these lived realities and not just to scriptural aspirations. Rather than interpret such actions as compromising of values, black churches could instead envision this as a means of walking with congregants through their day-to-day realities.

Meeting persons in their daily realities is yet another reason why faith-based sexuality ministries are successful. They use a variety of mediums to reach women where they are. Communities of faith must likewise be responsive. During my participation with the Pinky Promise and Wives in Waiting groups, and even while following Juanita Bynum's ministries, I received outreach multiple times a week. Whether that was an email, blog posting, text message, or invitation to a sisters' outing, I was regularly reminded to practice purity. This is not to suggest that churches mimic such potential harassment of black churchwomen to circumscribe their sexual agency but to point out that there are more opportunities for engagement and fellowship available to black churchwomen than they receive during Sunday services. If churches truly desire to meet people where they are, this needs to be ongoing work. Rather than take the quick-fix approach of castigation that does not actually help women create and sustain healthy relationships, churches are in a position to offer practical advice to black churchwomen that can enhance their lives.

This contemporary womanist sexual ethics is anchored in black church conversations. It is not necessary to remove women from the spaces in which they find solace; rather womanist sexual ethics pushes these spaces to provide real holistic support for women. While womanist concerns tend to be centered on Christianity, the decision to reflect back to the black church does not stem from this disciplinary comfort level. Instead it acknowledges that before dismantling support systems we must be aware that an adequate replacement may not be readily available, resulting in physical, emotional, and spiritual disruption for black women.[6] Thus instead of encouraging black women to leave black churches, a constructive womanist sexual ethics must empower them to seek transformation in the spaces in which they are already seeking answers.

This contemporary womanist sexual ethics is constructive because it is a means to imagine a new path that leads to sexual agency, pleasure, and love. It advocates for a practical application of religion, one in which black churchwomen are emboldened by their religious communities to make the best sexual decisions possible. This means considering the various experiences black churchwomen face, including being single, being celibate, dating, being sexually active, and getting married.

This book asserts the premise that black churchwomen are sexual agents. Their roles as sexual and moral agents begin with their critical consciousness of themselves as sexual beings, then moves on to their actual decision. Often the religious messages women receive obfuscate this first step. Perhaps this is one of the enticements of messages from Bynum and her ilk. Though they all begin with a declaration and affirmation of women as sexual, social beings, beyond this they take only one step: the call to celibacy. Celibacy ceases to be a free decision when it seems to be the only one available. A contemporary womanist sexual ethics highlights all consensual decisions while advocating for women to access all the possibilities they desire.

The book's next assertion is that, as fully embodied sexual agents, black churchwomen must equip themselves to negotiate the boundaries of intimacy and spirituality in ways that allow them to thrive. Whereas this contemporary womanist sexual ethics is an attempt to offer an ongoing process for black churchwomen to reflect on their decisions, there are numerous steps within this model for women to explore. For example, I have presented a model of womanist sexual ethics that promotes responsibility, celibacy, sexual hospitality and freedom, sexual generosity, and pleasure. Womanist sexual ethics is attentive to the plurality of religious messages that black churchwomen are receiving. Rather than assume black churches are the sole space to reform, this model extends critical analysis to faith-based sexuality ministries, noting that these messages can be negotiated in ways that promote black women's health and well-being.

One way of promoting thriving is to encourage black women's deconstruction of scripture, again mindful that it not beneficial to discount a source without providing an adequate alternative. The Hebrew Bible scholar Cheryl Anderson asserts that defining scripture is a deeply theological enterprise for black women, many of whom see the Bible as the mediator of God's presence in their lives.[7] Anderson's work explores what happens when minoritized community members read the Bible against their very bodies and their survival. The need for inclusive biblical interpretation reads black women's needs into the text and reminds the reader that the text is constantly being interpreted as people try to make the Bible meaningful in their lives.

Such theological education and redefinition is first achieved through a revamping of biblical interpretation. Douglas recommends integrating the works of black biblical scholars into current Bible studies because the expertise of scholars of color can help illuminate passages that have left women in unrealistic predicaments. One such scholar is Randall Bailey, who argues for a counternarrative to black churches that favor the King James Version of the Bible despite its being the most racist of all interpretations, which he argues ultimately leads readers to adopt meanings that are opposed to their own health and well-being.[8]

In this regard Marla Frederick observes that many of the women she interviewed possessed a more liberal interpretation of scripture than was preached in their church, which allowed them to be at ease with their sexual decisions.[9] However, these women are crafting these interpretations as they go along, without much help from scholars; hopefully this will become an unnecessary task as more womanist biblical scholars begin addressing sexuality. For instance, the womanist Hebrew scholar Renita Weems writes that the Song of Solomon has "eight chapters teeming with lust, love, sex, and passion in the middle of the Bible—and not once does the heroine or her beloved talk about marriage."[10] Rather than read this narrative as an allegory about God and Israel, Weems ponders what it might mean for churches to explore the sexuality positively expressed in this book. Imagine how revolutionary the act of admitting that a biblical text celebrates nonmarital sexual pleasure would be for women whose sexuality is dictated in particularly narrow ways. This type of biblical exploration reveals the well-kept secret that women like sex, even clamor for it, and can do so outside marital union without endangering their physical or spiritual selves. Getting to such a space of freedom may require letting go of theological constraints that stagnate black churchwomen's ability to make better sexual decisions for themselves.

However, this push for better sexual decision making does not reject outright celibacy as an option for black churchwomen. Despite some women in my focus groups seeing celibacy as an unwanted holding pattern until what they really desired came along, this model of womanist sexual ethics rejects this framing and instead shares biologist Winnifred Cutler's opinion that celibacy is not a "penance or a punishment. It represents an active choice, not a passive position."[11] For those choosing no sexual activity as a noncoerced, non-biblically mandated decision, they are choosing for their own reasons, and this decision should be respected. Some of the women actually practicing celibacy did so to strengthen their relationship with themselves, while others did so to strengthen their relationship with God.

Both these choices were subversive in rejecting external norms of sexual activity or even hypersexuality. While my interviews revealed women who were in the beginning stages of their celibacy choice (less than a year) and women who had been celibate for twenty-five years or more, each woman's decision to forgo sexual intimacy gave her more peace and well-being than other alternatives. Choices that amplify life and permit thriving are the telos for contemporary womanist sexual ethics, so if the option of abstaining provides this, then surely it is a moral good.

Similarly for those single black churchwomen who are sexually active, there also remains the push for relationships that enhance women's lives. Healthy sexual agents desire healthy relationships, and healthy relationships need not be monogamous, just honest and respectful. This is the cornerstone of a contemporary womanist sexual ethics. Healthy relationships are necessary because in this context selecting the wrong partner could have dire consequences, making it crucial that churches help women distinguish between unhealthy and healthy relationships. In his book *Crisis in the Village* the ethicist Robert Franklin challenges black churches to promote healthy dating as a means of producing healthy marriages. While the "date = marriage" formula and the compulsive heterosexuality found in black Christian sexuality is problematic, there is value in the desire to have churches endorse healthy relationships.

Franklin participated in a healthy marriage consultation that looked at the black clergy's attitudes toward healthy dating, and he discovered that many pastors admitted they were unable to get their congregants to understand the difference between casual dating, casual sex, and healthy relationships.[12] While Franklin's ultimate concern in increasing the number of black marriages is not the point of this work, his concern for healthy relationships is significant. Defining healthy relationships is a sacred work that takes place communally as well as individually. The individual may seek to grow into a better version of himself or herself and to become responsive to another's needs. By seeking relationship, the individual acknowledges a desire to become connected in intimate ways to another, which may not be a concern for those who engage in casual dating or casual sex.

There are multiple avenues for discussing healthy relationships. The majority of the faith-based sexuality ministries I monitored also advocated for healthy relationships, which their rhetoric revealed as God-given, male-headed relationships. If a woman rejects this narrative as her model for a healthy relationship, a counter or addition to this explanation is to bracket this conservative biblical understanding while supplementing or replacing it with a new measure for healthy relationships.

Healthy dating was a concern for many of the single black churchwomen in my focus groups. Yet there was a massive disconnect between these types of secular norms for healthy dating and participating in faith-based sexuality ministries that were marriage-driven and emphasized particular dating skills. For instance, both the Pinky Promise and Wives in Waiting groups devoted sessions to healthy dating or courtship as it is discussed within celibacy movements. Biblical courtship is discussed as having accountability partners and strictly enforced boundaries that respect the woman's desire to remain celibate. It was intriguing to find women in the focus group participating in biblical courtship ideals while simultaneously rejecting the emphasis on celibacy until marriage. These women considered a healthy relationship to be one that included sexual expression (although most groups required monogamous sexual expression) because God forgives and for some even blesses these nonmarital sexual encounters. The groups made interesting negotiations, like having "rules" against cohabitation. The boundaries established within these types of relationships were certainly attempts to create a healthy foundation on which to grow a relationship. Rather than reject these modifications as incomplete, a contemporary womanist sexual ethics posits that various healthy dating alternatives are useful.

There is a dearth of examples of healthy dating and healthy relationships after which single black churchwomen can pattern themselves. Many look to their pastor's family as an example to follow, but seeing a relationship from a distance makes it difficult to replicate their skills (assuming the pastoral couple is actually in a healthy relationship). Utilizing skills gained from faith-based sexuality ministries, contemporary womanist sexual ethics provides more concrete assistance than just glimpses of a relationship on Sundays. While faith-based sexuality ministries encourage those in biblical courtships to seek out married heterosexual accountability partners to serve as mentors for their relationship, womanist sexual ethics would require a couple of any sexual orientation to accept the responsibility of mentoring a new couple. This mentoring couple would be responsible for answering questions about sexuality without shaming the couple that is sexually active. A benefit of having them answer questions is that they can help young couples discuss a variety of relationship situations. For instance, a situation that contemporary couples often encounter is whether living together before marriage is a feasible option. One couple wrote to *Essence* magazine regarding their cohabitation. They felt "God is not looking at this [cohabitation] too favorably" but insisted they were doing what was right in their situation.[13] The female participant, caught between her love for her partner and the shame associated with "shacking," ultimately chose to live with her partner but acknowledged her angst about the decision. This conflict over living with her sexual partner could be an issue that she addresses with her relationship mentor.

Another value in the mentor relationship is the ability to assist new couples with determining when it is appropriate to express themselves sexually, that is, what criteria must be met.[14] This does not equate to the traditional wait-until-marriage mantra but instead involves listening to why the couple feels ready for such a step. The mentors are also needed to help encourage each individual in the relationship to respect his or her self-worth. Finally, the mentoring couple's role could be to encourage the couple to maintain a healthy relationship that includes sex. This relationship modeling is not meant to encourage couples into one standard example of success (e.g., marriage). It is meant to emphasize the values that should be present in any healthy relationship.

At its core the contemporary womanist sexual ethics presented in this book has articulated a way for women to advocate for the changes that are necessary for them to be reflective and healthy sexual agents. I gave readers concrete steps to reject the restrictions of black Christian sexuality by establishing norms besides marriage that match their reality. Womanist sexual ethics addresses more than the exploitation of black female sexuality. It asserts that a much more productive starting ground is to discuss black women's sexual agency. While the focus has remained on single black churchwomen and the influence of faith-based sexuality ministries on their sexual narratives, this constructive womanist sexual ethics is both a prophecy and a promise to help all black churchwomen continue the work of wrestling with their sexuality and spiritual walk with God.

INTRODUCTION

1 In this book the black church is defined as a predominantly black Protestant Christian body of believers. While discussions of the historical black church generally reference the seven major denominations, this study is not specific to any particular denomination, although the women I interviewed were predominantly Baptist. I adopt the womanist theologian Kelly Brown Douglas's assertion that while this discussion of the black church focuses more on the church's sexual silence and flaws, it "implicitly acknowledges that there are various black churches with more equitable views and practices" (*What's Faith Got to Do with It?*, 189). The term *black churchwomen* is used in scholarly discussions of black women, faith, and sexuality that seek not to homogenize women's voices but to amplify the diversity of experiences in black churches.

2 Kimberly Davis, "Sex and the Spirit : sos for Single Christian Sisters," *Ebony*, January 2005, 108.

3 Frederick, "'But It's Bible,'" 283.

4 Foucault, *The History of Sexuality*, 43.

5 Viefhues-Bailey, "Holiness Sex," 14. In this book I am particularly concerned with black evangelicals, so unless I want to distinguish between whites and blacks, the term *evangelicals* refers to blacks.

6 According to the historian Randall Balmer, *evangelical* refers broadly to conservative Protestants, including fundamentalists, Pentecostals, and charismatics (*Mine Eyes Have Seen the* Glory, xv–xvi).

7 Miller, "The Rise of African-American Evangelicalism in American Culture."

8 DeRogatis, *Saving Sex*, 8. Throughout the text the term *black Christian sexuality* is inclusive of both heterosexuality and same-sex desire. When it is relevant to the discussion, I note if the perspective is about heterosexuality specifically.

9 A notable exception is Marla Frederick's *Colored Television*.

10 Hammonds, "Black (W)holes and the Geometry of Black Female Sexuality,"138.

11 Hine, "Rape and the Inner Lives of Black Women in the Middle West," 915.

12 Butler, *Bodies That Matter*, 15. When the anthropologist Saba Mahmood explores the concept of agency to apply it to women's pietistic participation in Egyptian

mosques, she concurs that agency must be discussed in the "grammar of concepts within which it resides" while not being too preoccupied with finding resisters or certain types of resistance (*Politics of Piety*, 34).

13 Douglas, *Sexuality and the Black Church*, 36; Rose, *Longing to Tell*, 391. As pernicious today as it was in the nineteenth century, Jezebel is now represented by the image of the welfare queen, the sexually reproducing black woman whose redemption comes through state-sanctioned marriage to her children's father.

14 Higginbotham, *Righteous Discontent*, 196.

15 Quentin Schultze posits that American televangelists are more American than Christian, with their emphasis on personal experiences over collective faith expressions (*Televangelism and American Culture*, 132).

16 Sadly the field of womanist sexual ethics is still quite new, and there are not many competing discussions of black female sexuality going on in womanist scholarship. This is why Douglas's work remains so influential. Hers is the most in-depth study, but there is also promising work by the womanists Marcia Riggs, Katie Cannon, Karen Baker-Fletcher, Pamela Lightsey, Thelathia Nikki Young, and others.

17 Cornwall, *Theology and Sexuality*, 78–79.

18 Douglas, *Sexuality and the Black Church*, 66.

19 Guy-Sheftall, *Daughters of Sorrow*, 41.

20 DeRogatis, *Saving Sex*, 52.

21 Franklin, "Generative Approaches to Modernity, Discrimination, and Black Families," 112–13.

22 There is slim academic attention paid to the growing population of singles, and the discipline of Christian sexual ethics is woefully behind in discussing the sacred and sexual needs of singles. The ethicist Karen Lebacqz is a notable exception, as she counters the celibacy-in-singleness model by articulating that the moral norm in relationships should be appropriate vulnerability, not marriage. She contends that sexuality demands openness to another, which makes space for one to feel vulnerable; however, her theorizing does not provide a description of how to achieve this goal. See Lebacqz, "Appropriate Vulnerability," 132.

23 Silliman, *Undivided Rights*, 290.

24 Floyd-Thomas, *Mining the Motherlode*, 92.

25 Thomas, "Womanist Theology, Epistemology, and a New Anthropological Paradigm," 491–92. Thomas advises using focus groups and lengthy ethnographic study of the community, which I accomplished through virtual research and physical attendance in the communities. Relying on the tools of womanist ethnography to analyze these encounters, I did not mean these experiences to represent all black women in black churches. Instead they are used as examples that "point to the reality of all" by making black women's reality understandable. See Isasi-Díaz, *En La Lucha—In the Struggle*, 81.

26 Three of my focus group interviews were conducted in a library; one was conducted in a hair salon; and one was done in an otherwise empty Starbucks. We talked for around ninety minutes in each group, but women were free to stay and

speak with me after the group dispersed. Some did, and their recorded conversations with me were about thirty minutes each.

27 Melissa Harris-Perry quoted in Rebecca Traister, *All the Single Ladies*, 78.

28 Bernadette Barton has classified Bible Belt Christianity as it influences gays and lesbians, but my research concurred with the totalizing impact that religion had on the sociocultural lives of my interviewees. Barton's Bible Belt references both a region and a hegemonic religious ideology (*Pray the Gay Away*, 9–14). Regarding southern blacks being expected to find a church and facing sanctions for nonparticipation, see Ellison and Sherkat, "The Semi-Involuntary Institution Revisited."

29 While there are numerous southern stereotypes that counter this southern woman, it is typically the chaste southern female that is privileged in evangelical discourse. Juanita Bynum and Pinky Promise founder Heather Lindsey both maintain their ministries in Atlanta, Georgia. Wives in Waiting has more Sister Circles in the South than in any other region. These ministries reiterate the expectations of the southern woman described. See Lynxwiler and Wilson, "The Code of the New Southern Belle," 13.

30 Griffith, *God's Daughters*, 59. Similar to the women in Griffith's study, the women participating in these ministries decried the divisions within Christianity and saw the ministries as a way to bring about Christian unity.

31 While I expected them to participate entirely in a conservative evangelical world, many participants were deliberately engaging in religious messages from a variety of sources. For example, there has been a recent interest in depicting attitudes to religion and sexuality in reality TV shows that target black female audiences. *Mary Mary* ended season 4 with Tina Campbell rebuilding her marriage after her husband's infidelity; sex toys and STDs were highlighted on the now canceled *Sisterhood*, about pastors' wives; and in the 2014–15 season of the *Match Made in Heaven* reality TV series there was an emphasis on pastoral matchmaking.

32 First Lady Heather Lindsey founded the Pinky Promise Movement in 2012. This organization promotes abstinence in singleness and submission and fidelity in marriage. See chapter 3 for a more extensive discussion.

33 Rev. Chante Truscott founded the Wives in Waiting group in 2012. Her mission is to train women in their first marriage, the one they have with God in anticipation of their earthly nuptials. See chapter 3 for a more extensive discussion.

34 Burke, *Christians under Covers*, 3. Her work highlights scholars of digital and virtual ethnography, which validates the reliability of this research method.

35 I also made sure to use screen capture as website archiving to validate my data from the online ministries. While all of the ministries maintained publicly accessible websites, Pinky Promise also had a membership option where conversations were not public. Although my personal private page presented me as a researcher, the book only discusses in generalities data that came from my access to membership conversations out of respect for the members who may have been unaware that I was there solely as a researcher. I have changed names and not given demographic data to protect members' privacy.

36 In the field of Internet research ethics there has been attention to how researchers should determine when or if to intervene in a situation online. Because persons can post with pseudonyms or even provide less than accurate information, it can be difficult to gauge an appropriate action. There are recommendations available from the Association of Internet Researchers as well as books on ethics in virtual ethnography.

37 This methodology also created a larger buy-in from group participants, as they were able to choose their own pseudonyms and had the opportunity to approve their narratives for this book.

38 As examples of this white feminist theological model, I am influenced by the work of Beverly Harrison, Carter Heyward, Mary Hunt, Marvin Ellison, and Karen Lebacqz. These are exemplars because they represent the common themes of relational sexual ethics (e.g., privileging women's bodies, seeking interrelatedness and mutuality in sexual relationships, promoting intimacy and sexual expression). In the discipline of black feminist theory, this work is shaped by Audre Lorde, Patricia Hill Collins, Evelynn Hammonds, Michelle Wallace, and Tricia Rose. Two notable black feminist theorists who are exceptions in paying attention to religious experiences are bell hooks and Hortense Spillers. I made a deliberate effort to utilize scholars of color, feminists, and womanists as my main interlocutors to amplify the emphasis on black sexuality and black religion.

1 · SEXUAL PURITY AS PR

1 Megan McDonough, "On Love: Brelyn Freeman and Timothy Bowman Jr.," *Washington Post*, November 20, 2015. Timothy Bowman also attested that he was a virgin until their wedding night, yet most of the stories have followed his wife's presentation of her virginity. Their story was publicized on *Good Morning America* and in *USA Today, Essence, People, Christianity Today,* and elsewhere.

2 Viefhues-Bailey, "Holiness Sex," 7.

3 The historian Mark Jordan concurs and posits that evangelical discussions of sexual sins have included every erotic or quasi-erotic activity performed by humans (*The Ethics of Sex,* 78). Chapter 3 describes in greater detail specific ministries' discussions of sin.

4 Soul ties are not directly described in the Bible, but evangelicals infer that godly soul ties are referenced in 1 Samuel 18, where the soul of David was knit to Jonathan, as well as Genesis 2:24, when a married couple is believed to become one flesh. Ungodly soul ties are described in 1 Corinthians 6:16.

5 Bynum, *No More Sheets Devotional,* 65. Evangelical manuals suggest placing duct tape, which represents one's heart or soul, on an individual and then removing the tape and sticking it on another individual, typically demonstrating the bonding or soul tie that occurs during sex. The object lesson is that the tape will not stick by the time you meet your "soul mate" and is dirty from previous encounters.

6 Bynum, *No More Sheets Devotional,* 13.

7　DeRogatis, *Saving Sex*, 13, 3.

8　Moslener, *Virgin Nation*, 3.

9　Wolcott reads black sexual propriety as a public discourse on decency and a private strategy on protection from sexual violence (*Remaking Respectability*, 24–25).

10　Frederick, *Colored Television*, 91. Pentecostalism refers to the multiracial church bodies organized in the late nineteenth and twentieth centuries. They were part of the "Sanctified church" that encompassed Holiness, Pentecostal, and Apostolic movements. Important for all three bodies is the emphasis on experiencing a baptism of the Holy Spirit, which is evidenced by spiritual gifts like glossolalia (speaking in tongues), ecstatic worship, and the necessity of leading a godly life.

11　I am choosing to focus on COGIC because Prophetess Bynum was reared in a COGIC church, her parents were COGIC evangelists, and she graduated from a COGIC high school. COGIC is also a worthy denomination for analysis because it has explicit views on sanctification, sexual sin, and the submission of women. It is an apt example of the expectations of piety because it follows doctrines of sanctification.

12　Butler, *Women in the Church of God in Christ*, 66.

13　Living holy typically is associated with moral behaviors that are religiously and morally good. Evangelical Christians are called to be holy because they believe God commands it in 1 Peter 1:16. Ultimately, because God is holy, Christians should strive for holiness. *Purity*, *living holy*, and *chastity* are terms used interchangeably to describe the process achieved in sanctification.

14　In some denominations of black Christianity, the Holy Spirit represents God's ongoing presence among humanity. It is believed to be a transforming and sustaining force to help believers strive to do God's will or to follow God's blueprint for humanity. Miyon Chung asserts that evangelical Christians believe a person grows in holiness because she is already made holy by the work of Christ through the Spirit of God. This process requires complete submission to God and worshipping God with one's body and life. See Chung, "Conversion and Sanctification," 120–21. Sanctification is biblically referenced in 1 Thessalonians 5:23.

15　In both the COGIC and Baptist (the two largest black denominations) doctrines, sanctification is held in high regard for members. COGIC's official faith statement on sanctification is "We believe in the sanctifying power of the Holy Spirit, by whose indwelling, the Christian is enabled to live a Holy and separated life in this present world" (Church of God in Christ, "Statement of Faith"). In "What We Believe," the National Baptist Convention, USA, Inc., the largest black Baptist convention, states, "We believe the Scriptures teach that Sanctification is the process by which, according to the will of God, we are made partakers of his holiness; that it is a progressive work . . . that is carried on in the hearts of believers by the presence and power of the Holy Spirit."

16　This is an important distinction for black women, who, during slavery, were often dressed in inadequate and embarrassing clothing that offered no such protection. For further discussion, see Klassen, "The Robes of Womanhood."

17 1 Thessalonians 4:3–7 states that it is God's will that believers should be sanctified, avoid sexual immorality, and learn to control their own body in a way that is holy. Women are instructed to not wear clothing that highlights their body, to give only side hugs to avoid too much touching, and to be careful in how they walk and talk because they may tempt a man. See Anderson, *Damaged Goods*, 82.

18 DeRogatis, *Saving Sex*, 3.

19 Dianna Anderson argues that not all women are stumbling blocks. In the larger white evangelical audience, although men are deemed weaker because of their lust, it is believed they are particularly affected by thin, white, able-bodied women (*Damaged Goods*, 97–101). Yet black evangelical culture reiterates the idea of women as stumbling blocks, rehearsing the stereotypes of black women as sexual temptresses who must be controlled.

20 Sacrificing in relationship is a concept popularized by Bynum, who encourages her followers to kill their flesh. Killing the flesh or dying to the flesh refers to sacrificing one's desires in pursuit of following God's commandments. Heather Lindsey perpetuates this concept by noting that healthy marriages include a lot of death (death to old habits, former relationships, attitudes, etc.).

21 Burke offers a succinct distinction between complementarianism and mutual submission: the former refers to the "belief that men and women were created to fulfill different but equally important roles," and the latter is the "belief that both men and women should submit to God and to one other" (*Christians under Covers*, 42).

22 The women in Griffith's study found freedom by submitting to their husbands because in essence they were actually submitting to God, who grants all freedom. The women also believe they are rewarded as God's obedient daughters with marital bliss and self-fulfillment (*God's Daughters*, 179).

23 Frederick, *Colored Television*, 89–96.

24 Burke, *Christians under Covers*, 109–11.

25 DeRogatis, "What Would Jesus Do?," 112.

2 · READING "OUR" BYNUM AS TEXT

1 Bynum and her four siblings were raised in Chicago. She reports working as a hairdresser and a flight attendant and marrying and divorcing while still in her early twenties. In 2000 she was awarded an honorary doctorate in theology from Truth for Living Bible College in Jacksonville, Florida, and began promoting herself as Dr. Juanita Bynum. In 2012 she was named a goodwill ambassador of the Bayelsa State of Nigeria. In 2015 she was appointed a bishop in the Global United Fellowship. For details of her young adult life, see Valerie Lowe, "A Fiery New Army of African American Women Storms America's Pulpits," *Ministries Today*, July/August 1999. See also Saunders, "Bynum, Juanita 1959–."

2 During her interviews and publicity for her public birthday party she reported that the sword represented her desire to fight for every woman, connecting carrying the sword to her plan to lead a domestic violence ministry. Kenya Byrd,

"Juanita Bynum: I Will Never Allow Anyone to Misrepresent My Name," *Essence*, December 16, 2009, http://www.essence.com/2009/01/27/juanita-bynum-i-will-never-allow-anyone.

3 Frederick, *Colored Television*, 52. Frederick says that a "Dr." before their name establishes televangelists' authority, especially as viewers seldom question the accuracy of the title.

4 Bynum says the title "prophetess" refers to her prophetic anointing, which allows her to discern the dispensational time, or God's working in historical time for a certain group of people. Her prophecies tell what God is doing in this realm. Bynum publicly preaches as Ambassador Dr. Juanita Bynum but publishes solely as Dr. Juanita Bynum. After she legally changed her name to Juanita Bynum II, she changed her website information; the site now makes no mention of her role as a pastor or preacher, perhaps because they were too limiting compared to her role as CEO of Juanita Bynum Enterprises. Regardless of her title, her ministry continues to reflect her ongoing narrative of moving from "victim to victor" by undergoing "necessary" suffering.

5 John Fiske, "British Cultural Studies and Television," 132.

6 While I am concerned here with the popularity of black religious broadcasting specifically, I look at snapshots of the wider field of religious broadcasting as it relates to crafting a proper genealogy of Bynum. Concurring with Jonathan Walton that blacks have been marginalized in studies of religious broadcasting, I highlight yet another understudied arena: black female televangelism.

7 Hoover, *Mass Media Religion*, 21.

8 Goethals, "The Electronic Golden Calf," 141.

9 Byrd, "Juanita Bynum"; Bynum, *Walking in Your Destiny*, 66. These numbers vary so widely because the conference was part of Jakes's larger Woman, Thou Art Loosed ministry, so estimates sometimes include the attendance number for this ministry and not just the particular singles event.

10 Bynum, *No More Sheets* DVD.

11 Bynum, *No More Sheets: The Truth about Sex*, 174.

12 J. C. Christian, "Uncommon Beauty: A Mazza Exclusive," *Mazza International Hair Book*, July 2005, 30. Her reference to her Spirit is her connection to the Holy Spirit; at this time she could not be sure that she would follow God's plan for her life.

13 Bynum, *No More Sheets* DVD.

14 Thomas, "What the Mind Forgets the Body Remembers."

15 Bynum's successors also employ modesty ministries to deflect from their body, yet they too present conflicting messages in their portrayals. Eventually Bynum adopted a more contemporary and modest style. In a recent interview promoting a new CD, she responded to the reporter who commented on her new "sexy" look that she has always been an attractive woman who has worked hard to downplay that because of people's weaknesses, but now she feels she is no longer responsible for what goes on in another man's heart. She states that she is no longer going to deny how God made her. See Lee Bailey, "Diary of an Inspired Black Woman:

Prophetess Juanita Bynum on Music and 'Sexiness,'" *Jacksonville Free Press*, July 1–7, 2010.

16 Schultze, *Televangelism and American Culture*, 79.

17 Moultrie, "After the Thrill Is Gone," 245.

18 Bynum, *No More Sheets: The Truth about Sex*, 38.

19 Bynum, *No More Sheets* DVD. In *Saving Sex*, DeRogatis documents how evangelical sex manuals advocate great sex as a benefit of marriage, whereas seeking solely pleasurable sex without following the proper guidelines (e.g., within a heterosexual marriage) is detrimental to one's salvation and life.

20 Bynum, *No More Sheets: The Truth about Sex*, 173.

21 Bynum, *Pride vs. Proverbs 31 Woman*.

22 Fiske, "British Cultural Studies and Television," 143.

23 Christian, "Uncommon Beauty," 30. The language of blessing or being blessed by a ministry reflects God giving benefits or rewards to people. Christians believe blessings can be meant for the individual, family, or larger community; this concept has been emphasized most notably in prosperity gospel ministries, where any material, financial, or emotional benefits are gifts reflecting God's favor.

24 Schultze, *Televangelism and American Culture*, 56. This lack of formal education is heavily present in the leadership of faith-based sexuality ministries.

25 Bynum, *No More Sheets: The Truth about Sex*, 27.

26 Walton, "Response to Joseph de León," 272.

27 Bynum, *No More Sheets: The Truth about Sex*, 20.

28 Michelle Buford, "Carnal Knowledge," *Essence*, May 2001, 186.

29 Lee, *T. D. Jakes*, 150.

30 Lee, *T. D. Jakes*, 151; Bynum, "A Renewed Covenant."

31 Pope-Levinson, *Building the Old Time Religion*.

32 In her "No More Sheets" sermon she preaches that "men are projectors and women are receptors"; that is, the man deposits his spirit into the woman. Women are to prepare themselves for their spouse by learning to cook and clean while ridding themselves from the spirits of past men deposited in them.

33 Frederick, *Colored Television*, 115.

34 Nadiyah Jett, "Moving in the Spirit," *Upscale: For the Affluent Lifestyle*, August 2006, 70. Bynum's most recent CD was produced in a venture with Beyoncé's father's Music World Entertainment. In January 2015 she terminated her contract with Music World and solicited funds to relaunch her music label.

35 In July 2012 Bynum redefined her sexual testimony to include having been with women and experimented with drugs. While some in Christendom reeled from this news, others were reminded of the Bynum of old, whose ability to connect with her audiences was in direct relation to her ability to share in their struggles. See "Juanita Bynum, Televangelist: 'I've Been with Women,'" *Huffington Post*, July 18, 2012, accessed July 23, 2016, http://www.huffingtonpost.com/2012/07/18/juanita-bynum-ive-been-with-women_n_1683529.html.

36 Rosalind Bentley, "For 'Prophetess' of True Romance, Marriage a Mess," *Atlanta Journal-Constitution*, August 26, 2007. However, Pew Research Center and Ameri-

can Community Survey current data show that despite media portrayals, black men and black women over the age of twenty-five are equally unlikely to have married. Unmarried black women do outnumber unmarried black men (Wang and Parker, "Record Share of Americans Have Never Married"). According to U.S. Census data, only 13 percent of black women over the age of fifty-five have never been married (U.S. Census Bureau, Number, Timing, and Duration of Marriages and Divorces: 2009, May 2011.

37 Bynum, *No More Sheets* DVD.

38 Alexander, *Televangelism Reconsidered*, 23.

3 · BEYOND BYNUM

1 This is a popular conservative Christian reference to the union of Ruth and Boaz in Ruth 4. In some liberal interpretations, Naomi arranges for her daughter-in-law to sleep with Boaz in order to convince him to marry her and provide for their family. In most conservative interpretations of the text, Ruth and Boaz do not consummate their relationship until after marriage, providing further evidence of Boaz being a "man worth waiting for." The Hebrew Bible scholar Wil Gafney cautions Africana communities against reading this text as a romance without acknowledging how marginalized and sexually vulnerable Ruth is in both of her marriages ("Ruth," 250–52).

2 Downtown Atlanta has no shortage of gentlemen's clubs, otherwise known as strip clubs, and the decision to host that year's conference in downtown Atlanta seemed ironic given the focus on purity in an area seemingly saturated with sexual excess.

3 Perry, *Breaking Down Barriers*, 115–16.

4 U.S. Department of Health and Human Services, Family and Youth Services Bureau, Administration on Children, Youth, and Families, Community-Based Abstinence Education Program: Request for Proposals, 2006. See also Fine and McClelland, "Sexuality Education and Desire," 308

5 Christine Gardner posits that purity moves from the passive stage of waiting for a spouse to an active choice where one asks oneself "What would Jesus do?" in every aspect of life (*Making Chastity Sexy*, 31).

6 Cline, *Women, Celibacy, and Passion*, 143.

7 Kahan, *Celibacies*, 2. Kahan claims the literature shields against rendering celibacy as the sign of an unheeded same-sex or heterosexual desire, and presenting celibacy as a sexuality disrupts this binary. In the same way that asexuality, an orientation wherein a person does not experience sexual attraction, deconstructs the binary of heterosexual/homosexual desiring, celibacy can also be understood on this continuum. See the website of the Asexual Visibility and Education Network, which distinguishes celibacy, a choice, from asexuality, an intrinsic part of a person (http://www.asexuality.org/home/).

8 Kahan, *Celibacies*, 152–53.

9 Gardner, *Making Chastity Sexy*, 23–24.

10 Moultrie, "After the Thrill Is Gone," 247.

11 Kimberly Davis, "Sex and the Spirit: SOS for Single Christian Sisters," *Ebony*, January 2005, 106. McKinney Hammond describes her Heartwing Ministries as a love ministry given to her by God. Its goal is to give people scriptural principles to be freed from past pain, mistakes, and disappointments while giving the tools needed to give one the fullest life. See the ministry's website, http://www .michellehammond.com/heartwing-ministries/.

12 Swilley, "Christian and Single."

13 Camerin Courtney, "Why She's Sassy, Single, and Satisfied," *Today's Christian Woman*, March/April 1999, 98.

14 Ginia Bellafante, "Single Evangelical in Need of Advice? Books Have Plenty," *New York Times*, July 19, 2004.

15 Teresa Hairston, "Single? Christian? Seeking Your Soulmate?," *Gospel Today*, March/April 2008, 48.

16 Marilyn White, "A Heart to Heart: The Unspoken Rules of Love with Michelle McKinney Hammond," *Precious Times: The New Magazine for Today's Black Christian Woman*, June/July 2003, 17. This rhetoric should be read through the legacy of the black female stereotype of Sapphire, the sassy, uncontrollable black woman. Sapphire runs her household, is never submissive to her husband, and is too opinionated. See Townes, *Womanist Ethics and the Cultural Production of Evil*, 60–62.

17 Christine Ditchfield, "Michelle McKinney Hammond: Straight Talk," *Christian Mingle*, September 2001,15.

18 Wiley, *Soul Mate* DVD. Wiley touts the documentary as the first nationally distributed film written, produced, and directed by and for urban Christian women.

19 Wiley helped contribute to this demand by circulating a *Soul Mate* newsletter in which she encouraged fans of the film to sign up to earn money by becoming independent distributors. She also suggested asking hair salons to become independent distributors and to play the film in their shops. Her media guide describes the *Soul Mate* target audience as fans or frequent viewers of urban relationship films like *Waiting to Exhale*, *How Stella Got Her Groove Back*, *Woman, Thou Art Loosed*, and *Madea's Family Reunion*.

20 "Soulmate," *Precious Times Magazine*, Winter 2008, 36, http://www.soulmatefilm .com/pdf/PreciousTimesMag.pdf.

21 Jatika Hudson, "'Soulmate' Film Tells True Story of Unmarried Black Women," *Atlanta Voice*, October 12–18, 2006, 20.

22 Wiley, "What Women Need to Know about What a Man Wants.

23 The Adams Report, interview with Andrea Wiley.

24 Wiley, *Soul Mate* DVD.

25 Moultrie, "After the Thrill Is Gone," 250.

26 Chante Truscott started the ministry at age thirty, after God called her to preach. She is a licensed minister in the Foursquare Church. The Wives in Waiting ministry teaches that women were created as wives. Since Eve did not come to the world as a businesswoman, leader of a movement, or even a mother, a woman's first priority is to be a wife, first to God, her heavenly husband, then to a natural human

spouse. Participating in the ministry is mostly free, but there are costs associated with Truscott's products and services, such as annual membership fees ranging from $25 to $100, charges to hear the recorded webinars if not watched live via Google Hangout, and a six-week training program for engaged and married women that costs $300.

27 I have generalized some of their demographic data because the Wives in Waiting website provides actual names and contact information for Circle leaders. While the founder promotes celibacy and teaches on soul ties, the two Wives in Waiting Sister Circle leaders I interviewed said that unlike Pinky Promise, Wives in Waiting was not a purity ministry. Both women stated that celibacy could be an end result of strengthening one's relationship with Christ, but celibacy was not the goal. Kelli, another interviewee, shared this opinion that celibacy was about one's relationship with God and not church or biblical legalism.

28 Wives in Waiting, "Let's Talk about Sex 2." Because she is married, she shares that it is necessary to correct some of these misconceptions that women bring into their marriage if they do not heal from the guilt associated with their previous soul ties.

29 Volunteers run Sister Circles and coordinate local events to keep the sisters active and committed to a life of purity. Wives in Waiting is an international organization—it has a Sister Circle in Kenya—but its organizational structure is based in the United States. They can offer accountability regarding celibacy or any area of one's life.

30 Wives in Waiting, "Testimonials."

31 Wives in Waiting membership welcome packet, in author's possession.

32 The scriptures offered in support of this response are Psalm 37:4; Hebrews 11:6; Matthew 7:7–8. In these passages faithful women are simply to ask and be given their desires as if God operates as a genie granting wishes.

33 Wives in Waiting, "Frequently Asked Questions."

34 Weems, *What Matters Most*, 86.

35 Pinky Promise Movement website, accessed April 2, 2017, http://pinkypromise movement.com/about/.

36 My analysis of Pinky Promise includes an in-depth discussion of the organization and of its founder. While there is certainly a symbiotic relationship in that Lindsey's views are portrayed in the Pinky Promise Movement, Lindsey makes distinctions between herself as a brand and the organization. For example, she is a strict vegetarian and actively promotes this lifestyle, whereas Pinky Promise does not address this issue despite talking about topics beyond sexuality. Lindsey was raised in the United Church of Christ, and she and her husband founded the Gathering Oasis, a nondenominational church in Atlanta in 2013.

37 Since college is often the first time women choose to abstain from sex, alcohol, and so on outside the watchful eye of their parents, this could increase the need for accountability groups like Pinky Promise, which are collegiately based. See Pinky Promise Movement, "Who We Are" Lindsey, "How to Start a Business."

38 I question the membership numbers because I am personally counted as a member in three local groups (Nashville, Atlanta, and Boston). There does not appear to be

a mechanism to remove oneself from a local group when one changes location, so I imagine there are other members who are counted multiple times. I spent three years as a participant observer in the Pinky Promise community, where the experience of community is deeply felt and reciprocated. Even though I made my status as a researcher clear in my introduction to the community, I was called Sister Monique (MNM in the local Boston chapter). My opinions were solicited and my prayers encouraged even though I was there to observe. I introduced myself to the community and the founder as a researcher who expressed gratitude for their desire to serve God in this specific way, but we danced a tightrope between the community trying to convince me to sharing their opinions and me simply trying to be a silent observer.

39 Campbell, *Exploring Religious Community Online*.

40 An example is "Bedcheck: Anybody in your bed that shouldn't be there? Remember that he didn't pay the price for you, Jesus did. So send him home. Boyfriends don't get hubby treatment." Lindsey references Proverbs 4:23 to explain the necessity of gate checks.

41 Campbell, *Exploring Religious Community Online*, 181.

42 Bekkering, "From 'Televangelist' to 'Intervangelist,'" 103.

43 Nelson, *Black Woman Redefined*, 129.

44 Walker, *In Search of Our Mothers' Gardens*, ix.

45 Secondary virgins are persons who have been sexually active but are choosing virginity again; thus, the choice of sexual abstinence is always an option regardless of prior decisions. Gardner, *Making Chastity Sexy*, 33.

46 Nelson, *Black Woman Redefined*, 141.

47 Hill, "Who Are We for Each Other?," 348–49.

48 Frederick, *Between Sundays*, 196.

49 Wiley, *Soul Mate* DVD. Hale's description of God's anointing refers to the belief that God bestows on believers spiritual power to fulfill their purpose on earth. For many believers, the Holy Spirit grants an anointed person gifts and talents that are evident and acknowledged by the people. Thus losing God's anointing or God's power would be disastrous for a spiritual leader because it would mean being no longer closely connected to God.

50 Hale, *I'm a Piece of Work!*, 67. This is a paraphrase of Benjamin Franklin.

51 Williams, *Sensual Celibacy*, 20.

52 Williams, *Sensual Celibacy*, 74.

53 Williams, *Sensual Celibacy*, 19.

54 These steps are: (1) Begin decisively; (2) Know thy celibate self; (3) Set, then pursue goals; (4) Heal your soul; (5) Strengthen your celibacy practice; (6) Mind your body; (7) Get out of the house and mingle; (8) Give men the benefit of the doubt; (9) Model a healthy, happy, celibate lifestyle; and (10) End intelligently and decisively.

55 Williams encourages women to turn off the pastor in the pulpit and listen for their Christ consciousness to get direction and guidance. While a helpful correction, it was an improbable suggestion for women in my study. The introductory chapter

on sexual messages describes the impact of certain religious ideologies on single black churchwomen. An emphasis on maneuvering within traditional Christianity is key to this project, while admitting that Williams's freedom in her celibacy model perhaps comes from her ability to free herself of the limitations of traditional Christianity.

56 Tithing refers to the Christian practice of giving a tenth of one's earnings back to God. In evangelical communities, tithing is giving your best offering to God and this includes your time, body, and resources. Williams's reference to tithing sex refers to her sacrifice of abstinence as she described giving that part of herself up and in return receiving from God a greater sense of compassion, empathy, and love.

57 Williams, *Sensual Celibacy*, 204.

4 · "WHY I GOTTA BE GAY?"

1 For some evangelical Christians deliverance from homosexuality is a way of living either totally without same-sex desire or no longer acting on it. Symone's evidence of deliverance was that she married that man in February 2014. He knew her when she was dating her ex-girlfriend and expresses no discomfort in her discussing her lesbian past. Despite his acceptance, Symone recounted feeling shame and guilt surrounding her testimony, but, as is required for transparency, she felt it was her duty to share with others so that she could testify to her deliverance and tell others that they too could change.

2 "Calling All Sinners: Evangelist, National Best Selling Author and Playwright 'Ty Adams' Will Declare and Decree 'Sin City' to Be 'Win City' on August 11–12, 2006, *PRweb*, July 5, 2006, accessed July 23, 2016, http://www.prweb.com/releases/2006/07/prweb407283.htm.

3 Adams, *Single, Saved, and Having Sex?*, 18–19, 24–25.

4 Adams, *Single, Saved, and Having Sex?*, 41–42.

5 Lee, *Erotic Revolutionaries*, 87.

6 Shockley, *Say Jesus and Come to Me*, 20, 11.

7 Adams, *Single, Saved, and Having Sex?*, 36–37.

8 Coleman, *Making a Way out of No Way*, 155.

9 Griffin, *Their Own Receive Them Not*, 129–31.

10 Hammonds, "Black (W)holes and the Geometry of Black Female Sexuality," 136–37. She provides a historical critique of the coinage of queer theory as she addresses the failure of the white lesbian feminist Teresa de Lauretis to theorize queer theory in such a way that would include black lesbians. Hammonds asserts that in its early stages queer theory was structured in such a way as to doubly silence or erase black lesbian sexualities.

11 The American studies scholar and novelist Lashonda Barnett and the historian Eric Garber have written about the religious autonomy of black lesbians during the Harlem Renaissance; Rev. Irene Monroe writes about the religious ideologies of black lesbians supporting the past and current civil rights movements; and Rev.

Dr. Yvette Flunder is documenting the religious activism of lesbian and transgender persons participating in her international fellowship of fifty-six primarily African American Christian churches that practice radically inclusive Christianity.

12 Hammonds, "Toward a Genealogy of Black Female Sexuality," 181.

13 Baker-Fletcher, "The Erotic in Contemporary Black Women's Writings," 205.

14 Griffin, *Their Own Receive Them Not*, 140.

15 Griffin, "Black Churches, the Bible, and the Battle over Homosexuality," 195.

16 Frederick, *Between Sundays*, 205–6.

17 There was an entire discussion thread dedicated to the topic "So why I gotta be gay?" that enabled women to share their disdain for those opposed to believing that they were heterosexual and celibate.

18 Frederick, *Between Sundays*, 208.

19 Irene Monroe quoted in Comstock, "Rev. Irene Monroe," 69.

20 Richardson, "No More Secrets, No More Lies," 63–76.

21 The ethicist Kathy Rudy discusses how this coerced monogamy urges gays and lesbians to mimic heterosexual relational structures and re-create the nuclear family in ways such as marriage, procreation, and even following traditional gender roles within relationships (*Sex and the Church*, 75).

22 Walker, *In Search of Our Mothers' Gardens*, xi.

23 Hill, "Who Are We for Each Other?," 346.

24 In Kelly Brown Douglas's *Sexuality and the Black Church* and subsequent works, she acknowledges the prevalence of homophobia in the black church and warns that heterosexism threatens the full humanity of black gays and lesbians. The ethicist Katie Canon urges womanist ethicists to pass on strategies for the church that unmask compulsive heterosexuality ("Sexing Black Women," 17).

25 Hill, "Human Sexuality," 185.

26 Best, "Are the Gods Afraid of Black Sexuality." Best asks what it means to paint the picture of heterosexual expression without engaging in heterosexual sex as he tries to move conversations on black sexuality and religion to include the closet as a location of choice.

27 Anderson, "The Black Church and the Curious Body of the Black Homosexual," 311.

5 · "THE LORD STILL HAS WORK FOR ME TO DO"

1 Cornelius et al., "Adaptation of an HIV Prevention Curriculum for Use with Older African American Women," 16.

2 Muzacz and Akinsulure-Smith, "Older Adults and Sexuality," 4.

3 Zeiss and Kasl-Godley, "Sexuality in Older Adults' Relationships," 24.

4 The Christian ethicist Marvin Ellison discusses the eroticization of power and control as he notes how certain bodies are infantilized while the culturally normative able-bodied paradigm finds contempt for other bodies. This hierarchy also occurs with race and age as the social construction of sexuality has imbued young white

affluent men with the means to manage the bodies of all others. This system makes "male gender supremacy" feel natural and even pleasurable or the moral thing to do. See Ellison, *Erotic* Justice, 41–55.

5 Laura Carstensen cited in Portmann, *The Ethics of Sex and Alzheimer's*, 42.

6 Townes, *Womanist Ethics and the Cultural Production of Evil*, 31. See also Douglas, *Sexuality and the Black Church*, 36–45. Contemporary popular culture versions of Mammy tend to be black men in drag (Tyler Perry as Madea and Martin Lawrence as Big Momma), but when elderly women are given actual roles they reiterate the same asexual persona, for example, Miss Claire in the 2015 film *War Room*.

7 Cheryl Townsend Gilkes notes that the role of church mother has historic roots in the Baptist, Methodist, and Sanctified (Pentecostal, Holiness, Apostolic) denominations, but only the Sanctified tradition had a fixed structural power attached to the position. In other black denominations, those chosen to be church mothers had great moral influence in their religious community. See Townsend Gilkes, *If It Wasn't for the Women*, 103.

8 Yet when the data for race are broken out, blacks tended to consume less technology than their peers of other races. See Smith, "Older Adults and Technology Use"; Madden, "Older Adults and Social Media."

9 Thumma, "Virtually Religious."

10 Women in this age range have been shaped by different historical moments; for example, some experienced birth control as a revolution and others view it as normative.

11 Dickerson and Rousseau, "Ageism through Omission," 320. The Administration on Aging found that in 2013, 44 percent of older African Americans were married, 31 percent were widowed, 16 percent were divorced, and 9 percent had never been married. See U.S. Department of Health and Human Services, Administration for Community Living, "A Statistical Profile of Older African Americans."

12 This lack of partners was also discussed by older Pinky Promise members, who moaned that dating was tedious because even Christian men did not respect their decision to remain chaste.

13 Postmenopausal women experience a loss of estrogen, which results in a thinning of the vaginal walls, decreasing vaginal lubrication; they can also experience more difficulty with vaginal penetration as the labia may not fully extend during sexual arousal and make entrance into the vagina more difficult (Zeiss and Kasl-Godley, "Sexuality in Older Adults' Relationships," 19).

14 Since the FDA approved Osphena in 2013, advertisements for it have included no women of color. While it is being marketed as "pink Viagra," its ads seem to target an older white woman of means and leisure. This parallels the delayed marketing of Viagra to men of color.

15 Loe describes sexual relationships as usually occurring in the context of marriage or dating and nonsexual intimacies as social and physical connections with others (even connections with pets); caretaking involves self-care as well as care for others; and intellectual stimulation refers to personal satisfaction associated with

thinking and problem solving individually or with a group ("Pleasure in Old Age," 279).

16 Irene Henderson, a pastoral counselor, suggests that menopause is a time in which women face "who I have become" while simultaneously acknowledging "who I did not become" ("Betwixt and between Again," 219).

17 Conway-Turner, "Sex, Intimacy, and Self Esteem," 91.

18 Fisher et al., "Sex, Romance, and Relationships." Psychologist Luciana Laganá's exploration of African American older women's sexuality confirms these data; she found that even when there was decreased sexual activity, the quality of the sex was better, as it had become more meaningful for the female participants.

19 Fishel and Holtzberg, *Still Doing It*, 104, 106.

20 Minority Nurse Staff, "Preventing HIV/AIDS in Older African American Women."

21 Conway-Turner, "Sex, Intimacy, and Self-Esteem," 100.

22 Frederick, *Between Sundays*, 189.

23 Jenkins, "Warrior Chicks," 247. In the Pinky Promise chat room one discussion forum suggested that more older women needed to take on the task of mentoring younger women.

24 In his argument for mash-up religion, McClure posits that just as mash-up songs are created out of parts of other songs, lived religion today borrows from a variety of sources to make meaning in one's life (McClure, *Mashup Religion*, 1).

25 Westfield, "Influences of Sexism in Black Church Worship," 49.

26 The SISTA curriculum curriculum, "Women Informing Women on Topics about AIDS," invited women fifty and older who self-reported being in heterosexual relationships to join their study. They recruited from black Baptist and Methodist churches, and their intent was to get input on how to modify the CDC curriculum for women in their age range.

27 Cornelius et al., "Adaptation of an HIV Prevention Curriculum for Use with Older African American Women," 24.

28 The Presbyterian Church's statement frames the denial of elderly sexual needs by stating that institutions for the aging and medical professionals neglect the need for intimate relationships, as do family members. This often results in older persons "lacking social permission to express their attraction to another person, afraid of appearing ridiculous or immature if they were to reveal their sexual needs, overwhelmed with confusion and guilt feelings about sexual desires, [so] they deny themselves their own sexuality." It concludes with an argument for rethinking sexual relationships outside of marriage, including masturbation and other means of experiencing sexual pleasure. See "Older Adults, Office of the General Assembly, Presbyterian Church U.S.A.," 297–304.

29 McKoy and Petersen, "Reducing African American Women's Sexual Risk," 1151.

30 Portmann, *The Ethics of Sex and Alzheimer's*, 138.

31 Portmann traces the idea of sexual generosity throughout the book; in an earlier chapter he cautions against the trap of sexual selflessness, whereby women especially were expected to follow the model of Queen Victoria, who never remarried after her husband died. With regard to black churchwomen, Coretta Scott King

is the exemplar of sexual selflessness. Portmann argues that following sexual selflessness can lead to abusive scenarios where only the male spouse's needs are considered and the female never expects that her own needs will be met.

32 Walker, *In Search of Our Mothers' Gardens*, xi–xii.

33 Brown, "Constructing a Doctrine for the *Ecclesia Militans*," 68.

34 Fishel and Holtzberg, *Still Doing It*, 5. Chapter 1 explores the concept of sexual sin in more depth.

35 Newman, *Oh God!*, 160.

6 · HORNY AND HOLY

1 Hammonds, "Black (W)holes and the Geometry of Black Female Sexuality," 134.

2 Hammonds lists Cheryl Clarke, Jewelle Gomez, and Barbara Smith as contemporaries of Lorde in their efforts to theorize black female sexuality and desire ("Toward a Genealogy of Black Female Sexuality," 181).

3 Rose, *Longing to Tell*, 395.

4 Pinn, "Embracing Nimrod's Legacy," 161.

5 Hammonds, "Black (W)holes and the Geometry of Black Female Sexuality," 131.

6 Lee, *Erotic Revolutionaries*, x.

7 Guy-Sheftall, *Daughters of Sorrow*, 41.

8 Higginbotham, *Righteous Discontent*, 193; Mark et al., "What Has Changed about Vaginal Douching among African American Mothers and Daughters?," 419.

9 Zaggata, "Paradox in Discourse on Sexual Pleasure," 7.

10 Douglas, *Sexuality and the Black Church*, 120.

11 Foucault, *The History of Sexuality*, 19–20.

12 Bynum, *Pride vs. Proverbs 31 Woman*.

13 Bynum, *No More Sheets: Starting Over*, 181. Bynum and her successors discuss sexual pleasure outside of marriage as spiritual warfare between the Holy Spirit within and Satanic forces striving to lure the believer away from God. In these ministries Satan is a real and active agent in the world that women must guard themselves against.

14 Bynum, *No More Sheets: Starting Over*, 183.

15 Bynum, *No More Sheets* DVD.

16 Frederick, *Between Sundays*, 200.

17 Adams, *Single, Saved, and Having Sex?* (revised and updated edition), 172–73.

18 Adams also believes that being manually stimulated by another is sexually prohibited (*Single, Saved, and Having Sex?* [revised and updated edition], 26).

19 Lorde, *Sister Outsider*, 57.

20 Lindsey, "Secret Sins."

21 Grant, *The Best Kind of Loving*, 157.

22 That other surveys of black women and masturbation report much lower participation in self-pleasure has been correlated to strong beliefs that masturbation is immoral. See Dodge et al., "Sexual Health among U.S. Black and Hispanic Men

and Women," 336; Shulman and Horne, "The Use of Self-Pleasure," 263. These studies note that researchers often inquired about masturbation when surveying low-income women from Planned Parenthood or HIV prevention programs. This indicates the survey teams associated masturbation with other risks of sexually transmitted infections, a bias I do not share.

23 Williams, *Sensual Celibacy*, 127.

24 Gudorf, *Body, Sex, and Pleasure*, 85.

25 Dodge et al., "Sexual Health among U.S. Black and Hispanic Men and Women," 336. Gail Wyatt's 1997 study of black women's sexuality, *Stolen Women*, did include qualitative responses; she reported being struck by the disparate number of women (45 percent of her participants) who were not performing oral sex despite their partner's willingness to perform oral sex on them.

26 Adams, *Single, Saved, and Having Sex?* (revised and updated edition), 104.

27 Adams, *Single, Saved, and Having Sex?* (revised and updated edition), 227.

28 Wives in Waiting, "Let's Talk about Sex"; and "Let's Talk about Sex 2."

29 Covenant Spice, accessed July 23, 2016, http://covenantspice.com. Kelsy Burke's *Christians under Covers* explores this topic is great detail; however, these sites typically cater only to married Christian couples, not Christian singles.

30 Dugas, *Who Told You That You Were Naked*, 42–43.

31 During my follow-up interview with Michelle, her views had modified and she spoke of finding the "one" and getting married. Now thirty years old, she admitted her views had changed, which she attributed to getting older and currently dating someone she and her parents found marriage-worthy.

32 Hill Collins posits that honest bodies accept all components of themselves celebrating the totality of mind, body, and spirit. This redirects focus on how a person experiences her body as sexually autonomous because using one's honest body engages all forms of sexuality that bring pleasure and joy and for Hill Collins this freedom is intertwined with sexual responsibility. Hill Collins, *Black Sexual Politics*, 283–89.

33 Walker, *In Search of Our Mothers' Gardens*, xii.

34 Turman's womanist ethic of incarnation envisions black women as made from the same substance of God; thus their bodies are divine and human. The flesh cannot be divorced from the God incarnate (*Toward a Womanist Ethic of Incarnation*, 161).

35 Douglas, *Black Bodies and the Black Church*, 56.

36 Ellison, *Erotic Justice*, 82.

37 Lorde, *Sister Outsider*, 58. While Lorde's essay is a foundation of feminist and womanist discussions of the erotic, introducing a black feminist lesbian's perspective that is not Bible- or God-centered may pose a problem for many black church-women. I concur with Baker-Fletcher that the erotic satisfies more than just bodily needs as it can represent humanity's desire for the sacred; however, I do not want to overemphasize such a perspective because this can be seen as solely spiritual and ignore these women's bodily desires. See Baker-Fletcher, "The Erotic in Contemporary Black Women's Writings," 202–3.

38 Nelson, *Black Woman Redefined*, 149.

39 Ellison, *Erotic Justice*, 92.

40 Cooper, "Single, Saved, and Sexin'."

41 Newman, *Oh God!*, 162.

42 McCarty, *Sexual Virtue*, 223.

43 Wyatt, *Stolen Women*, 227–28.

44 Nelson, *Black Women Redefined*, 144.

45 Chevonne Harris, "Single, Saved—and Having Sex," *Essence*, May 2012, 91–92.

46 Baker-Fletcher, "The Erotic in Contemporary Black Women's Writings," 208.

47 "#BlackChurchSex: A Dialogue about Faith and Female Pleasure." These dialogues grew into a graduate student–led conference, Love Thyself: Black Bodies and Religious Space, that was cosponsored by the Center for Black Church Studies at Princeton Theological Seminary and Columbia University's Center for African-American Religion, Sexual Politics, and Social Justice. In this regard the public media was brought into academic discourse and vice versa as the conference was broadcast live online.

CONCLUSION

1 Walker, *In Search of Our Mothers' Gardens*, xi–xii.

2 Marcia Dyson, "Can You Love God and Sex?," *Essence*, February 1, 1999, 173.

3 In "Identifying Theo-Cultural Malpractice," Rev. Eugene Se'Bree's discussion of theocultural malpractice refers to the mogul Tyler Perry, but I find his description applies to depictions that distort the representations of blacks, blocking their agency while simultaneously re-presenting their religious culture in ways that serve those in power. This argument is relevant to my project because it takes seriously the symbiotic relationship of media in black religious culture and how people of faith interpret their faith through their media.

4 Davis-Carroll, "An Ethic of Resistance," 225.

5 Daniels, "Let's Pray for Sexually Active Daughters," 15.

6 Nelson, *Black Woman Redefined*, 132.

7 Anderson, *Ancient Laws and Contemporary Controversies*, 141.

8 Bailey, "The Danger of Ignoring One's Own Cultural Bias in Interpreting the Text," 76–78.

9 Frederick, *Between Sundays*, 194.

10 Weems, *What Matters Most*, 17–18. The biblical scholar David Carr calls the Song of Solomon one of the most read and commented on parts of the Christian biblical canon, with more Latin manuscripts than any other book (*The Erotic Word*, 4).

11 Winnifred Cutler, quoted in Williams, *Sensual Celibacy*, 45. The feminist bell hooks writes about the stigma associated with women who chose sexual inactivity. She contends that sexual agency that gives women the right to say yes to sex also can empower women to say no (*Communion*, 41).

12 Franklin, *Crisis in the Village*, 67. He defines unhealthy dating as when a person's body, mind, emotions, or values are disrespected.

13 Adrienne Samuels, "To Shack or Not to Shack: Is Living Together Still Taboo?," *Essence*, May 2007, 180.

14 I would like to thank Laquinta Yokley Ward for her insight on constructive steps black churches could take to embrace single black women who are sexually active.

Adams, Ty. *Single, Saved, and Having Sex?* Detroit: Heaven Enterprises, 2003.

———. *Single, Saved, and Having Sex?* Rev. and updated ed. New York: Warner Books, 2006.

The Adams Report. Interview with Andrea Wiley. Accessed July 23, 2016. http://www .theadamsreport.com/Profile_Andrea_Wiley_Soulmate.html.

Alexander, Bobby Chris. *Televangelism Reconsidered: Ritual in the Search for Human Community.* American Academy of Religion Studies in Religion. Atlanta: Scholars Press, 1994.

Anderson, Cheryl B. *Ancient Laws and Contemporary Controversies: The Need for Inclusive Biblical Interpretation.* New York: Oxford University Press, 2009.

Anderson, Dianna. *Damaged Goods: New Perspectives on Christian Purity.* New York: Jericho Books, 2015.

Anderson, Victor. "The Black Church and the Curious Body of the Black Homosexual." In *Loving the Body: Black Religious Studies and the Erotic*, edited by Anthony Pinn and Dwight Hopkins, 297–314. New York: Palgrave Macmillan, 2004.

Augustine. *Confessions.* Translated by Henry Chadwick. New York: Oxford University Press, 2008.

Bailey, Randall. "The Danger of Ignoring One's Own Cultural Bias in Interpreting the Text." In *The Postcolonial Bible*, edited by R. S. Sugirtharajah, 66–85. Sheffield, U.K.: Sheffield Academic Press, 1998.

Baker-Fletcher, Karen. "The Erotic in Contemporary Black Women's Writings." In *Loving the Body: Black Religious Studies and the Erotic*, edited by Anthony Pinn and Dwight Hopkins, 199–216. New York: Palgrave Macmillan, 2004.

Balmer, Randall. *Mine Eyes Have Seen the Glory: A Journey into the Evangelical Subculture in America.* New York: Oxford University Press, 2014.

Barton, Bernadette. *Pray the Gay Away: The Extraordinary Lives of Bible Belt Gays.* New York: New York University Press, 2012.

Beauvoir, Simone de. *The Coming of Age.* Translated by Patrick O'Brian. New York: Norton, 1996.

Bekkering, Dennis. "From 'Televangelist' to 'Intervangelist': The Emergence of the Streaming Video Preacher." *Journal of Religion and Popular Culture* 23.2 (2011): 101–17.

Best, Wallace. "Are the Gods Afraid of Black Sexuality?" Institute for Research in African-American Studies, Columbia University. *Livestream*, October 23, 2014. http://livestream.com/accounts/5576628/events/3490564/videos/65824457.

Beyoncé. "Single Ladies (Put a Ring on It)." *I Am . . . Sasha Fierce.* CD. Sony, 2008.

"#BlackChurchSex: A Dialogue about Faith and Female Pleasure." *YouTube*, May 21, 2015. https://www.youtube.com/watch?v=INo1Q_Rtwqw.

Boyd, Julia. *Embracing the Fire: Sisters Talk about Sex and Relationships.* New York: Dutton Books/Penguin Group, 1997.

Brown, Michael Joseph. "Constructing a Doctrine for the *Ecclesia Militans.*" In *Loving the Body: Black Religious Studies and the Erotic*, edited by Anthony Pinn and Dwight Hopkins, 53–72. New York: Palgrave Macmillan, 2004.

Burke, Kelsy. *Christians under Covers: Evangelicals and Sexual Pleasure on the Internet.* Berkeley: University of California Press, 2016.

Butler, Anthea. *Women in the Church of God in Christ: Making a Sanctified World.* Chapel Hill: University of North Carolina Press, 2007.

Butler, Judith. *Bodies That Matter: On the Discursive Limits of Sex.* New York: Routledge, 1993.

Bynum, Juanita. *Matters of the Heart.* Lake Mary, Fla.: Charisma House, 2002.

———, producer. *No More Sheets.* DVD. Waycross, Ga.: Juanita Bynum Ministries, 1998.

———. *No More Sheets: Starting Over.* Rev. ed. Shippensburg, Pa.: Destiny Image, 2010.

———. *No More Sheets: The Truth about Sex.* Lanham, Md.: Pneuma Life, 1998.

———. *No More Sheets Devotional: My Accident.* Lanham, Md.: Pneuma Life, 1998.

———, producer. *Pride vs. Proverbs 31 Woman.* DVD. Duluth, Ga.: Global Destiny Ministries, 2007.

———. "A Renewed Covenant." *YouTube*, January 12, 2008. https://www.youtube.com/watch?v=BCH_6zin2WU.

———. *Walking in Your Destiny.* Lake Mary, Fla.: Charisma House, 2006.

Campbell, Heidi. *Exploring Religious Community Online: We Are One in the Network.* New York: Peter Lang, 2005.

Cannon, Katie. "Sexing Black Women: Liberation from the Prisonhouse of Anatomical Authority." In *Loving the Body: Black Religious Studies and the Erotic*, edited by Anthony Pinn and Dwight Hopkins, 11–30. New York: Palgrave Macmillan, 2004.

Carr, David. *The Erotic Word: Sexuality, Spirituality, and the Bible.* New York: Oxford University Press, 2003.

Centers for Disease Control and Prevention. "HIV among African Americans." March 6, 2017. https://www.cdc.gov/hiv/group/racialethnic/africanamericans/index.html.

Chung, Minyon. "Conversion and Sanctification." In *The Cambridge Companion to Evangelical Theology*, edited by Timothy Larsen and Daniel Treier, 109–24. Cambridge: Cambridge University Press 2007.

Church of God in Christ. "Statement of Faith." Accessed April 2, 2017. http://www.cogic.org/our-foundation/our-statement-of-faith/.

Cline, Sally. *Women, Celibacy, and Passion.* London: Andre Deutsch, 1993.

Coleman, Monica A. *Making a Way out of No Way: A Womanist Theology.* Innovations: African American Religious Thought. Minneapolis: Fortress Press, 2008.

Comstock, Gary. "Rev. Irene Monroe." In *A Whosoever Church: Welcoming Lesbians and Gay Men into African American Congregations*, 59–71. Louisville, Ky.: Westminster John Knox, 2001.

Conway-Turner, Katherine. "Sex, Intimacy, and Self Esteem: The Case of the African American Older Woman." *Journal of Women and Aging* 41 (1992): 91–103.

Cooper, Anna Julia. *A Voice from the South*. New York: Oxford University Press, 1998.

Cooper, Brittany. "Single, Saved, and Sexin'." *YouTube*, March 15, 2013. https://www.youtube.com/watch?v=ejKj9Ii6q9E&feature=plcp.

———. "Single, Saved, and Sexin': The Gospel of Getting Your Freak On." *Crunk Feminist Collective*, February 3, 2011. http://www.crunkfeministcollective.com/2011/02/03/single-saved-and-sexin-the-gospel-of-gettin-your-freak-on/.

Cornelius, Judith, Linda Moneyham, and Sara LeGrand. "Adaptation of an HIV Prevention Curriculum for Use with Older African American Women." *Journal of the Association of Nurses in AIDS Care* 14 (2008): 16–27.

Cornwall, Susannah. *Theology and Sexuality*. London: SCM Press, 2013.

Daniels, Cora. "Let's Pray for Sexually Active Daughters." In *Impolite Conversations: On Race, Politics, Sex, Money, and Religion*, 9–21. New York: Atria Books, 2014.

Davis-Carroll, Hilda. "An Ethic of Resistance: Choosing Life in Health Messages for African American Women." *Journal of Religion and Health* 50 (2011): 219–31.

DeRogatis, Amy. *Saving Sex: Sexuality and Salvation in American Evangelicalism*. New York: Oxford University Press, 2015.

———. "What Would Jesus Do? Sexuality and Salvation in Protestant Evangelical Sex Manuals, 1950s to the Present." *Church History* 74 (2005): 97–137.

Dickerson, Bette, and Nicole Rousseau. "Ageism through Omission: The Obsolescence of Black Women's Sexuality." *Journal of African American Studies* 13 (2009): 307–24.

Dodge, Brian, Michael Reece, Debby Herbenick, Vanessa Schick, Stephanie Sanders, and J. Dennis Fortenberry. "Sexual Health among U.S. Black and Hispanic Men and Women: A Nationally Representative Study." *Journal of Sexual Medicine* 7, supplement 5 (2010): 330–45.

Douglas, Kelly Brown. *Black Bodies and the Black Church: A Blues Slant*. New York: Palgrave Macmillan, 2012.

———. *Sexuality and the Black Church: A Womanist Perspective*. Maryknoll, N.Y.: Orbis, 1999.

———. *What's Faith Got to Do with It? Black Bodies/Christian Souls*. Maryknoll, N.Y.: Orbis, 2005.

Dugas, Candi. *Who Told You That You Were Naked: Black Women Reclaiming Sexual and Spiritual Goodness*. CreateSpace Independent Publishing Platform, 2012.

Ellison, Christopher, and Darren Sherkat. "The Semi-Involuntary Institution Revisited: Regional Variations in Church Participation among Black Americans." *Social Forces* 73.4 (1995): 1415–37.

Ellison, Marvin Mahan. *Erotic Justice: A Liberating Ethic of Sexuality*. Louisville, Ky.: Westminster John Knox Press, 1996.

Erzen, Tanya. *Straight to Jesus: Sexual and Christian Conversions in the Ex-Gay Movement*. Berkeley: University of California Press, 2006.

Fine, Michelle, and Sara McClelland. "Sexuality Education and Desire: Still Missing after All These Years." *Harvard Educational Review* 76.3 (2006): 297–338.

Fishel, Deidre, and Diana Holtzberg. *Still Doing It: The Intimate Lives of Women over Sixty.* New York: Penguin, 2008.

Fisher, Linda L., Gretchen Anderson, Matrika Chapagain, Xenia Montenegro, James Smoot, and Amishi Takalkar. "Sex, Romance, and Relationships: AARP Survey of Midlife and Older Adults." AARP, April 2010. Accessed July 23, 2016. http://assets.aarp.org/rgcenter/general/srr_09.pdf.

Fiske, John. "British Cultural Studies and Television." In *What Is Cultural Studies? A Reader*, edited by John Storey, 115–46. New York: Arnold, 1997.

Floyd-Thomas, Stacey M. *Mining the Motherlode: Methods in Womanist Ethics.* Cleveland: Pilgrim Press, 2006.

Flunder, Yvette. *Where the Edge Gathers: Building a Community of Radical Inclusion.* Cleveland: Pilgrim Press, 2005.

Foucault, Michel. *The History of Sexuality: An Introduction.* Vol. 1. New York: Vintage Books, 1990.

Franklin, Jentezen. "The Boaz Family Tree." *YouTube*, December 31, 2013. https://www.youtube.com/watch?v=3hXnIaJwWY4.

Franklin, Robert M. *Crisis in the Village: Restoring Hope in African American Communities.* Minneapolis: Fortress Press, 2007.

———. "Generative Approaches to Modernity, Discrimination, and Black Families." In *American Religions and the Family: How Faith Traditions Cope with Modernization and Democracy*, edited by Don S. Browning and David A. Clairmont, 104–23. New York: Columbia University Press, 2007.

Frederick, Marla. *Between Sundays: Black Women and Everyday Struggles of Faith.* Berkeley: University of California Press, 2003.

———. "'But It's Bible': African American Women and Television Preachers." In *Women and Religion in the African Diaspora*, edited by R. Marie Griffith and Barbara Dianne Savage, 266–82. Baltimore: Johns Hopkins University Press, 2006.

———. *Colored Television: American Religion Gone Global.* Stanford: Stanford University Press, 2016.

Gafney, Wil. "Ruth." In *The Africana Bible: Reading Israel's Scriptures from Africa and the African Diaspora*, edited by Hugh Page, 249–54. Minneapolis: Fortress Press, 2010.

Gardner, Christine. *Making Chastity Sexy: The Rhetoric of Evangelical Abstinence Campaigns.* Berkeley: University of California Press, 2011.

Goethals, Gregor. "The Electronic Golden Calf." In *Religion and Popular Culture in America*, edited by Bruce David Forbes and Jeffery Mahan, 125–44. Berkeley: University of California Press, 2000.

Grant, Gwendolyn Goldsby. *The Best Kind of Loving: A Black Woman's Guide to Intimacy.* New York: HarperCollins, 1995.

Griffin, Horace. "Black Churches, the Bible, and the Battle over Homosexuality." In *Walk Together Children*, edited by Dwight Hopkins and Linda E. Thomas, 193–209. Eugene, Ore.: Cascade Books, 2010.

———. *Their Own Receive Them Not: African American Lesbians and Gays in Black Churches.* Cleveland: Pilgrim Press, 2006.

Griffith, R. Marie. *God's Daughters: Evangelical Women and the Power of Submission.* Berkeley: University of California Press, 1997.

Gudorf, Christine. *Body, Sex, and Pleasure: Reconstructing Christian Sexual Ethics.* Cleveland: Pilgrim Press, 1994.

Guy-Sheftall, Beverly. *Daughters of Sorrow: Attitudes toward Black Women, 1880–1920.* Brooklyn: Carlson, 1990.

Hale, Cynthia. *I'm a Piece of Work! Sisters Shaped by God.* Valley Forge, Pa.: Judson Press, 2010.

Hammonds, Evelynn. "Black (W)holes and the Geometry of Black Female Sexuality." *Differences: A Journal of Feminist Cultural Studies* 6 (1994): 126–45.

———. "Toward a Genealogy of Black Female Sexuality." In *Feminist Genealogies, Colonial Legacies, Democratic Futures*, edited by Jacqui M. Alexander and Chandra Talpade Mohanty, 170–82. New York: Routledge, 1997.

Henderson, Irene. "Betwixt and between Again: Menopause and Identity." In *In Her Own Time*, edited by Jeanne Stevenson-Moesnner, 213–25. Minneapolis: Fortress Press.

Higginbotham, Evelyn Brooks. *Righteous Discontent: The Women's Movement in the Black Baptist Church, 1880–1920.* Cambridge, Mass.: Harvard University Press, 1993.

Hill, Renee. "Human Sexuality—The Rest of the Story." In *Walk Together Children: Black and Womanist Theologies, Church, and Theological Education*, edited by Dwight Hopkins and Linda E. Thomas, 183–92. Eugene, Ore.: Cascade Books, 2010.

———. "Who Are We for Each Other? Sexism, Sexuality and Womanist Theology." In *Black Theology: A Documentary History*, Vol. 2: *1980–1992*, edited by James Cone and Gayraud Wilmore, 345–54. Maryknoll, N.Y.: Orbis Books, 1993.

Hill Collins, Patricia. *Black Sexual Politics: African Americans, Gender, and the New Racism.* New York: Routledge, 2004.

Hine, Darlene Clark. "Rape and the Inner Lives of Black Women in the Middle West: Preliminary Thoughts on the Culture of Dissemblance." *Signs* 14.4 (1989): 912–20.

hooks, bell. *Communion: The Female Search for Love.* New York: William Morrow, 2002.

Hoover, Stewart M. *Mass Media Religion: The Social Sources of the Electronic Church.* Communication and Human Values. Newbury Park, Calif.: Sage, 1988.

Isasi-Díaz, Ada María. *En La Lucha—In the Struggle: A Hispanic Women's Liberation Theology.* Minneapolis: Fortress Press, 1993.

Jenkins, Kathleen. "Warrior Chicks: Youthful Aging in a Postfeminist Prosperity Discourse." *Journal for the Scientific Study of Religion* 51 (2012): 247.

Jordan, Mark. *The Ethics of Sex.* Oxford: Blackwell, 2002.

Kahan, Benjamin. *Celibacies: American Modernism and Sexual Life.* Durham, N.C.: Duke University Press, 2013.

Klassen, Pamela. "The Robes of Womanhood: Dress and Authenticity among African American Methodist Women in the Nineteenth Century." *Religion and American Culture: A Journal of Interpretation* 14 (2004): 39–82.

Lebacqz, Karen. "Appropriate Vulnerability: A Sexual Ethics for Singles." In *Sexuality*, edited by Karen Lebacqz and David Sinacore-Guinn, 129–35. Cleveland: Pilgrim Press, 1999.

Lee, Shayne. *Erotic Revolutionaries: Black Women, Sexuality, and Popular Culture*. Lanham, Md.: Hamilton Books, 2010.

———. *T. D. Jakes: America's New Preacher*. New York: New York University Press, 2005.

Lindsey, Heather. "How to Start a Business: God's Way and Up and Comers." May 24, 2012. *Heather's Official Blog*. http://www.heatherllindsey.com/2012/05/how-to-start-business-gods-way-up.html#.VR3K5UJE-bA.

———. "Secret Sins: Masturbation and Pornography." *Heather's Official Blog*, July 10, 2013. http://www.heatherllindsey.com/search?q=masturbation+and+pornography#.VXkxYs5E_8k.

Loe, Meika. "Pleasure in Old Age." In *Sex for Life: From Virginity to Viagra, How Sexuality Changes throughout Our Lives*, edited by Laura Carpenter and John DeLamater, 278–98. New York: New York University Press, 2012.

Lorde, Audre. *Sister Outsider*. Berkeley: Crossing Press, 1984.

Lynxwiler, John, and Michele Wilson. "The Code of the New Southern Belle: Generating Typifications to Structure Social Interaction." In *Southern Women*, edited by Caroline Dillman, 113–25. New York: Hemisphere, 1988.

Madden, Mary. "Older Adults and Social Media." Pew Research Center, August 27, 2010. http://pewinternet.org/Reports/2010/Older-Adults-and-Social-Media.aspx.

Mahmood, Saba. *Politics of Piety: The Islamic Revival and the Feminist Subject*. Princeton: Princeton University Press, 2005.

Mark, Hayley, Susan Sherman, Joy Nanda, Tracey Chambers-Thomas, Mathilda Barnes, and Anne Rompalo. "What Has Changed about Vaginal Douching among African American Mothers and Daughters?" *Public Health Nursing* 27.5 (2010): 418–24.

McCarty, Richard W. *Sexual Virtue: An Approach to Contemporary Christian Ethics*. New York: State University of New York Press, 2015.

McClure, John. *Mashup Religion*. Waco, Texas: Baylor University Press, 2011.

McKoy, Jacintha, and Ruth Petersen. "Reducing African American Women's Sexual Risk: Can Churches Play a Role?" *Journal of the National Medical Association* 98 (2006): 1151–59.

Miller, Albert G. "The Rise of African-American Evangelicalism in American Culture." In *Perspectives on American Religion and Culture*, edited by Peter W. Williams, 259–69. New York: Blackwell, 1999.

Minority Nurse Staff. "Preventing HIV/AIDS in Older African American Women." *Minority Nurse*, March 30, 2013. http://minoritynurse.com/?s=preventing+hiv.

Morrison, Toni. *Beloved*. New York: Plume, 1987.

Moslener, Sarah. *Virgin Nation: Sexual Purity and American Adolescence*. New York: Oxford University Press, 2015.

Moultrie, Monique. "After the Thrill Is Gone: Married to the Holy Spirit but Still Sleeping Alone." *Pneuma* 33 (2011): 237–53.

Muzacz, Arien, and Adeyinka Akinsulure-Smith. "Older Adults and Sexuality: Implications for Counseling Ethnic and Sexual Minority Clients." *Journal of Mental Health Counseling* 35 (2013): 1–14.

National Baptist Convention, USA, Inc. "What We Believe." Accessed July 23, 2016. http://www.nationalbaptist.com/about-us/what-we-believe.html.

Nelson, Sophia. *Black Woman Redefined: Dispelling Myths and Discovering Fulfillment in the Age of Michelle Obama.* Dallas: BenBella Books, 2011.

Newman, Susan D. *Oh God! A Black Woman's Guide to Sex and Spirituality.* New York: One World/Ballantine Books, 2002.

"Older Adults, Office of the General Assembly, Presbyterian Church U.S.A.)." In *Sexuality and the Sacred: Sources for Theological Reflection*, edited by James Nelson and Sandra Longfellow, 297–304. Louisville, Ky.: Westminster John Knox Press, 1994.

Perry, Dwight. *Breaking Down Barriers: A Black Evangelical Explains the Black Church.* Grand Rapids, Mich.: Baker Books, 1998.

Pinky Promise Movement. "About Us." Accessed April 2, 2017. http://pinkypromisemovement.com/about/.

Pinn, Anthony. "Embracing Nimrod's Legacy: The Erotic, the Irreverence of Fantasy, and the Redemption of Black Theology." In *Loving the Body: Black Religious Studies and the Erotic*, edited by Anthony Pinn and Dwight Hopkins, 157–78. New York: Palgrave Macmillan, 2004.

Pope-Levinson, Priscilla. *Building the Old Time Religion: Women Evangelists in the Progressive Era.* New York: New York University Press, 2015.

Portmann, John. *The Ethics of Sex and Alzheimer's.* New York: Routledge, 2014.

Richardson, Mattie Udora. "No More Secrets, No More Lies: African American History and Compulsory Heterosexuality." *Journal of Women's History* 15.3 (2003): 63–76.

Rose, Tricia. *Longing to Tell: Black Women Talk about Sexuality and Intimacy.* New York: Farrar, Straus and Giroux, 2003.

Rudy, Kathy. *Sex and the Church: Gender, Homosexuality, and the Transformation of Christian Ethics.* Boston: Beacon Press, 1997.

Saunders, Shellie. "Bynum, Juanita 1959–." *Contemporary Black Biography*, 2002. Accessed July 23, 2016. http://www.encyclopedia.com/topic/Juanita_Bynum.aspx.

Schultze, Quentin J. *Televangelism and American Culture: The Business of Popular Religion.* Grand Rapids, Mich.: Baker Book House, 1991.

Se'Bree, Eugene. "Identifying Theo-Cultural Malpractice: Redefining through the Cultural Lens of Identity Politics." Master's thesis, Vanderbilt Divinity School, 2013.

Shockley, Ann Allen. *Say Jesus and Come to Me.* New York: Hearst, 1982.

Shulman, Julie, and Sharon Horne. "The Use of Self-Pleasure: Masturbation and Body Image among African American and European American Women." *Psychology of Women Quarterly* 27.3 (2003): 262–69.

Silliman, Jael Miriam. *Undivided Rights: Women of Color Organize for Reproductive Justice.* Cambridge, Mass.: South End Press, 2004.

Smith, Aaron. "Older Adults and Technology Use." Pew Research Center, April 3, 2014. http://www.pewinternet.org/files/2014/04/PIP_Seniors-and-Tech-Use_040314.pdf.

Swilley, Stephanie. "Christian and Single: What's a Person to Do?" Touch of Faith Ministry, 2012. Accessed July 23, 2016. http://www.touchoffaith.org/sermons /christiansingle.htm.

Thomas, Linda. "What the Mind Forgets the Body Remembers: HIV/AIDS in South Africa—A Theological and Anthropological Issue." *Currents in Theology and Mission* 35.4 (2008): 276–86.

———. "Womanist Theology, Epistemology, and a New Anthropological Paradigm." *Cross Currents* 48.4 (1998): 488–99.

Thumma, Scott. "Virtually Religious: Technology and Internet Use in American Congregations." Hartford Institute for Religious Research, March 2011. Accessed July 23, 2016. http://www.hartfordinstitute.org/research/technology-Internet-use.html.

Townes, Emilie. *Womanist Ethics and the Cultural Production of Evil.* New York: Palgrave Macmillan, 2006.

Townsend Gilkes, Cheryl. *If It Wasn't for the Women: Black Women's Experience and Womanist Culture in Church and Community.* Maryknoll, N.Y.: Orbis, 2001.

Traister, Rebecca. *All the Single Ladies: Unmarried Women and the Rise of an Independent Nation.* New York: Simon and Schuster, 2016.

Turman, Eboni Marshall. *Toward a Womanist Ethic of Incarnation: Black Bodies, the Black Church, and the Council of Chalcedon.* New York: Palgrave Macmillan, 2014.

U.S. Census Bureau, "Number, Timing, and Duration of Marriages and Divorces: 2009." May 2011. Accessed April 2, 2017. https://www.census.gov/prod/2011pubs /p70-125.pdf.

U.S. Department of Health and Human Services, Administration for Community Living. "A Statistical Profile of Older African Americans." Accessed July 23, 2016. http://www.acl.gov/NewsRoom/Publications/docs/A_Statistical_Profile_of_Older _African_Americans.pdf.

Viefhues-Bailey, Ludger H. "Holiness Sex: Conservative Christian Sex Practices as Acts of Sanctification." *Journal of Men, Masculinities, and Spirituality* 6.1 (2012): 4–19.

Walker, Alice. *In Search of Our Mothers' Gardens: Womanist Prose.* New York: Harcourt Brace Jovanovich, 1983.

Walton, Jonathan L. "Response to Joseph de León." In *Creating Ourselves: African Americans and Hispanic Americans on Popular Culture and Religious Expression*, edited by Anthony Pinn and Benjamin Valentín, 231–48. Durham, N.C.: Duke University Press, 2009.

———. *Watch This! The Ethics and Aesthetics of Black Televangelism.* Religion, Race, and Ethnicity. New York: New York University Press, 2009.

Wang, Wendy, and Kim Parker. "Record Share of Americans Have Never Married." Pew Research Center, September 24, 2014. http://www.pewsocialtrends.org/2014/09/24 /record-share-of-americans-have-never-married/.

Weems, Renita. *What Matters Most: Ten Lessons in Living Passionately from the Song of Solomon.* New York: Walk Worthy Press, 2004.

Westfield, Nancy Lynne. "Influences of Sexism in Black Church Worship." In *Black Religion and Aesthetics: Religious Thought and Life in Africa and the African Diaspora*, edited by Anthony Pinn, 37–52. New York: Palgrave Macmillan, 2009.

Wiley, Andrea, producer. *Soul Mate*. DVD. Los Angeles, Clean Heart Productions, 2006.

——. "What Women Need to Know about What a Man Wants." *Beliefnet*. Accessed July 23, 2016. http://www.beliefnet.com/Love-Family/Relationships/Galleries/What -Women-Need-to-Know-about-What-a-Man-Wants.aspx.

Williams, Donna Marie. *Sensual Celibacy: The Sexy Woman's Guide to Using Abstinence for Recharging Your Spirit, Discovering Your Passion, Achieving Greater Intimacy in Your Next Relationship*. New York: Simon and Schuster, 1999.

Wives in Waiting. "Frequently Asked Questions." Accessed July 23, 2016. http://www .wivesinwaiting.com/#!faq/t6bjv.

——. "Let's Talk about Sex." *Google Hangout*, December 26, 2014. https://www .youtube.com/watch?v=7iclupZPnso.

——. "Let's Talk about Sex 2, Part 2." *YouTube*, January 30, 2015. Accessed July 23, 2016. https://www.youtube.com/watch?v=UgSFlgTcIEg.

——. "Testimonials." Accessed July 23, 2016. www.wivesinwaiting.com.

Wolcott, Victoria. *Remaking Respectability: African American Women in Interwar Detroit*. Chapel Hill: University of North Carolina Press, 2001.

Wyatt, Gail Elizabeth. *Stolen Women: Reclaiming Our Sexuality, Taking Back Our Lives*. New York: John Wiley, 1997.

Zaggata, Elizabeth R. "Paradox in Discourse on Sexual Pleasure: A Feminist Pastoral Theological Exploration." PhD diss., Vanderbilt University, 2011.

Zeiss, Antonette, and Julia Kasl-Godley. "Sexuality in Older Adults' Relationships." *Generations* 25 (2001): 18–25.